From Business Strategy
to IT Action

*Right Decisions for a
Better Bottom Line*

Praise for
From Business Strategy to IT Action

The authors provide us a most insightful approach to industry's toughest problem: on what IT investments should we invest our scarce resources? More importantly, their framework can be applied to any and every discretionary corporate investment. Linking corporate investments to strategic objectives is critical to remaining or becoming a viable and vital business—and this book gives us the roadmap for the journey. Particularly helpful are the provocative sets of questions and helpful tools to address this complex issue.

—*Francisco A. Figueroa, CFO and Vice President,*
Sandia National Laboratories

This is a dynamite book of practical advice for companies that do not fully understand IT, and should become required reading for both business and IT management. It is a "gem" of disciplines and practices and of business-based ways to manage IT and to get the biggest and most important value from IT investments.

—*Cecil O. Smith, Senior Vice President and CIO, Duke Energy*

I've worked with Bob for several years. This book, which outlines his practical yet elegant approach for aligning IT action plans with the overarching business strategy, is a must read for anyone who wants to get more impact from their IT dollar!

—*Brian Gill, Vice President and CIO, Sunlife Canada*

I like this book very much. It offers an extraordinary set of insights on how to take IT planning, innovation, and performance measurement to the bottom line. For more than two decades I struggled, as a CIO, to tie IT management decisions to business outcomes. Finally, I found in this book a consistent framework for guiding IT and business leaders alike, in maximizing the business value of their IS capabilities and technology investments.

—*Doron J. Cohen, Ph.D. CIO, The BrassTacks*

To bridge the chasm between business and IT, concise and clearly defined business and financial decision processes and metrics need to be created and articulated. This book provides a precise and simple to follow methodology that IT executives can use to better align themselves with CFOs and their business partners.

—*Mark Popolano, CIO, Vice President, AIG, Inc.*

This book tells you all you need to know about strategy and execution related to developing IT strategies, making the right investment decisions, and implementing the strategies that will lead to creating greater impact to business performance. A great insight shared by the authors for those who are concerned with IT investment and return.

—*Swee-Cheang Lim, Director, Institute of Systems Science, Singapore*

In 1988, *Information Economics* proposed a way of thinking and a method about the value of IT. In this new book, based on their broad business-based experience, the authors further develop the framework and process. It is the combination that lays the foundation for increasing the bottom-line results of IT investments.

—*Prof. dr. Pieter Ribbers, Faculty of Economics,*
Tilburg University, The Netherlands

Within ING there is continuous pressure to ascertain that all discretionary IT-related business investments generate a stable earnings stream that is significantly higher than the weighted average cost of capital. Following on the valuable insights of Information Economics, this book may contribute to the firm's ability to enhance IT's contribution to its value creation process by ameliorating project risk.

—*Dr. John FA Spangenberg, Head of IT Performance &*
Investment Management, ING Group

From Business Strategy
to IT Action

Right Decisions for a
Better Bottom Line

ROBERT J. BENSON

THOMAS L. BUGNITZ

WILLIAM B. WALTON

WILEY

John Wiley & Sons, Inc.

Copyright © 2004 by John Wiley & Sons. All rights reserved.

Published by John Wiley & Sons, Inc., Hoboken, New Jersey
Published simultaneously in Canada

For general information on our other products and services, or technical support, please contact our Customer Care Department within the United States at 800-762-2974, outside the United States at 317-572-3993 or fax 317-572-4002.

Wiley also publishes its books in a variety of electronic formats. Some content that appears in print may not be available in electronic books.

Library of Congress Cataloging-in-Publication Data

Benson, Robert J.
    From business strategy to IT action : right decisions for a better
bottom line / by Robert J. Benson, Tom Bugnitz, William Walton
    p.   cm.
Includes index.
    ISBN 0-471-49191-8
    1. Business planning.   2. Business enterprises—Computer networks.
3. Information technology—Management.   4. Information resources
management—Economic aspects.   I. Bugnitz, Thomas L.   II. Walton,
William, 1951–   III. Title.
HD30.28.B4533   2004
658.4'03—dc22   2003020204

Printed in the United States of America.

10 9 8 7 6 5 4 3 2 1

*Bob Benson thanks his wife, Noreen Carrocci,
for her continuous and constant support
and dedicates this effort to her and our families.*

*Tom Bugnitz dedicates his work on this book to
Diane Dimeff, who has supported, helped,
encouraged, and most of all put up with him
and his many idiosyncrasies for the last ten years.*

*Bill Walton dedicates his work to his wife Eliza
and children, Mac, Jas, and Grace.
Together, you are both my why and my how.*

*Miraculously, we have all three ended up with women
who are much better than we deserve.*

about the authors

Bob Benson is a Principal with The Beta Group. He has served as CIO, financial executive, dean, professor, author, and consultant for over 40 years. His consulting and research deals with the business value of IT, business and IT strategic planning, methodology and process development, IT governance, and facilitation. He has conducted executive seminars and performed and managed consulting engagements on these subjects throughout the world (in 20 countries and 40 states) and has taught graduate courses in schools of business and engineering in Europe and the United States. For over 10 years, he has consulted full time in his areas of interest.

He has keynoted numerous international conferences, created and managed academic programs and organizations, developed large-scale computer systems, and consulted with a wide range of companies and government agencies. Mr. Benson is coauthor of several books and numerous book chapters, articles, and monographs, including *Information Economics: Linking Information Technology and Business Performance* (Prentice-Hall, 1988) and *Information Strategy and Economics: Linking Information Systems Strategy to Business Performance* (Prentice-Hall, 1989).

Mr. Benson is an affiliate professor of computer science at Washington University in St. Louis, where he also served as senior executive for computing and communications, institutional financial planning, and professor, dean, and center director. He is currently a professor of information management (part-time), Faculty of Economics, Tilburg University, The Netherlands. He served as founding managing director of the E-Business Forum.

Tom Bugnitz has been the President of The Beta Group, a consulting firm he cofounded with Bob Benson, for the past 15 years. Mr. Bugnitz has consulted and lectured widely in the United States on the subject of the business-IT connection, and has codeveloped a number of consulting methodologies for improving IT management. In addition, he is closely associated with Washington University in St. Louis as an adjunct professor of computer science and participates actively in the development and execution of research in the field of information management. He is coauthor of several books on systems and computer programming. Mr. Bugnitz brings practical experience to bear on his consulting and teaching assignments, having worked at all levels of information systems organizations, including 10 years managing large data centers and telecommunications operations.

Bill Walton is a Principal with The Beta Group. His areas of special interest and expertise include Performance Measurement, Alignment, Integrated Strategic Planning, IT/Business Value, Organizational Change Management, and Technology-Driven Change.

Before joining The Beta Group Mr. Walton was with Gartner and Real Decisions for 17 years. He spent his final 5 years at Gartner as the Vice-President of R&D for Gartner Measurement where he was directly responsible for the development of numerous innovative benchmarking and IT performance measurement services and their associated analytical methods. These included the use of organizational and technical complexity as IT cost drivers, the application of the Balanced Scorecard to IT, and the development of IT management process models. Most recently, with The Beta Group Mr. Walton has been responsible for the development of a set of management frameworks and tools that support IT strategic alignment and planning processes.

Mr. Walton has been active in the information and technology management field since 1977. He has worked with a large number of clients in the USA, Canada and Europe on critical IT measurement and management issues. Mr. Walton applies a combination of active research and practical experience to each of his consulting engagements.

about the beta group

The Beta Group consults to Fortune 500 companies and government agencies in North America and Europe, focusing on improving IT's bottom-line impact and controlling IT spending. Beta Group consulting practices cover the IT planning-to-execution cycle, starting with strategic planning and budgeting through investment prioritization, alignment, performance measurement, and portfolio management. For more information on the company or its methods, visit *www.the-beta-group.com* or *www.beta-books.com*.

about the website

As a purchaser of *From Business Strategy to IT Action: Right Decisions for a Better Bottom Line,* you have access to the companion website. The Notes that are provided on the Website provide additional information and background on IT value strategies including the Strategy-to-Bottom-Line Value Chain, New Information Economics, the five practices, and Portfolio Management and Assessment. To access the website, go to *www.wiley.com/go/ITAction.*

NOTES

1   IT and Economic Cycles
2   IT's Value—A Definition
3   IT, Bottom-Line Impact, and Government
4   Tests for Connected Business and IT
5   Modern Portfolio Management
6   One Company's View of Portfolio Management
7   Constructing Portfolios
8   Gap Analysis: Closing Disconnects between Business and IT
9   Building an IT Profit Model
10 Stage Theory and Management Culture
11 Right and Wrong in Management Culture
12 Value and Values
13 Our Use of Shareholder Value
14 Scoring for Portfolio Assessment
15 The CFO's Role
16 What about IT's Performance
17 Other Portfolio Classifications
18 ROI and the IT Value Life Cycle

contents

Notes are available on this book's website: *www.wiley.com/go/ITAction.*

preface

Almost 20 years ago, Bob Benson of Washington University and Marilyn Parker of IBM, with the help of Ed Trainor, broke new ground in understanding the value relationship between IT and business. As co-principal investigators in a research project sponsored by the IBM Los Angeles Scientific Center and Washington University in St. Louis, Bob and Marilyn described a process and framework for assessing the business value of IT investments in any company. Their first book, *Information Economics: Linking Business Performance and Information Technology,*[1] established the view that, to be effective and valuable to the enterprise, IT has to fundamentally improve how a business[2] performs; to do this, business management must be directly involved in IT decision-making.

This insight defined performance improvement in strategic and operational terms, in the areas strategically relevant to the company and not merely as measured in traditional bottom line or ROI terms. Their book established a practical methodology for prioritizing IT investments, and it demonstrated that focusing new investment on achieving explicit business strategies and operational excellence helped maximize the bottom line impact of new investments for the business.

Over the past two decades, Information Economics has served as the foundation for consulting by The Beta Group and research and teaching by Bob Benson, Tom Bugnitz, and Bill Walton (Beta Group Principals). Through these experiences, the authors have extended the original Information Economics concepts and gained a number of key insights that form the foundation for this new book.

This new book, *From Business Strategy to IT Action,* applies the original Information Economics philosophy to all of the activities in which business and IT management are engaged together—planning, innovation, prioritization, alignment, performance measurement, and portfolio and culture management. The concepts around *IT action* are a crucial enhancement to the original ideas.

---

[1] Marilyn M. Parker and Robert J. Benson, with E.H. Trainor, *Information Economics: Linking Business Performance to Information Technology* (Prentice-Hall, 1988).

[2] While the terminology here and throughout the book is presented in "business" terms, the concepts and practices apply with equal force to government and nonprofit organizations. While business is concerned with competitive strategy and financial outcomes, government is just as concerned with strategy and performance to organizational mission.

This addition takes the philosophy of IT/business connection from a passive prioritization to an active let's-get-the-job-done viewpoint. Without action that produces bottom-line impact, nothing else matters. But even that isn't sufficient; the action must produce business results in line with business strategies. That's the message of "Right Decisions for a Better Bottom Line."

However, "action" also requires that we address issues of culture, process maturity, and disconnects between business and IT. Toward this end, we introduce the Strategy-to-Bottom-Line Value Chain, a framework that integrates the five NIE practices and three support areas. In this framework, Culture Management provides tools for understanding and changing a company's current culture with respect to business and IT cooperation. Portfolio Management establishes information and analysis tools for prioritizing, aligning, and assessing the company's entire IT investment. IT Impact Management establishes the IT culture and performance models for the IT/Business connection.

We use the expression "Right Decisions/ Right Results" throughout the book as a shorthand expression to convey all of this. The five NIE practices lead to the best decisions about the company's IT investments; the Strategy-to-Bottom-Line Value Chain leads to the necessary actions. Taken together, the company achieves the right results: a powerful impact on its bottom-line.

The original Information Economics concepts applied in the first book represented only one of the five NIE practices described in this book. By surrounding those concepts with a complete planning and management framework, we are again establishing a new way for business and IT managers to understand and use IT to produce better bottom-line results.

CONTINUING DEVELOPMENT

This book is a work in progress. Further research and experience in companies in the United States and Europe will continue to develop these ideas. We expect to update chapter information on a regular basis.

Our websites, *www.NewInformationEconomics.com* and *www.beta-books. com,* contain directions on how to obtain future updates. We can be reached individually by e-mail at:

Bob Benson	*bbenson@aismail.wustl.edu*
Tom Bugnitz	*tbugnitz@aismail.wustl.edu*
Bill Walton	*wwalton@lincoln.midcoast.com*

BOB BENSON
TOM BUGNITZ
BILL WALTON
March 2004

acknowledgments

We have benefited from the advice and suggestions of a number of people. We are grateful that Jon Shapiro, Rodney Alsup, Cecil Smith, Francois Wouters, Larissa Moss, Dennis Smith, Camille Appledorn, Ed Curvey, David Reo, Tony Salvati, and Nicholas Nash gave us the benefit of their thoughts and reviews of early drafts. We are especially grateful for the work we have done with Joe Barkley and Bruce Schneider of AIG and the many insights they gave us in the course of writing this book.

We recognize the many people who have influenced our professional lives and our thinking over the last twenty years and more. These include: Bill Smith and the late Hardy Fuchs at Washington University, the best "IT guys" we've ever known; Marilyn Parker, Bob's coauthor of *Information Economics* and a prime influence; Ed Trainor, who contributed the practical foundation for *Information Economics;* Piet Ribbers of Tilburg University, with whom we always have great ideas; Ken Orr, who always inspires; John Zachman and Dick Nolan, who set the standard for what we try to do; Mike Nicholson, our first client and a faithful supporter, and Bob Rouse, associates in the Beta Group; Linda Bastoni of Gartner and Regina Paolillo of Creditek, always encouraging better from us; Chuck Lybrook, who has supported us all these years; Greg Sullivan, whose constant friendship and good humor means so much; Mary Ann Gibson, whose business sense, intelligence, and support have pointed the way in building our business; Mike Luby, who possesses a first-rate executive mind connected to an exquisite sense of humor; Phil Andrews, Swami Viswanathan, Jason Grant, and the rest of our other clients and good friends (many of whom are both). Students in our Washington University and Tilburg University courses also have had a considerable impact on our thinking, as they have often heard our ideas first and served as a valuable crucible in improving how we express them.

CHAPTER 1

Define the Goals

This book is based on a very simple idea: A company should only spend money on IT[1] that directly supports its business strategy and its operational effectiveness, and should not spend money on IT that doesn't. The management team can control IT budgets and investments, and at the same time improve IT's bottom-line impact, by consistently and persistently selecting the best IT investments, and eliminating underperforming existing IT activities. This book shows how to do that.[2]

Right Results: The "right results" we want are controlled IT costs and at the same time improved bottom-line impact.

Right Decisions: The "right decisions" lead to the management actions needed to produce the right results. These right decisions lead to:

- Creating better investment alternatives—or, in IT terms, creating better ideas for development projects.
- Choosing the right investments and projects from the alternatives.
- Eliminating nonperforming and poorly performing existing IT resources from current spending.
- Improving the performance of the remaining existing IT resources.
- Implementing and following through on the right investments and performance improvements.

Our Right Results goals of controlled IT costs and improved bottom-line impact work together. As new projects enable the business to improve its products,

1

services, and quality, and at the same time reduce operating costs, higher impact on the company's bottom line will result. As management focuses on controlling ongoing operational costs, overall costs may decline. This combination allows the company to move from today's cost and bottom-line position to a future controlled-cost and improved bottom-line impact position.

To accomplish this, business executives and IT managers balance new IT investments with the ongoing assessment of the performance of committed IT resources. Money saved in one area can be applied to the other. From senior management's perspective, this all adds up to the "IT spend." From IT management's perspective, this all represents the resources that must be managed effectively. Working together, the goals of controlled IT costs and improved bottom-line impact can be realized.

This is the goal of this book, as illustrated in Exhibit 1.1. Companies can work toward goals in the IT Improvement Zone by examining and improving both new project impact and ongoing costs.

EXHIBIT 1.1   Our Goal Is the IT Improvement Zone

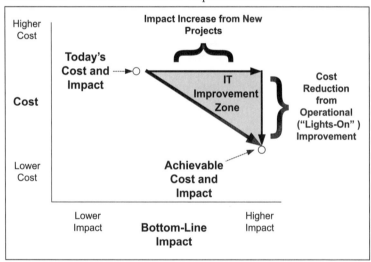

TODAY'S REALITY

Companies spend as little as 2 percent and as much as 10 to 15 percent of revenue on IT, including the ongoing cost of keeping the existing IT operational activities going as well as new investment in development and enhancement projects. As shorthand, we call the first the "lights-on" budget,[3] and the second, the "projects" budget.

We are interested in the entire IT spend, the sum of lights-on and project budgets. Most of the spending is connected to ongoing operational costs, often 70 or 80 percent of the total. To be serious about controlling cost and increasing IT's impact on the bottom line, we have to address the entire spend.

However, with IT as in many other parts of the business, simply reducing IT costs does not by itself improve the bottom line. But with the right management frameworks and management practices, companies can successfully control the growth of IT costs and at the same time improve the business bottom-line impact of those costs and investments.

Historically, company executives have spent a great deal of time evaluating and prioritizing new IT projects and investments. Considerable management energy is spent prioritizing and dealing with the politics of project selection. However, this effort applies to perhaps 20 or 30 percent of the overall IT spend. The other 70 or 80 percent, the lights-on budget, is larger but attracts almost no attention from management. In many ways, the lights-on budget is a black box with no visibility to management.

An "entitlement" mentality tends to apply to the lights-on budget, where each business manager expects that the information systems now in place will continue with current or improved levels of support, and the CIO tends to expect that the base budget for current applications support, including infrastructure, will continue at current or increased levels. This entitlement mentality also affects project prioritization (managers fight for "their" projects to be done by "their" project people) as well as the ongoing costs of supporting each manager's applications. It can be very difficult to reduce support for existing individual applications, making it difficult to control and possibly reduce the lights-on budget over time.

As a result, rather than pursuing the goals of both reduced cost *and* improved bottom-line impact, managers focus on one or the other. This leads to one of several unfortunate scenarios, as shown in Exhibit 1.2.

1. **Lower lights-on cost *and* reduced bottom-line impact,** where companies focus solely on cost reduction, without considering the specific impact the cost reduction has on IT's contribution to the bottom line. A typical outsourcing arrangement fits this scenario.

2. **Higher lights-on cost combined with *no* improvement in bottom-line impact.** This is the entitlement situation, where managers assume that lights-on budgets will regularly increase and new projects are chosen that do not produce enough bottom-line impact to overcome increased costs. Companies that rely on traditional budget methods and traditional business-case and prioritization methodologies often end up here.

3. **Higher lights-on cost *and* higher bottom-line impact.** This scenario is common where business conditions are improving or where the business is rapidly growing. Business growth obscures the fact that better management scrutiny of both projects and the lights-on budgets can make the result even better, and perhaps even move the scenario into the sweet spot of both lower costs and higher bottom-line impact. In times of rapid growth, higher cost may be unavoidable, but it does not have to be uncontrolled or unreasonable.

EXHIBIT 1.2   Current Patterns for Many Companies

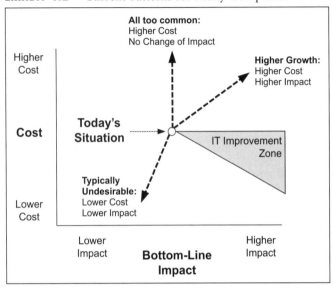

THE ENTIRE IT SPEND: REDUCING COST AND IMPROVING BOTTOM-LINE IMPACT

We want to be very clear on this: Getting the Right Decisions/Right Results means dealing with both IT's cost and IT's impact on the bottom line. Of course, if we reduce IT's cost, then some of that cost reduction will filter down to the bottom line. But that is not what we mean when we talk about IT's impact on the bottom line. Bottom-line impact, both short- and long-term, comes from the cost reductions, quality improvements, and so forth that IT enables in the rest of the company, and from making sure that *these* IT business impacts flow to the bottom line. Over time, we want management teams to be able to dramatically improve *both* cost and bottom-line impact.

To accomplish this, we propose three possible objectives, shown in Exhibit 1.3, that a company may pursue, depending on its current circumstances:

1. **A Reduced Cost Objective**[4]—By applying the frameworks and five management practices, company management can reduce IT costs and retain the contribution that IT makes to the bottom line. IT can perform just as well as before, but at reduced cost.

2. **A Stable Cost Objective**—Company management can continue to grow IT use and keep up with the growth of the business, and yet control the overall IT spend. IT can increase its support of the business and its impact on the bottom line, but at current cost levels.

EXHIBIT 1.3 Possible Outcomes for Companies

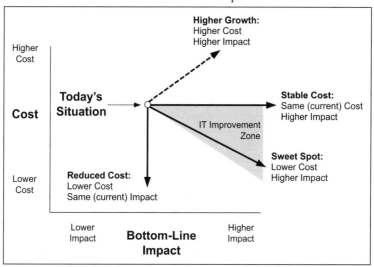

3. **A "Sweet Spot" Objective**—This combines cost reductions with better bottom-line impact. IT can both lower its cost and also improve its performance in terms of bottom-line impact.

A fourth "Higher Growth" Objective (mentioned in the previous section) may apply to companies experiencing rapid change and/or growth. In this case, the higher IT costs, though controlled, are justified because they produce even greater bottom-line impact. Even in these cases, we can reduce the overall cost increases, thus increasing the bottom-line impact even further.

THE STRATEGY-TO-BOTTOM-LINE VALUE CHAIN

What does it take to control IT costs and produce higher bottom-line impact? Simply, we need effective planning processes, appropriate resource decisions, and workable budgets and plans. We need them to work together consistently.

But companies already do this, managers may say. They work to improve the bottom-line performance of their company.[5] From year to year, they set budgets for ongoing operations and invest in projects or initiatives to change or add to the business. Managers then expect that new budgets will support better bottom-line performance than prior-year budgets, and that investments in projects or initiatives will produce better bottom-line performance (see Exhibit 1.4).

The practical problem is that most companies carry out planning, prioritization/resource decisions, budgets, performance measurement, and so forth, in silos or stovepipes. We mean this in two ways. First, in management process terms, business planning, IT planning, prioritization, budgets, and performance

EXHIBIT 1.4   Strategy-to-Bottom-Line Value Chain

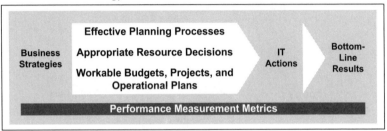

measurement are poorly connected. For example, a company may have strategies, but its management performance measurement is not consistent with those strategies. Similarly, business and IT planning may not be coordinated. These management processes operate, but not consistently or from a common base of information, and are disconnected. Second, many companies are organized in silos or stovepipes, and the various management activities—such as planning, prioritization, budgets, and so forth—do not take an enterprise perspective nor do they coordinate across the barriers between silos or stovepipes. The business units are disconnected.

Yet, IT has many aspects that, to control costs and assure IT's bottom-line impact, have to operate across silos or stovepipes. IT's infrastructure is a simple example, but the idea extends to the coordination/integration of information systems across silos and to the exchange and integration of information across silos. Certainly, planning, prioritization, budgeting, and so forth have to connect across these silos to be effective.

DISCONNECTS

Although we need effective planning, appropriate resource decisions, workable budgets, and so on, whether we get them depends on how well the management processes work across silos, both process silos and organizational silos. Operational budgets and future projects result in an improved bottom line only when managers and staff perform budget-setting and project selection well. Budgets and projects themselves are only as good as the planning that produces them. Budgets and projects produce results only when managers and organizations perform effectively, without silos and disconnects getting in the way.

Most companies and organizations have a loose collection of disconnected management processes around IT. For example, in a large consumer products company, business planning does not directly connect to IT planning, which does not connect to company budget processes and management performance assessments. The consequence is that the company's IT investments and ongoing expenditures do not clearly support business strategies; the CEO cannot tell what the company is getting for its investment; and IT managers are frustrated at their inability to communicate what IT is up to and why, to business managers and the CEO. These disconnects are the problems we need to solve in order to put the necessary management practices into action.[6]

As it has been more than three decades since these problems first became apparent, there must be more to the problem than management process disconnects. We often find:

- Business plans do not drive IT plans.

- IT plans focus on technology rather than directly addressing business strategies.

- Business managers do not see IT as supporting their strategies.

- IT projects do not support business strategies. IT spending on infrastructure and application maintenance does not support strategy.

- Company budgets do not reflect the results of IT planning.

- IT plans are shelfware that does not guide management decisions, projects, or budgets.

- IT governance practices do not direct IT from a business perspective.

These symptoms are characteristic of companies with disconnects. What gets in the way, fundamentally, is different views among business and IT managers about the role that IT plays in the business, the value that IT can bring, and the management practices that are needed to effectively bring IT to bear on business strategies. These different views result from, and in, the failure to plan, align, prioritize, innovate, and measure performance for IT consistently from a business strategy perspective. This failure results from management cultures in business and IT that are incompatible with using a business perspective to manage IT.

Companies need their own version of a Strategy-to-Bottom-Line Value Chain. Readers may recall Michael Porter's work on competitive analysis.[7] He proposed that enterprises have a *value chain* of connected, coordinated activities that individually and in concert add value to the products and services that an enterprise produces. We take that basic idea and apply it to the management processes that connect the company's planning and strategies to IT planning, budgets, and actions, and to performance management that tracks the results. This is a Strategy-to-Bottom-Line Value Chain where, as in Porter's model, each individual management process both adds value and, working consistently with the other processes, works in concert to reduce or control IT costs and simultaneously improve IT's contributions to the company's bottom line. By examining each management process and applying the tools and practices contained in this book to those processes, a company can "connect the dots" in terms of its processes and optimize its Strategy-to-Bottom-Line Value Chain.

CRITICAL SUCCESS FACTORS

Effective planning processes, appropriate resource decisions, and workable budgets, projects, and plans are the foundation, working consistently across process and organizational silos. Based on these, we can produce the right IT actions to control costs and, in turn, impact the bottom line. We can control costs at the same time as improving IT's contributions. The problem is, these three elements are bound up in the existing management culture and processes.

We can tell how well a company does in producing our five outcomes (better projects, right project choices, reduced nonperforming spending, improved performance of existing spending, and right management actions) by examining whether:

- Business and IT planning processes are fully connected and integrated.

- IT-enabled innovations impact business planning and result in new business strategies and improved ways to implement current business strategies.

- IT investments are prioritized against business strategy.

- The entire IT spend—including development, operations, maintenance, and services—is aligned with business strategy.

- IT business and technical performance is tracked.

- Business and IT management teams consistently execute the management processes that improve IT's contribution to the business's bottom-line performance.

- Planning and management processes focus on the entire IT investment, including both Lights-On and Projects.

- IT and business managers participate effectively in these management processes.

To the extent that the above statements are not true in a company, its effective planning processes, appropriate resource decisions, and workable plans simply will not be effective, appropriate, and workable. The IT actions will not be connected to business strategy, and costs will not be controlled, nor will the right results be produced.

These are the Critical Success Factors[8] for getting Right Decisions/Right Results. We want better projects, we want to choose the best projects, we want to eliminate nonperforming and poorly performing assets and resources, and we want to improve the performance of existing assets and resources. Overall, we want to reduce costs and, at the same time, improve IT's contribution to bottom-line performance. To do this requires attention to these critical success factors.

COMPLETING THE PICTURE: THE NEW INFORMATION ECONOMICS PRACTICES

We have developed five basic management practices that flesh out the Strategy-to-Bottom-Line Value Chain. More specifically, these practices create "yes" answers to the eight CSF questions stated above. These five practices, shown in Exhibit 1.5, are the basis for connecting strategy and results.

EXHIBIT 1.5   New Information Economics Practices

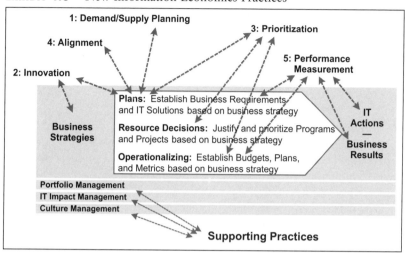

We call this set of five practices "New Information Economics" (NIE) to reflect that they are outgrowths of the original *Information Economics* work described in our first two books. Briefly, we have had almost two decades of experience in applying Information Economics in companies in the United States, Europe, and the Pacific Rim. This experience and our research has led to the five practices, which have been applied in business and government environments.

The five practices in NIE make up a set of tools for IT and business managers to use, embedded in management processes, to translate a company's business strategies into programs and initiatives that IT can implement. This book describes each of these practices in detail, and gives the reader complete details about what is needed to implement these practices, in whole or in part, in the reader's company. The five practices are briefly defined as:

NIE Practice 1: Strategic Demand/Supply Planning—Translates business strategies into terms that give IT clear direction on what the company intends to do (the company's "strategic intentions"). Business and IT managers achieve consensus on where the company is going and what IT can do to help. They do this by establishing the business drivers as expressed through management's strategic intentions, and translating them into the strategic IT requirements needed to fulfill the strategic intentions. Management's strategic intentions establish the drivers for IT; the strategic IT requirements establish the business's strategic "demand" for IT, for which IT strategic planning must deliver technology solutions as the strategic "supply." The result is a strategic agenda for the use of IT in the business that can be translated into IT plans and, ultimately, action.

NIE Practice 2: Innovation—Changes the business strategies through IT capabilities. IT usually responds to business needs. Less frequently, business changes its directions based on the things that IT makes possible. This practice explicitly drives business management to uncover the business opportunities that IT makes possible and also provides a way to feed those opportunities into business strategic and tactical planning. The result is a more robust and competitive set of business opportunities.

NIE Practice 3: Prioritization—Assesses the business impact of proposed IT initiatives, prioritizes those projects, and assigns resources to the highest value projects. The company should spend money only on projects that directly relate to its strategic intentions. This practice tells managers which IT projects strongly support strategic intentions, ranking them by future business impact. As a result, money is spent in the right places, for the right reasons, with business and IT managers agreeing on the decisions.

NIE Practice 4: Alignment—Assesses the business impact of existing IT activities. A dollar spent on maintaining existing systems is a dollar not spent on new development. This practice lets business and IT managers together decide which existing IT initiatives should get resources, rather than assuming that everything currently operating is critical for the business and should be supported at existing levels. The result is a more reasoned approach to spending money for existing activities, which often results in money made available for new development.

NIE Practice 5: Performance Measurement—Measures IT performance in ways that relate to the business. It is easy to measure IT's performance in operational and tactical terms. It is hard to measure IT's impact on the business. This practice blends the two and allows IT to determine what to measure, how to manage IT based on those measures, and how to communicate its performance to business managers in ways that they can understand. The result is improved IT performance and improved communication with business management.

Practice Support: IT Impact, Portfolio, and Culture Management

The five practices are supported through value, portfolio, and culture management concepts. IT Impact Management deals with one part of the company's management culture and offers a framework and vocabulary to state what is important to the company. Portfolio Management makes it possible to consider the entire IT spend, providing an holistic framework for making priority and investment management decisions. Culture Management enables the company to deal with its existing culture in the company in order to remove barriers to management process change.

Business Value Maturity Model™

Company management culture, along with limitations on the company's ability to execute NIE practices, are significant constraints on management's success in adopting new management processes based on NIE practices. The Business Value Maturity Model™ helps a company to identify and overcome the two factors of culture and limitations on the company's ability to execute. We describe desired business outcomes for each NIE practice area and we use "maturity" as the measure of whether the company can produce the outcomes based on a combination of culture barriers and company capability to act on the results.

Strategy-to-Bottom-Line Value Chain

Each NIE practice creates outcomes that help a company better connect its IT investments to its business strategies. For example, the *prioritization* practice connects IT investments to business strategic intentions; the *performance measurement* practice tracks progress in producing the desired business results. Getting these outcomes from NIE practices is half the battle. The other half is to follow through with the right actions in the business and IT organizations to actually produce the desired business results. This requires an unbroken string of company business and IT management processes that consistently apply the outcomes of NIE practices. NIE practices may be embedded in the company's existing management processes, and practice outcomes should result in changing how those processes operate.

Exhibit 1.6 expresses this embedding as a value chain of connected management processes leading from business strategy to action. The value chain is expressed as 12 specific deliverables produced from the management processes. Each process adds value to the overall Strategy-to-Bottom-Line chain by means of these deliverables, ensuring that the following processes and their deliverables are consistent and remain focused on business strategy. The connections and deliverables ensure that the necessary IT and business actions become part of business and IT organization annual plans, and that those actions will occur. Moreover, if relevant performance measurement metrics are established, management can track the actions and their results. The connection to the annual plan, and to the performance measurement metrics, is critical to assuring that the right action occurs and the right results are produced.

Twelve elements make up the Strategy-to-Bottom-Line Value Chain.[9] They start with the company's strategic intentions (Strategic Business Plan) and continue up to the Operational Plans covering the actions of each business unit, both business and IT. Exhibit 1.6 symbolizes the goal for Right Decisions/Right Results in terms of the NIE practices providing the foundation and connections for producing the elements in the Strategy-to-Bottom-Line Value Chain. The key point, however, is that most of the underlying management processes or deliverables will already exist in a company. The trick is to coordinate and connect them using the NIE practices.

EXHIBIT 1.6   Strategy-to-Bottom-Line Value Chain

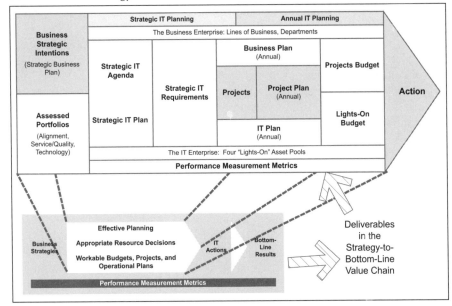

The value chain is a management process view of how things need to work. There is a lot more to it than just getting the management processes right. Specifically, a company's existing management culture determines whether or not such a value chain can be successful. Whether the company's leadership teams can play the roles, and support and carry out the results, is critical.

This book outlines how all elements of the company's activities, including management culture, can consistently apply the concepts and principles of Right Decisions/Right Results and New Information Economics practices. Our goal is to enable a company to achieve an effective Strategy-to-Bottom-Line Value Chain. We describe the five key New Information Economics practices and the role they play in management processes. We outline the value chain in the company's management processes, and the roles that the company's senior, business, and IT leadership teams play in it. We examine management culture and how management culture supports each practice. We introduce the Business Value Maturity Model™ as a tool for assessing where the company currently stands in its Strategy-to-Bottom-Line Value Chain. Through Culture and IT Impact Management, assisted by the Business Value Maturity Model™, we address process and culture change issues.

Right Decisions/Right Results: Getting to the Right Actions Is the Key

Too often, we find companies that do have good planning practices, do alignment and prioritization well, and employ good enterprise architecture practices, yet fail to get it all together in the form of action. Action, after all, is what produces results. In our view, action that produces the right results is all that really matters.

What do we mean by "right action"? An easy way to think of it is: For every business strategy, whether corporate, line of business, or functional, IT should have a clear idea of *exactly* what it is doing to further the strategy. IT should also have a clear idea that those things it is doing that do not connect to strategy should *not* be done. This is the basis, ultimately, for controlling cost at the same time as improving bottom-line impact.

SUMMARY OF THE BOOK

This book is about controlling spending and choosing the right things on which to spend. This problem applies to every part of the business. In every case, managers need to control spending, choose the right things to invest in, and thereby control costs and improve impact.

Controlling spending means controlling the total of all spending, the aggregate of all IT spend for a company. This includes everything from operational costs to project costs. It includes expense and capital, as well as depreciation and amortization. The goal is to understand what the company spends and then keep that total spend within parameters established by management.

Choosing the right spend means, within the total of all spending, making the best choices about the detailed expenditures. While "controlling spending" means keeping the total within the desired parameters, "choosing the right spend" focuses on each line item, determining its performance and contribution to the bottom line.

You are likely to be reading this book because you believe your organization must improve how it directs and applies IT. You believe that IT should produce greater value and have a greater impact on organizational performance. You want to know that you are spending IT resources on the right problems, and you need assurance that the IT resources produce value. You want to get action and produce the right results from IT.

Further, you are interested in understating how your company can get Right Decisions and Right Results, as shown in Exhibit 1.7. Ideally, you want to achieve the "sweet spot."

This book describes the framework, the NIE principles and management practices for applying them, and the changes in management culture that result. The book is the outcome of the authors' consulting, research, and teaching engagements over the past 20 years.

Beyond merely describing these elements, this book explains in practical terms what it takes to implement the principles and practices in the business environment. Using a Business Value Maturity Model™ framework, the book also addresses ways to assess an organization's readiness for implementing and utilizing the tools, and gives practical advice for implementing the cultural and process changes required. The book also explains the "takeaways" for business

EXHIBIT 1.7   Our Goal Is the IT Improvement Zone

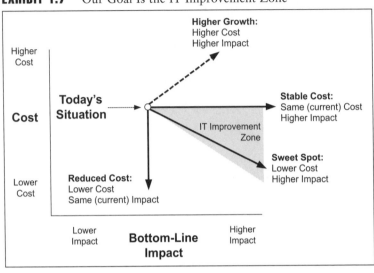

and IT management, detailing the overall benefits that the management team will realize from adopting these frameworks.

DEFINE THE GOALS: MANAGEMENT AGENDA

The following is a self-examination for the critical success factors for Right Decisions/Right Results.

Management Question	Yes or No?	If No, What Is Our Plan for Correcting This?
Are business and IT planning processes fully connected and integrated?		
Do IT-enabled innovations impact business planning and offer new business strategies?		
Are IT investments prioritized against business strategy?		
Does the entire IT spend, including development, operations, maintenance, and services, align with business strategy?		
Is IT business and technical performance tracked?		
Do business and IT management teams consistently execute the management processes that improve IT's contribution to business bottom-line performance?		

Management Question	Yes or No?	If No, What Is Our Plan for Correcting This?
Do planning and management processes focus on the entire IT spend, both lights-on and projects?		
Do both IT and business managers participate effectively in these management processes?		

The balance of this book provides answers to the question: "What is our plan for correcting this?"

ADDITIONAL READING

The book's website contains additional information:

Website Note 8: Gap Analysis: Closing Disconnects between Business and IT

Website Note 9: Building an IT Profit Model

The appendices also contain related information for Chapter 1:

Appendix C: The Development of Strategic Intentions, with Examples

NOTES

1. Our European friends prefer the more inclusive term Information and Communications Technology (ICT). Our use of "IT" includes communications technologies.

2. As we noted in the preface, while the terminology used here and throughout the book is in business terms, the concepts and practices apply with equal force to government and nonprofit organizations. While business is concerned with competitive strategy and bottom line outcomes, government is just as concerned with strategy and performance to organizational mission.

3. Our thanks to Joe Barkley and Fabrice Forsans for introducing this term to us as it applies to the ongoing operational component of the IT spend.

4. Our objective is the effective management of overall IT costs. Cost objectives, as we apply them in the scenarios, take unit cost reductions and demand changes into account. We do not focus directly on unit costs but rather on macro-level IT costs. We focus on demand in terms of increasing high-value activities and reducing low-value activities.

5. Executives for government and nonprofit agencies also work to improve performance. Rather than "bottom line," they work to improve agency mission performance. Throughout this book, we typically use "bottom line" terminology. However, our concepts and practices work equally well for "mission performance" and "mission impact."

6. For an extended discussion of the origins and challenges of business/IT disconnects, see Website Note 8, "Gap Analysis: Closing Disconnects between Business and IT."

7. Michael E. Porter, *Competitive Strategy: Techniques for Analyzing Industries and Competitors* (New York: Free Press, 1980) and *Competitive Advantage: Creating and Sustaining Superior Performance* (New York: Free Press, 1985).

8. J. Rockart, "Chief Executives Define their Own Data Needs," *Harvard Business Review,* March–April 1979.

9. See Chapter 6 for a complete description of the 12 Value Chain deliverables.

CHAPTER 2

Ask the Right Questions

The purpose of this chapter is to explore how management can most effectively address basic questions about IT and business, and thereby set the stage for effectively controlling the IT spend and maximizing IT's bottom-line impact.

Managers ask tough questions about IT spending, particularly at budget time. Here are typical questions we have heard:

CEO: Can we afford what we're spending on IT? Do we even know how much we're spending on IT? How can I tell if IT is helping with our strategies? Are we getting bottom-line impact from our IT investments, and how will I know that? Are we making as much use of the technology in our business as we should? How can I get all of my managers to agree on our technology strategies and plans?

CFO: Are we controlling our IT expenses? Do our IT managers understand the financial implications of their decisions? How do we justify new IT investments?

Control Spending and Maximize Impact on the Bottom Line	
1	Define the Goals
2	**Ask the Right Questions**
3	Connect to the Bottom Line
4	Understand Costs and Resources
5	Focus on the Right Things
6	Adopt Effective Process to Produce Action
7	Tackle the Practical Problems
8	Make the Right Decisions
9	Plan for the Right Results
10	Keep Score
11	Deal with Culture
12	Chart the Path to Implementation
13	Define What's Next
14	Answer the "So What?" Question

How do we balance our resources between requests for new investment and the needs of existing activities? How do I know IT is contributing to our business success? Can we justify spending what we are, on IT?

CIO: I've got $75 million in IT project proposals and $30 million in IT budget . . . how do we as a company decide which are the best $30 million of projects to do? What is the correct balance between infrastructure support and new projects? How do I get business and IT people on the same page

17

about IT initiatives, priorities, and expectations? How do I get business managers to agree on IT's priorities? How does IT communicate its performance and its impact on the business in terms business understands?

Business Unit Manager: How can I help control my IT costs? How do I figure out how to use IT to improve my business and competitive edge? My direct reports all have good technology ideas . . . how do I choose? How do I get IT working on the things the business needs, as opposed to the things that individuals need? How do I build a business case for the IT investments we need?

IT Managers and Professionals: How do we explain to the business what we are doing and why it costs what it does? How do we cut costs and still provide good services to the business? How can we work most effectively with our peers in the business, to assure that we are addressing the right problems and producing the right solutions? How do we know that the infrastructures and applications we manage are making a difference for the company?

These are the questions managers feel they have to answer to get to Right Decisions/Right Results. The questions address management process (e.g., "How can I get IT working on things the business needs") and outcomes (e.g., "How do I know we're getting value from IT?"). However, we propose a simpler set of questions that address all of these concerns while focusing the company's attention on the most effective IT actions.

THE RIGHT QUESTIONS FOCUS
ON AFFORDABILITY AND IMPACT

Businesses feel three pressures when trying to control IT spend while producing bottom-line impact. First, the overhang of existing IT activities (legacy systems, infrastructure, personnel, etc., which we will call the "lights-on" expense) usually requires annual spending increases. Second, each year business defines new IT investments ("projects"), increasing the budget requests for future periods. Finally, business managers continue to put downward pressure on IT costs, forcing hard examination of lights-on expenses and new investments.

From a practical perspective, we see these pressures play out in the annual IT budget cycles. First, companies develop future lights-on budgets with pro-forma increases, with little examination of the underlying bottom-line impact of the activities and expenses. Second, new IT investment proposals are developed (often as business wish lists), and combined with the lights-on expenses to complete the overall IT budget proposal. Finally, business management places spending constraints on the organization, forcing a close examination of all IT expenses.

In many companies, the lights-on budget (up to 85% of IT expense in some companies) is treated as an entitlement, with little examination of the value of those continuing expenses. Consequently, controlling IT spending means controlling the costs of new investment, squeezing new projects out rather than reducing existing activities. In effect, the amount of new IT investment is the difference between overall budget targets and the budgeted lights-on expenses.

We propose that the role of management in this context is to force the examination of all IT expenses, using the yardstick of bottom-line impact, and creating IT spending patterns and budgets that are affordable for the business, given budget constraints and guidelines, while supporting the new IT activities that the business needs. To do this, management must address two complementary sets of questions:

Affordability Questions

- What can we afford to spend on IT?
- Can we reduce unnecessary IT costs?
- Can we redeploy expenses to support needed projects?

These questions address management's judgment on where, and how, to spend company resources on its operations, of which IT is but a part.

Impact Questions

- Are we investing IT resources in the right places?
- Do our business strategies drive our IT actions and produce bottom-line impact?
- Are we getting bottom-line impact from our lights-on resources?
- Are we balancing our strategic and tactical investments?

These questions address the alignment of what IT spends with the company's basic strategies and goals. The questions also get at IT's performance with respect to doing the "right" projects and the "right" way to allocate IT resources.

We also want to point out a question we are *not* asking: We are *not* being distracted by the "IT Value" question. Considerable energy has been expended throughout the IT industry to answer the "What is the Value of IT?" question. We do not believe that at this stage of business and IT development, this is the right question, because it does not lead to the appropriate management actions. We are focused on the *actions* needed to control IT spending and improve IT's impact on the bottom line.

To ask and answer these questions effectively, we need to engage senior managers in discussing and resolving the basic Affordability and Impact Questions, in order to take the actions that effectively control the IT spend and improve

IT's bottom-line impact. Senior managers should be responsible for a number of actions:

- *Establishing spending targets and specific justification criteria for IT spending.* IT spending is like any other business expense, and managers need to set affordable and realistic IT spending targets.

- *Understanding investments.* Senior managers should understand where and why money is being spent for new projects and ongoing IT.

- *Understanding the business impact.* Senior managers should know the connection between IT investments and accomplishing what is important to the business (reflected in the company's strategic intentions).

By considering affordability and impact, the management team can most efficiently focus its own activities and drive the actions of the IT management group.

AFFORDABILITY QUESTIONS: THE STARTING POINT FOR THE RIGHT ACTIONS

Over the last 15 years, we have conducted many management exercises in prioritization and alignment intended to answer the Impact Questions about IT's value: Are we spending our money in the right place, can we support our strategy, and so forth. These exercises generally succeeded in getting management groups to understand what they were doing with IT, and renew or redirect their commitment to their IT strategic and tactical plans.

However, in almost all cases, there was a subtext to the management teams' discussion: that the company had implied limits to what it could spend on IT. In effect, an "affordability"[1] factor enters into management's concerns. Consequently, for many companies, the "strategic" questions are not the first ones to ask. The management actions needed are not only to decide on IT investment to support strategy, but also to decide, in the context of that company and industry, what is the *right level* of IT spending, and how should the company allocate those dollars between ongoing activities and new investment as effectively as possible.

By starting with affordability, we start with reality. We are explicitly stating that the issue is not one of garnering new budget support for every new idea, but allocating a scarce resource between new needs and existing activities, so that the mix produces the best bottom-line impact for the company.

The three Affordability Questions are simple to state but complex to answer. Each question contributes a critical piece of understanding to managers making resource decisions.

1. *What can we afford to spend on IT?* From a CEO's perspective, IT is but one of a number of business expenses that must be managed and controlled.

From the business unit or CIO perspective, IT expenses are often entitlements (lights-on budgets) and new spend (project budgets) that need to grow if services and functions are to continue. We propose that each company has an implied target for IT spend, which may or may not be articulated throughout the company. The issue for management is to identify and understand that constraint, and allocate IT resources within that number to the best and highest-impact activities.

What is the right level for IT expenditures for a given company? "Lights-on" should be stable at worst, given the constant decline in unit costs of hardware and the many alternatives available for reducing software costs. Project money should be dependent on the strength of the individual project business cases, offset by the risks involved, and represented in total by the project portfolio. Our starting point is to look for stronger projects with larger bottom-line impact. Overall, the right level for IT expenditures is based on executives' judgments on what the company can afford, dependent on industry conditions and company capabilities, rather than line management's beliefs about what they need.

2. ***Can we reduce unnecessary IT costs?*** For the most part, this question deals with lights-on budgets and ongoing IT activities. First, it implies that we know what the costs for IT are. However, we have learned that in many companies neither business nor IT managers truly understand the extent or detail of the costs that make up ongoing activities. While gross bottom-line budgets are known, such important issues as the cost to run a given application (or even what the inventory of applications is), the people dedicated to particular systems, and the overall infrastructure component costs (and what is driving those costs) are completely unknown. Second, it also implies that companies are examining these costs, but we have found there is very little examination of ongoing costs (beyond anecdotal cases for outsourcing, systems replacement with new purchased software, etc.). The issues for management are to identify these costs, understand their bottom-line impact, and eliminate (or redeploy) costs that are not contributing to the bottom line.

3. ***Can we redeploy expenses to support needed projects?*** Given limited resources (first question) and understanding of overall and especially unnecessary costs (second question), this question implies that we can redeploy poor-performing assets and resources to new projects. Assuming flat or slightly increasing budgets, redeployment allows an overall higher impact from all IT dollars, while supporting more "strategic" projects that might otherwise go unfunded.

By starting with and answering the Affordability Questions, we set the ground rules for spending and resource allocation, and provide the basis for using the Impact Questions to drive the right actions from IT.

IMPACT QUESTIONS: THE ROADMAP
FOR THE RIGHT ACTIONS

The Strategy-to-Bottom-Line Value Chain is a series of connected management processes that produce projects and project budgets and ongoing operations. In the processes, management makes decisions about strategies, projects, and plans; those decisions are then implemented in terms of the projects and operational budgets. The result is a roadmap for getting the right IT actions. See Exhibit 2.1.

EXHIBIT 2.1   The Impact Questions

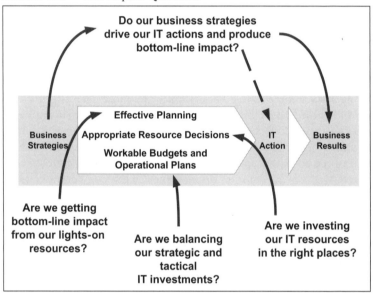

Senior managers know they need effective and timely information technology support for their key business strategies. What the Impact Questions do is allow them to drive IT actions directly from those business strategies, and focus IT and business line management on using resources to deliver bottom-line impact.

1. *Are we investing IT resources in the right places?* Given a company's strategies and operational issues, are the IT resources devoted to the most important things? This can mix resource allocation questions (which investments should we make?), impact questions (are we spending on and supporting old IT activities that are no longer important?), and planning questions (are we generating the best ideas for using IT in the business; are we contributing solutions to our business strategies?). Business and IT management teams must answer this question together, with a clear view of the business strategies

being supported and an equally clear view of the opportunities that IT presents to meet those strategies. (Typically, management disconnects between IT and business get in the way. If business and IT management are not working from a common philosophy, and a common set of cultural values in making these decisions, they simply add to the problem rather than answer the questions.)

2. ***Do our business strategies drive our IT actions and produce bottom-line impact?*** The question implies that management agrees on a common statement of business strategy and understands the kind of actions IT is taking to support that strategy. In many companies, merely asking the question forces a rearticulation of the strategies, in terms that are *actionable* by line management. IT is then able to understand more fully what management is intending and what actions it can take to support those intentions.

   We often see companies that do a good job of connecting their IT planning to business strategy but then fail to implement the best projects. The culture forces projects with high short-term ROI to the top of the priority list, or emphasizes short-term operational goals in setting budgets and choosing projects. This illustrates the importance of having a common basis for answering the question: *"Do our business strategies drive our IT actions?"* The answer is important, but the culture and practice to do something about the answer are important as well.

3. ***Are we getting bottom-line impact from our lights-on resources?*** This question implies that we know in detail what our current IT resources are, and how they are being used. Additionally, the answer depends on the intended outcomes from the investments in IT assets and resources. For example, if they are competitive in nature, then the question is about the impact that the investments have on competitiveness, market share, customer retention, and so forth. If the outcomes relate to cost or productivity, then the question is about the impact that the investments will have on costs and on operational performance.

   Disagreements about IT value can occur when business and IT management have different views on the actual business outcomes needed. For example, business management may look for substantial ROI or, alternatively, substantial competitive edge, as the basis for IT's value. If IT looks for competitive edge, and business is marching to the ROI drum, a serious disconnect exists. Disconnects can also occur in culture, which may resist changing existing business practices or focus on immediate bottom-line performance. Disconnects can also exist in management processes, where nothing in the annual planning or budgeting activities requires connecting the business strategies to the IT planning practices.

4. ***Are we balancing our strategic and tactical IT investments?*** People typically think of lights-on budgets as tactical, and "new" projects as strategic. However, in most IT activities there is a mix of tactical and strategic spending in both lights-on and new project budgets. The question for management is balancing the amount spent on each so that the strategic needs of the company

are met, as well as the tactical needs (usually meaning productivity and cost reduction). The answer to this question also demands a clear and common view of overall company objectives and strategies. IT managers need a common view with the senior manager team, and typically this is difficult to achieve.

For example, in a large consumer products company, the IT management team works closely with individual vice-presidents who are responsible for the major functional areas of the business. These functional managers do not have a clear consensus among themselves or with senior management on what the enterprise strategies are or, more importantly, the implications of those strategies for each functional area and their use of IT. Without a clear and common view of the company's strategic directions, IT does the tactical things demanded by the individual vice presidents preventing the productivity and competitive advances the company needs. (We will pay close attention to the ideas of balancing investments in our portfolio management discussions in subsequent chapters. The notion of "balance" covers not only strategic/tactical but also back-office versus front office, infrastructure versus applications, and risk management.)

These questions have been around in one form or another since IT entered mainstream business discussions. In the past, senior management teams looked to IT management for answers to the IT Impact Questions, but the questions are not simply about IT; they are connected to business as well. This is the core problem for the senior leadership team. While it may be convenient to look at IT as the silver bullet to produce results for the company, it is clear that IT is merely an enabler. For significant bottom-line results to occur, business management has to be intimately engaged. IT produces value by enabling business to make transformational changes—in internal processes, in products, and in outreach to the customers. In every case, the underlying business process has to change in order to produce value. Business and IT management have to work together on a common vision and in tandem to produce the technical solutions and business process changes. This is how value is produced.

EXAMPLES: ANSWERING THE QUESTIONS

Consider the example of a company that defines its strategic intentions[2] as: (1) growing sales and revenue through market share increase, (2) reducing product manufacturing cost, and (3) strategic acquisitions in its industry. In analyzing the company's IT "lights-on" budget, the result was shown to management with Exhibit 2.2.

The chart shows that only 42 percent of the ongoing lights-on budget strongly supports the company's three strategic intentions, while 39 percent of the budget has from no support to weak support of the strategic intentions. (This is in response to the question: "Are we getting sufficient value from our current IT resources?")

This also means that only 42 percent of the actions IT takes, in dollar terms, strongly support the company's three strategic intentions, while 39 percent weakly support those intentions.

What we see here is a company that is not taking the right actions and, therefore, not getting the right results from its IT investments. The management team now has decisions to make and actions to take. These decisions can take the form of reviewing where those poorly performing IT activities are and how they could be improved or abandoned or, alternatively, how the business units could improve their utilization of the IT *resources* being provided. The key is that questions are asked, answers are provided, and action can result. Of course, if no action actually occurs, then the exercise is not helpful.[3]

EXHIBIT 2.2   Application Portfolio Support for Strategic Intentions

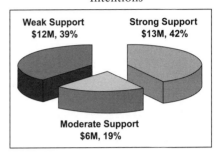

Consider another company that asked the question: "Are we investing our new IT resources in the right places?" In this case, the question focused on the new development budgets for projects. Exhibit 2.3 shows six strategic intentions for the company, and shows their relative importance to one another (expressed as a "weight"). The exhibit then shows the project investment dollars that strongly support those strategic intentions.

EXHIBIT 2.3   Investment Dollars in Strong Support of Strategic Intentions

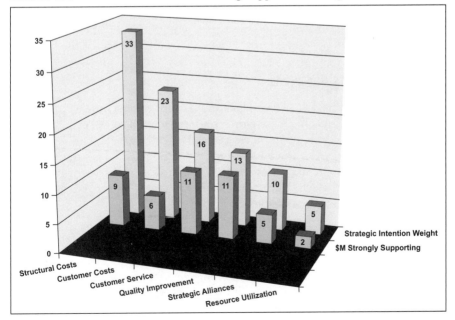

The interpretation is that the most project dollars, in terms of strong support of business strategic intentions, occurs for the middle two strategic intentions, and that the most important ones are not getting as much support. The good news is that the projects are supporting the company's strategic intentions. The bad news is that the proportion may not be as appropriate as company management might wish.[4]

One consequence is that the set of IT actions represented by the projects and their impact on strategic intentions is not optimally established. Management may wish to take action on the mix of projects to be undertaken. Another consequence is that management does understand what the IT actions will accomplish, in terms of bottom-line impact.

THE CONTEXTS FOR MANAGEMENT QUESTIONS ARE PLANNING AND BUDGETING PROCESSES

Management teams generally focus on IT when it comes time to plan and budget for IT spending. This comes to a head during the annual planning and budgeting cycles. As we ask the Affordability and Impact Questions, we must provide answers by working within the context of planning and budgeting, and link the process of answering the questions to those processes.

Planning Processes

As management establishes strategic and annual operating plans, IT affordability and impact is an important factor. From each business unit's perspective, it is a question of what IT will do for that unit with new projects and ongoing operations. From the enterprise perspective, it is a question of whether the overall costs are appropriate and affordable and how well IT supports the business.

Workable Budgets and Plans

A basic premise of this book is that plans and resources mean little until IT management takes the right actions, either by implementing new capabilities or supporting the directions the business takes. The rubber meets the road when budgets are available and actions are taken. For development projects, this means effective prioritization and project selection. For ongoing IT activities, it means appropriate support levels, infrastructure maintenance, and maintenance and support of the existing applications.

WHY ASK AFFORDABILITY AND IMPACT QUESTIONS?

The questions we posed above look at the company's strategies, ask about whether the strategies are being supported, and result, generally, in redressing gaps in spending. The questions' thrust is strategy first, then decisions, and then action.

IT is approaching 50% of many companies' capital budgets.[5] The proportion of corporate resources devoted to IT is rapidly rising, to 15% or more of revenues in some industries.[6] In many industries, IT-enabled services and processes have the capability to change the competitive landscape: consider the experiences of Wal-Mart, FedEx, and Charles Schwab. IT can remain a dominating issue for the senior management team for years, as evidenced by the experiences of many companies struggling with ERP, consuming enormous amounts of money and staff energy, and yet promising an impact across the board on business practices. Even in difficult economic times, IT is on the agenda, if for no other reason than when the economy is down, there is increased interest in controlling the costs of IT, which gives rise to assuring the most efficient use of IT resources, cost reduction, and validation of IT's value. In today's competitive and rapid paced economy, companies simply must get the maximum value from their IT investments.

There are also other views in the industry that we should consider. Nicholas Carr introduced a new point into the relationship between IT and the business, in an article in the *Harvard Business Review* titled "IT Doesn't Matter."[7] Carr suggests that IT is a commodity in most businesses, rather than a unique component of the company's strategic position in the industry. IT remains important, to be sure, as most businesses completely rely on IT for the conduct of their core business activities. But every business has access to IT, and the competitive, "strategic" advantage to be obtained from IT may no longer be a realistic objective for most management teams. In other words, there is no substantial reason for major investment in IT except to further enable the basic conduct of the business. Carr essentially recommends that management treat IT as a commodity and manage it accordingly. Among other things, this means "spending less" rather than spending more as a starting point for the management of IT. It also means focusing on cost and resulting efficiency of business processes, as well as addressing the risks.

This really is not a completely new idea. For example, Paul Strassmann wrote persuasively about his research that found little correlation between the level of expenditures competitors make in IT and their relative profitability. His "shotgun" charts documented, by industry, where each company stood in plotting bottom-line performance against IT investment levels. The charts were completely random.[8]

Jack Keen and Bonnie Digrius wrote an excellent book[9] that focused on finding ROI in every IT investment. As Keen and Digrius put it, for an individual project, everything is in the ROI. As a practical matter, this means finding the specific way the IT commodity (in project terms) reduces cost, finds some direct impact on revenue, or finds a connection to management goals.

We do not believe that "IT doesn't matter." IT is vital to most companies. The things IT enables—effectiveness and efficiency, new products, new means to markets—are certainly critical to the competitive health of companies. What does matter is that a company's investments in new IT projects and ongoing IT operations are consistent with management's strategies and effective in carrying them out.

We propose that, to be effective in managing IT, *companies need good answers to the questions about IT's affordability and impact, especially when IT is such an important part of senior management's agenda.*

But what if the answers to the IT Impact Questions are *"no"* or *"we don't know"?*

This often happens in even the most successful companies, when their management processes do not focus sufficiently on the questions and their answers, or fail to deal with their implications. This book is about five management practices that address the IT Impact Questions. These five NIE practice areas cover planning, innovation, prioritization, alignment, and performance measurement, and apply concepts of value, portfolio, and culture management.

TAKING ACTION

We have developed a simple business/IT stage model that describes where a company is in its management and use of IT. Our view is that the "right questions" depend on whether the company management can do anything with the answers, and this depends on the stage at which the company finds itself. Briefly, companies move through five stages with respect to IT. Stage 1, where the performance of ongoing IT activities such as the infrastructure and running existing applications, is at an acceptable service and quality level. If current infrastructure or applications are unreliable or of low quality in terms of accuracy, then asking questions about strategic support or affordability are irrelevant. This is because management will not be capable of responding effectively to the answers to the questions. The Stage 1 performance issues must be addressed first. See Chapter 4 for the ideas on how assessment of Operational Processes and Tasks can be done.

Stage 2 has to do with the performance of systems development. If current development efforts are substantially behind schedule or over budget, or if the results of development are ineffective in meeting business requirements, then asking questions about strategy are largely irrelevant, and questions of affordability are limited to operational tasks. See Chapter 6 for ideas on how to assess Development Processes and Tasks.

Stage 3 deals with the capability of the IT organization to respond to current tactical requirements, making the changes and doing the projects necessary to respond to those changing tactical requirements. If IT is unable to respond effectively, then asking questions about strategy is not relevant. Affordability issues are not helpful either, if the work being paid for cannot respond to tactical requirements.

Stage 4 deals with the ability to articulate and respond to strategic requirements. This includes the dimension of process change and change management. Again, if IT is not performing this well, then issues of strategic alignment are not as helpful as when they can perform well.

Stage 5 deals with IT's leadership in providing new strategies and directions to the company.

Filtering the "right questions" through the stages laid out helps define the agenda for addressing Right Decisions/Right Results. The goal is to control IT spending, and spend on the right things that will produce bottom-line impact.

The Impact Questions should drive down from the top of the model. We cannot get to the strategy-level issues (Stages 4 and 5) without dealing with the first-level questions. If IT is not performing, then asking about strategic investments is a waste of effort.

The Affordability Questions should drive up from the bottom, starting with operations, then development, then the tactical and strategic projects undertaken. This is because, first, that's where the money is, and second, that's where actions can be taken.

CHAPTER SUMMARY

Companies achieve great things when IT actually supports what company management thinks is important. This is critical, because it is not just IT acting alone, it is IT enabling what management thinks it wants to accomplish. This is the heart of what we want to accomplish in finding consistency and connection in management activities—to connect business strategy to IT action.

Our thrust is to connect IT investments to what is important to management, in ways that actually connect to the bottom line by consistently and persistently applying key ideas from planning through to performance management. By seeking the answers to the right questions, management is able to control IT expenses and improve IT's bottom-line impact.

Impact

- We translate our business strategies into IT actions that produce the right results.
- We invest in new IT resources in the right places.
- We get results, and sufficient value, from our current IT assets and resources.
- We balance our strategic and tactical investments.

Affordability

- We spend what we can afford.
- We reduce unnecessary IT costs.
- We redeploy unnecessary expenses to support needed projects.

The Strategy-to-Bottom-Line Value Chain and the NIE practices enable management to produce these answers to the right questions.

ASK THE RIGHT QUESTIONS: MANAGEMENT AGENDA

	Questions	Yes or No?	If No, What Is Our Plan for Correcting This?
Right Decisions	Are we investing new IT resources in the right places?		
	Do we know what we can afford?		
	Can we reduce unnecessary IT costs?		
	Can we redeploy expenses to support needed projects?		
Right Actions	Are we able to reduce the cost of poorly performing activities?		
	Are we able to translate our business strategies into IT actions that will produce the right results?		
Right Results	Are we getting results—and sufficient value—from all our lights-on resources?		
	Are we able to effectively control our IT costs?		

ADDITIONAL READING

The book's website contains additional information related to Chapter 2:

Website Note 1: IT and Economic Cycles

Website Note 2: IT's Value—A Definition

Website Note 3: IT, Bottom-Line Impact, and Government

Website Note 18: ROI and the IT Value Life Cycle

NOTES

1. We are indebted to Joe Barkley for putting words and meaning to this issue.
2. "Strategic Intentions" is a framework we use to define a company's objectives and strategies. The framework is described in detail in Chapter 3. See also Appendix C, "The Development of Strategic Intentions, with Examples."
3. This example is from the Alignment practice, described in Chapter 8.
4. This example is from the Prioritization practice, described in Chapter 8.
5. Capital spending data from Morgan Stanley Technology Research, March 2002.
6. Percentage revenue data from META Group and Metricnet 2002.
7. Nicholas G. Carr, "IT Doesn't Matter," *Harvard Business Review,* vol. 81, no. 5, May 2003, pp. 41–49.

8. See, for example, Paul Strassmann, *The Business Value of Computers* (New Canaan, CT: Information Economics Press, 1990), and, by the same author, *Information Productivity* (New Canaan, CT: Information Economics Press, 1999).

9. Jack Keen and Bonnie Digrius, *Making Technology Investments Profitable: ROI Road Map to Better Business Cases* (Hoboken, NJ: John Wiley and Sons, 2003).

CHAPTER 3

Connect to the Bottom Line

Managers improve IT's impact on the company's bottom line by controlling IT spending and evaluating all parts of the IT spend according to bottom-line impact. We define three basic ways that the total IT spend connects to the bottom line.

First, and most obviously, company money expended on IT is a cost to the company, so eliminating project work or reducing lights-on costs affects the bottom line. Business-driven prioritization and alignment exercises can achieve this.

Second, a new IT investment can directly produce revenues or reduce expenses, and thereby directly connect IT to the bottom line. The financial analyses on project business cases highlight this direct financial return. If management increases directly measurable ROI by choosing the right projects, the result shows directly on the bottom line. Doing so requires selecting only those projects with achievable cost reductions or revenue enhancements. Business-driven prioritization can achieve this, with appropriate selection of prioritization factors.

Control Spending and Maximize Impact on the Bottom Line	
1	Define the Goals
2	Ask the Right Questions
3	**Connect to the Bottom Line**
4	Understand Costs and Resources
5	Focus on the Right Things
6	Adopt Effective Process to Produce Action
7	Tackle the Practical Problems
8	Make the Right Decisions
9	Plan for the Right Results
10	Keep Score
11	Deal with Culture
12	Chart the Path to Implementation
13	Define What's Next
14	Answer the "So What?" Question

Third, and most critically, an IT expenditure can enable or support a business activity that itself impacts the bottom line. There also can be a direct cause-and-effect relationship between an IT expenditure and the success or failure of management's efforts to change the business in some way. This is the most powerful bottom-line connection, because to the extent that IT enables the success of management's strategies, it becomes a direct contributor to the overall efforts of the business to impact the bottom line.

The first and second categories, though real, are very much in the minority of opportunities in companies today. The biggest challenge, and opportunity, is controlling IT spend and improving bottom-line impact when projects and lights-on budgets do not produce their promised cost reduction or yield immediate financial returns. IT is at least one step removed from direct bottom-line impact. Business units apply IT in their business processes, and it is through those business processes that the company's expenses are reduced or revenues improved. In other words, IT's bottom-line impact is filtered through the activities of other functional areas of the business.

For new IT project investments, direct bottom-line impact is normally addressed in each project's business case. Jack Keen and Bonnie Digrius's book on business cases[1] deals effectively with this, laying out a powerful method for expressing a business case and defining bottom-line impact for an individual project. The method is based on making the strongest possible business case by connecting the project to the business through a variety of techniques including financial measures.

Our focus, however, is on the total IT spend, including all projects and lights-on expenses. The challenge is to use a *common* method to connect to the bottom line for all new projects and all components of the ongoing IT spend, and to determine how to control spending for the total IT spend.

We assume that acceptable business cases have been made for new IT projects. Our objective is to examine the complete new project portfolio *after* business cases for individual projects have been made and select the best ones from all the opportunities. For the lights-on portion of the IT spend, we assume that all the activities have relevance to the business, but this is an opportunity to eliminate or renew the lowest performing activities. We need tools and methods to work with the complete IT budget. The problem is not to justify an individual project; the problem is to choose the best portfolio of projects. Similarly, the problem is not to justify an individual line item in the lights-on budget; the problem is to allocate the ongoing lights-on budget to the best line items, and thereby improve overall bottom-line impact. This is how we control IT spending and improve bottom-line impact.

Our basic approach for connecting to the bottom line has three elements:

1. By prioritizing all IT investments in terms of bottom-line impact (including risk), the company improves overall bottom-line performance by choosing the high-impact investments and eliminating or reworking low-impact investments.

2. By aligning the lights-on IT spend (e.g., infrastructure, existing applications) to the business, the company improves overall bottom-line performance by changing or eliminating the low-impact activities.

3. By understanding the cost of elements of the IT spend and by assessing the performance of the lights-on IT spend in terms of technology, architecture, quality, and service level, the company improves overall bottom-line performance by eliminating costly, poorly performing IT activities.

In simpler times, managers would use financial analysis alone (e.g., ROI) to determine bottom-line impact for a proposed project. By extension, a portfolio of projects could be ranked solely by ROI results. But the problems with ROI and similar financial analysis techniques are well known, particularly in a portfolio context for ranking projects. Risk is not easily assessed on a consistent basis within a portfolio by solely using an ROI methodology. ROI is not easily computed on a consistent basis across widely different projects, particularly when nonfinancial benefits (e.g., improvements in quality or customer satisfaction) are included. Additionally, ROI is also not applicable to lights-on costs for applications and infrastructures. But the most critical problem with exclusive reliance on financial analysis is that ROI measures do not easily connect to management's strategies for the company's future.

We do not downplay ROI or other financial analysis, but treating "enabling" projects with financial evaluation methods alone will lead to serious decision errors. We do, however, put ROI into a larger context of overall IT spend and overall total impact of the complete portfolios of IT activities. We apply a more effective way to connect to the bottom line, one that includes financial computations such as ROI as one factor in evaluating IT investments. This way is based on a financial philosophy of shareholder value and is founded on the basic idea of cause and effect.

In this chapter, we lay out the basic principles of connecting to the bottom line based on cause and effect. (In the next chapter, we introduce the specifics of portfolio management, which is the framework within which we implement this basic approach.)

BOTTOM-LINE IMPACT BASED ON CAUSE AND EFFECT

The key to assessing bottom-line impact is determining cause and effect. Because IT is one step removed from the bottom line, we look for the chain of connection between the IT expenditure (whether project or lights-on expense) and direct bottom-line impact. "If we do project A, then we will cause a change in business process B, which then will translate into reduced expenses C and/or improved revenue D." This is the logical flow of cause and effect. Or, for a "strategic" investment, "if we do project A, then we will cause a change in our business process B or a new business process C, or create a new product D, which will cause our customers to buy more from us or allow us to raise the price, etc., which creates improved revenue E." This is strategic cause-and effect thinking.[2] See Exhibit 3.1.

The key to cause and effect on the bottom line is management action. The cause-and-effect logic above exists only in an ideal world. Of course, the real-world causality is "If we *successfully* do project A, then we will *hopefully* cause a change in business process B, which *if successful and if the result effectively connects* with the rest of the things going on with the business, will translate into reduced expenses C and/or improved revenue D." The words in italics reflect risk and the vagaries of whether and how individual business units actually apply new tools and harvest the resulting benefits. This is the crux of the issue. Whether IT investments, either projects or ongoing, produce bottom-line impact is completely dependent on the behavior of the management team and individual business units. Simply buying infrastructure, building IT systems, or purchasing software means nothing by itself unless business units take action and managers actually change what they do. Action is key.

EXHIBIT 3.1   Cause-and-Effect to the Bottom Line

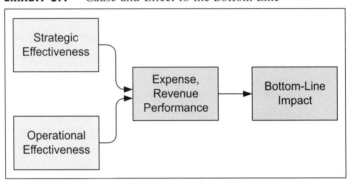

*The key to bottom-line impact is **future** management action.* What counts is what management will do in the future with a new IT investment, or with existing IT resources. At a low level, this is the basis of change management: to successfully cause the needed change in a business process or business behavior, and to achieve the cost reduction or revenue improvement. The key, however, is that business cases for projects and justification for ongoing expenses are completely dependent on estimating the future actions of management. It does not matter what the business case says, if management doesn't do anything or, more realistically, doesn't do enough to actually accomplish the goals of the project. It doesn't matter what the expense justification is for infrastructure or ongoing applications, if management doesn't effectively use the IT capability and apply it effectively in the business. Future management action is a moving target, greatly affected by changing business conditions and, more fundamentally, changing management teams.

CAUSE AND EFFECT IS BASED ON MANAGEMENT'S INTENTIONS

Fundamentally, by focusing on strategic intentions, we are predicting what management will do in the future in order to use IT in the business in the ways that create bottom-line impact. Management's intentions apply to the use of a given new IT project, and to the use of ongoing IT resources such as applications and infrastructures.

We use the term *intentions* to reflect what management will do in the future. (In Chapter 5, we define the specifics of tools using strategic intentions as the base. Here, we establish what management intentions are based on.)

The Shareholder Value financial philosophy provides a strong platform for management intentions.[3] Briefly, a company performs better if it improves its performance of its strategies (strategic effectiveness) or improves the performance of its operations (operational effectiveness). By extension, bottom-line impact is created when the company improves its strategic and operational effectiveness. *Therefore, what management intends to do in terms of improving strategic or operational effectiveness should impact the bottom line.* We call this *strategic intentions.*

Our approach is to show the cause and effect between the IT spend, both projects and lights-on expenditures, and the bottom line by measuring IT's cause-and-effect connection to management's strategic intentions.

This addresses the key problem of predicting management's intentions for the future. By obtaining agreement on what those intentions are, and by using performance measurement to track this, we can directly establish IT's cause-and-effect impact on the bottom line.

MANAGEMENT'S STRATEGIC INTENTIONS

Management's strategies and plans to improve strategic and operational effectiveness are its strategic intentions.[4]

Senior management teams make decisions and allocate resources according to their vision and commitments to a set of strategies, whether explicit or informal. These strategies are intended to increase the company's success, ultimately measured in terms of profitability Companies can have formal and explicit strategy statements, or they can have an informal set of strategies that are implied by management's decisions. (We typically find a set of formal strategies that are explicitly stated and saluted (often in a slick publication) but, in reality, are subordinate to the unstated strategies that drive actual decisions and actions.)

We like Michael Porter's general definitions for operational and strategic effectiveness, and use them to define management's strategic intentions:

- **Operational effectiveness** means performing similar activities better than rivals perform them.

- **Strategic effectiveness** means performing different activities from rivals' or performing similar activities in different ways.[5]

Operational Effectiveness includes:	Strategic Effectiveness includes:
☐ Efficiency	☐ Product/service development and positioning
☐ Process improvement	
☐ Quality improvement	☐ Customer access
☐ Management information	☐ Targeting customer segments

Operational and Strategic Effectiveness

For example, an insurance company has strategic intentions of: (1) increasing its sales performance through partnering with other financial service firms, (2) adding to customer loyalty through improved service and improved products, and (3) reducing administrative overhead through innovative uses of technology and consolidation of headquarter locations. The management team will take actions based on these strategic intentions; if the strategies are successful, they will result in improved revenues and/or reduced costs, and improved financial performance.

As Michael Porter's definition states, operational effectiveness includes efficiency (meaning cost and productivity), quality improvement, and process improvement. Strategic effectiveness includes customer and product/service issues.

We go beyond Porter's definitions of strategic effectiveness to a more general definition. Consider an example of strategic intentions as shown in Exhibit 3.2. These are the strategic intentions of a company engaged in the production and sale of a basic commodity.

EXHIBIT 3.2   Examples of Strategic Intentions

Strategic Intention Name	Strategic Intention Goals	Strategic Intention Metrics	Weight
Focus on Specific, Narrow Markets	• Focus on markets in which the company can profitably compete • Build strategic partnerships with key customers	• Market share in specific markets • Profitability in specific markets	30
Improve Efficiency through Common Business Practices	• Employ best practices throughout the company • Reduce the unique systems and processes in each operating location	• Percent of standard systems used throughout company • Percent of standard processes in use throughout the company	10
Be the lowest-cost supplier in focused markets	• Reduce the administrative, manufacturing, and operations costs of the company • Optimize purchasing power	• Production throughput • Net delivered cost of product	40
Grow through Acquisition	• Increase the capability of the company to rapidly integrate new applications and operations, with decreased cost	• Time to integrate a new acquisition or operation	20

These strategic intentions conform with Porter's definition of strategic effectiveness. But the point is that IT will connect to the bottom line *to the extent that IT's current applications, new projects, and infrastructures support the achievement of these strategic intentions.*

When IT makes the company more successful in achieving its strategic intentions, which improve the company's operational effectiveness and strategic effectiveness, then IT impacts the bottom line.

PRINCIPLES OF IT'S BOTTOM-LINE IMPACT

This section builds the base for cause and effect to the bottom line. (Note that "agency mission performance" can be used as a government and nonprofit organization's surrogate for bottom line, or profitability.)

- *Bottom-Line Principle 1:* IT's bottom-line impact is based on its direct contribution to improved profitability.

- *Bottom-Line Principle 2:* IT's direct contribution to improved profitability is based on improving the company's operational and strategic effectiveness.

- *Bottom-Line Principle 3:* IT improves strategic and operational effectiveness by carrying out management's strategic intentions.

◆

Bottom-Line Principle 1: IT's *bottom-line impact is based on its direct contribution to profitability.*

Of course, improved bottom-line performance—that is, profitability—is the fundamental goal for companies. Whatever we do with IT, at the heart of it, we do it to directly or indirectly improve bottom-line performance. This is the result that is always being sought by the management team. For government or nonprofit entities, the equivalent goal is mission performance; whatever we do with IT, we do with the expectation of improving the agency's mission performance.

The problem is: What constitutes direct contribution to profitability? The easiest answer may be direct cost reduction; when IT reduces costs, then it directly contributes to profitability. IT could produce revenue directly by offering services directly to the customer, as well. For example, IT could be the mechanism for selling information from a database. But beyond these simple examples, the idea of direct contribution to profitability becomes murkier. Where IT's direct contribution to cost reduction or revenue improvement can be measured, it should be, reflecting IT's financial contribution. However, this is the minority of situations. In most cases, IT's contribution is reflected in improvements in some aspect of the business's organizational performance.

The reason for this is that IT is, fundamentally, an *enabler* of business activity. IT may enable managers to manage better, or marketers to target more profitable markets or customers. IT may enable reengineering of business processes to reduce time cycles, and therefore reduce errors, or improve service quality, or increase customer satisfaction. But in all these cases, IT's contribution is to *enable* a more efficient or effective business activity, which *in turn* results in improved profitability. IT is a partner in the bottom-line result, but it isn't the only factor.

Traditional IT financial analysis works to translate IT's enabling character into concrete estimates of reduced cost or increased income and thereby produce a measure of IT's contribution to profitability, or ROI.[6] This is laudable but it confuses IT's basic contribution of enabling and improving business activity with the financial measure of its contribution.

Bottom-Line Principle 1 states that IT's bottom-line impact is based on contribution to profitability, with the understanding that directly measuring it may be difficult.

◆

Bottom-Line Principle 2: *IT's direct contribution to improved profitability is based on improving the company's operational and strategic effectiveness.*

IT can certainly enable improvements in a company's operations. Improvements can take the form of cost reduction, time reduction, improved flexibility, increased quality, and so forth. If these business operational improvements reduce cost or improve revenue, IT will have contributed to profitability. Such improvements may be measured by estimating the amount of cost reduction or revenue improvement, and consequently an ROI can be calculated. In other cases the process improvement can be measured (e.g., in terms of time, quality, error rate, etc.) but the connection to profitability may be less clear (e.g., improves customer satisfaction, or customer loyalty, etc.).

IT also can enable the success of a company's strategy. For example, for a medical insurance company, a key strategy is increasing customer loyalty through improved customer service. If IT provides the environment and information for improved customer service, or if IT enables the reengineering of business processes to improve customer service, then IT has bottom-line impact because it enables the success of the strategy which, in turn, will result in improved profitability.

To reiterate, IT's bottom-line impact is based on: (1) improving the company's operational effectiveness and (2) improving the company's strategic effectiveness. In the first case, the operational performance improvement in some cases is measurable, and possibly directly connected to profitability. In the second case, the strategic effectiveness is connected to the bottom line through management's intentions—through the strategy—to improve company performance.

The underlying idea is, again, cause and effect, based on a bottom-line impact chain concept. The direct cause of an improvement may be IT enabling a basic capability, such as management information or reduced time cycle for a process. The effect of this capability is improving a business process (e.g., in terms of cost or cycle time reduction) or achieving a strategy (e.g., improved customer retention). The critical element is the definition of the cause/effect connection, or bottom-line impact chain, between the things IT enables, as well as the ultimate connection to the bottom line.

Over the past two decades, there has been a remarkable convergence of thinking on this point. For example, the original *Information Economics* focused on justifying and prioritizing IT investments based on management factors[7] such as strategic match, competitive advantage, competitive response, and management information in conjunction with ROI or other financial measures. These management factors were adopted precisely because a company's financial performance is most directly improved through improving these performance drivers.

Shareholder Value and Economic Value Added (EVA), emerging in the late 1980s, expressed this idea directly. Although these are financial disciplines, they recognize the cause-and-effect linkages of activities such as product development, marketing initiatives, and cost reduction programs as the drivers of financial performance. McTaggart states, "Managing to improve shareholder bottom-line impact means generating, choosing, and implementing the best alternatives for any business strategy or operational issue."[8] This is a key point for us as well: generating (via Strategic Demand/Supply Planning and Innovation), choosing (via Prioritization and Alignment), and implementing (via Culture Management and Performance Measurement) the *alternatives* with the best bottom-line impact.

These alternatives fall into two general categories: *strategic effectiveness factors* and *operational effectiveness factors*. These are the causes, and financial performance is the effect.

In our work with clients, we frequently use a diagram (shown in Exhibit 3.1) which is adapted from bottom-line impact management and shareholder bottom-line impact literature that illustrates this relationship. What matters are those things that most directly influence strategic effectiveness and operational effectiveness. By managing to improve those effectiveness factors (the causes) through information technology, we will have contributed to the company's overall financial performance (the effects). By prioritizing, aligning, planning, and measuring IT's performance with strategic and operational effectiveness as the focus, we can improve and communicate the bottom-line impact of IT to the enterprise.

We cannot overstate the importance of this point. The identification of the cause-and-effect factors affecting strategic effectiveness and operational effectiveness is the basis for defining strategic intentions for the NIE prioritization and alignment practices; this underlies our approach to integrated planning. See Exhibit 3.3, which emphasizes the cause-and-effect relationships.

Other authors have reached similar conclusions. Kaplan and Norton's work on the Balanced Scorecard is based on cause-and-effect linkages between customer-, internal process- and people-related measures, and financial performance. Their notion of "leading" and "lagging" indicators is, at heart, an elaboration of cause-and-effect relationships. Also consider Michael Porter's contributions to the understanding of competitive strategy. He defined generic strategies of cost-leadership, differentiation, and focus. In developing these ideas in his 1996 *Harvard Business Review* article, Porter remarked on the difficulty companies have in defining and executing strategy: "The root of the problem is the failure to distinguish between operational effectiveness and strategy. The question of productivity, quality, and speed has spawned . . . management tools . . . and bit by bit, (they) have taken the place of strategy."[9] His point is that operational effectiveness—things like productivity, quality, and speed—are important, but strategy (and, in our words, strategic effectiveness) is equally important. Porter echoes McTaggart's point: "The essence of strategy is in the

EXHIBIT 3.3   Improvements in Effectiveness Produce
Revenue/Expense Improvement which
Produces Bottom-Line Impact

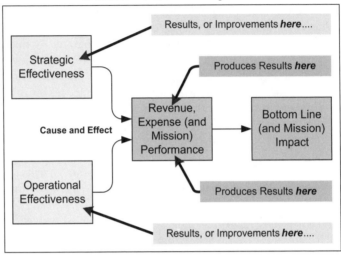

activities—choosing to perform activities differently or to perform different activities than rivals."[10] The key is *choosing* among alternatives, which is the heart of integrated planning, and following through on the cause-and-effect chain to implement IT solutions that support and enable those choices.

This defines the cause and effect between IT enabling improvements in operational effectiveness or strategic effectiveness, and the company's bottom line.

◆

Bottom-Line Principle 3: IT improves strategic and operational effectiveness by carrying out management's strategic intentions.

By focusing on strategic and operational effectiveness, management is encouraged to focus on the company's bottom-line impacts. That is, management has to define its strategic intentions and what it intends to do to improve the company's performance through those strategic intentions. At the same time, management defines the basis for its operational goals—the improvements in cost, performance, customer satisfaction, product quality, and all the other dimensions of the company's activities. Again, management defines its objectives for such improvement, always with an eye toward improving financial performance by improving operational effectiveness.

This is bottom-line impact-based management. By extension, the NIE practices apply these ideas to IT and the contributions IT makes toward strategic and operational effectiveness.

For example, in prioritization, the management team assesses how each IT project increases strategic effectiveness or operational effectiveness. (See, for example, Exhibit 3.4. In this exhibit, the six strategic intentions cover the company's intentions about both strategy and operational improvement.) In Alignment, the management team considers how the IT lights-on spend connects to strategic and operational effectiveness. (Chapter 8 describes both the Prioritization and Alignment practices.) In Strategic Demand/Supply Planning and in Innovation, the objective is to define exactly what IT can do to promote improvised effectiveness. (Chapter 9 describes the Strategic Demand/Supply Planning and Innovation practices.)

EXHIBIT 3.4   Dollars in New Development, in Support of Strategic Intentions

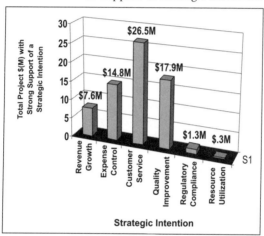

SUMMARY AND ADDITIONAL IMPLICATIONS

We have made four basic points. First, our objective is to control the IT spend and improve IT's bottom-line performance. Second, we do this through improving the company's operational and strategic effectiveness. Third, these improvements are represented by management's strategic intentions, and fourth, we connect IT to the bottom line by directly supporting those strategic intentions. We can have direct connections through immediate cost reduction or revenue enhancement, but the real challenge and opportunity is to make the connection for the entire IT spend.

Implications for Project Business Cases

Improving the company's operational and strategic effectiveness is the key to IT's bottom-line impact. Management's strategic intentions express how the company intends to improve them. Therefore, the business case justification for each development and enhancement project needs to clearly state exactly how the project supports management's strategic intentions and exactly how the project will therefore improve the company's operational or strategic effectiveness. This, of course, is connected to performance measurement, with the metrics that track operational and strategic effectiveness and management's strategic intentions. This also is connected to planning in terms of how strategic intentions are defined, and to prioritization in terms of making project investment decisions.

All this illustrates the importance of a common framework like the Strategy-to-Bottom-Line Value Chain, and the basic alignment and affordability goals expressed in Chapter 1.

Connections to Financial Performance

Of course, IT can produce direct impact to the bottom line. ROI computations (or the many variants of ROI) hope to exactly measure this impact, and where direct cost reductions or revenues are created, this is appropriate and encouraged by NIE practices. But the other connections, made by cause and effect, are equally or more important. The real leverage that management has in improving financial performance is through its strategic intentions. Right Decisions/Right Results through NIE practices makes both a reality. The opportunities to use financial measurements for bottom-line impacts, including using the new advances in option theory, risk management, and similar developments, can be included in the NIE practices.

Business Process and Operations: A Big Opportunity

It should be obvious that when we talk about "controlling IT spend," we are only talking about from 2 percent to maybe 10 percent of the total corporate budget. Most of our interest focuses on the impact IT has on the rest of the company, in terms of reducing those company costs and improving strategic effectiveness.

One major IT impact, of course, is on the back-office company activities. These can be from 10 percent to as much as 50 percent or more of the company's total expense budget. In this chapter, we express this impact in terms of improving operational effectiveness. That presumably results in lower cost and, consequently, *bottom-line* impact.

The big opportunity is to apply Right Decisions/Right Results concepts and the five NIE practices *directly to the company's business processes* which have many of the same characteristics as IT systems and applications. We can construct portfolios of business processes and apply alignment and portfolio assessments such as service and quality to them. We can prioritize changes to them, and we can put performance measurement metrics on them. In short, we can apply the same kind of management decisions directly to business processes and accomplish substantial impact on the company bottom line.

This is beyond the immediate scope of this book. But the implications, and direct applicability, of the Value Chain and NIE practices to business process is a big opportunity.

The Connection to Performance Measurement

For Right Decisions/Right Results, Performance Measurement is critical in validating and verifying the cause-and-effect relationships that were assumed during the strategy and planning processes. Historically, IT performance measurement has focused on the operational aspects of IT, with measures that report performance in IT terms. For NIE, performance measurement focuses on IT's performance relative to business operational and strategic effectiveness. The role of performance measurement is to track IT's contributions in *financial* terms and in strategic and operational effectiveness terms. Both are important, and the latter are important in establishing the strategic connection to financial performance.

CONNECT TO THE BOTTOM LINE: MANAGEMENT AGENDA

Questions for management about IT's connection to, and impact on, the bottom line:

Management Question	Yes or No?	If No, What Is Our Plan for Correcting This?
Do we know our strategic intentions?		
Does IT demonstrably support our strategic intentions?		
Are IT investments prioritized against strategic intentions?		
Does the entire IT spend, including development, operations, maintenance, and services, align with strategic intentions?		
Can IT reduce unnecessary expenditures?		
Are we evaluating lights-on budgets against strategic intentions?		
Do both IT and business managers participate effectively in these management processes?		

ADDITIONAL READING

This book's website contains additional information for Chapter 3:

Website Note 8: Gap Analysis: Closing the Disconnect between Business and IT

Website Note 9: Building an IT Profit Model

Website Note 13: Our Use of Shareholder Value

There is also related information for Chapter 3 in the appendices:

Appendix C: The Development of Strategic Intentions, with Examples

NOTES

1. Jack M. Keen and Bonnie Digrius, *Making Technology Investments Profitable: ROI Road Map to Better Business Cases* (Hoboken, NJ: John Wiley and Sons, 2002).

2. We do not ignore "mandatory" investments, enabling infrastructure investments, and so forth. We are setting up the cause-and-effect logic, which can be applied in all these cases.

3. See Website Note 13 on Shareholder Value. Our use of shareholder value focuses on the cause-and-effect relationship between management actions and ultimate bottom-line impact. As the note points out, we do not require the financial decisions components of shareholder value.

4. See Gary Hamel and C.K. Prahalad, "Strategic Intent," *Harvard Business Review*, May–June 1989. Our use of "strategic intentions" began as "management factors" in the original *Information Economics* work in the mid-1980s, and is parallel to the work on strategic intent reported in this article.

5. Michael E. Porter, "What Is Strategy?" *Harvard Business Review*, November–December 1996, p. 62.

6. For most of this book, we use the term *ROI* as a generic label covering financial computations of expense, revenue, and return.

7. See Appendix C for examples of strategic intentions in business and government. See Chapter 4 for further description of strategic intentions/management factors and an example of their application in prioritization.

8. James M. McTaggart, Peter W. Kontes, and Michael C. Mankins, *The Value Imperative: Managing for Superior Shareholder Returns* (New York: The Free Press, 1994), p. 49.

9. Michael E. Porter, "What Is Strategy?" *Harvard Business Review*, November–December 1996, pp. 113–118.

10. Ibid., p. 115.

CHAPTER 4

Understand Costs and Resources

This chapter describes portfolio management and introduces some of its uses in the Strategy-to-Bottom-Line Value Chain and the New Information Economics practices.

The idea of managing IT as a set of portfolios has been around for three decades. Most prominently, Warren McFarlan advanced the idea in a *Harvard Business Review* article in 1981,[1] where he focused on investment decisions, risk management, and portfolio classifications. NIE practices use portfolios as a tool for obtaining and managing information about applications, infrastructure, services, and management activities.

Control Spending and Maximize Impact on the Bottom Line	
1	Define the Goals
2	Ask the Right Questions
3	Connect to the Bottom Line
4	**Understand Costs and Resources**
5	Focus on the Right Things
6	Adopt Effective Process to Produce Action
7	Tackle the Practical Problems
8	Make the Right Decisions
9	Plan for the Right Results
10	Keep Score
11	Deal with Culture
12	Chart the Path to Implementation
13	Define What's Next
14	Answer the "So What?" Question

INTRODUCTION

Portfolios are collections of resources. Portfolio Management, applied in NIE practices, is a powerful tool for planning and decision-making about IT investments and resources.

In the financial world, a portfolio is a set of financial investments and resources such as stocks and bonds, held by an individual or organization. The portfolio also contains information about the investments and resources, such as number of shares, current value, and when the asset was acquired. In IT, a portfolio is a set of IT investments and resources, together with information about them. Each line item in the portfolio is a separate investment or resource, such as an application, an infrastructure component, an IT service, or a management activity.

Exhibit 4.1 is an example of a template for portfolio information.[2] Each row is an individual member of the portfolio, such as an application or an IT service. In addition to basic information about the line item (name of line item, a size or quantity indicator, and costs/resources consumed), information about service and quality, the risks, and bottom-line impact is specified in the template.

Exhibit 4.2 is an example of an application portfolio. Each line item is an application currently in use by the company. The purpose of portfolio management is to enable management analysis and decision-making about the individual elements of the portfolio. For example, in the portfolio listing shown in

EXHIBIT 4.1 Basic Portfolio Template

Basic Information			Service and Quality				Risk and Uncertainty				Value/State		
(A Portfolio line item is an individual application, infrastructure component, service, or management activity)	Quantity	Costs or Resources Consumed ($ or FTE)	Functionality	Accuracy	Availability	Responsiveness	Business	Technology	Organizational	Project	Technical Assessment	Strategic Alignment	ROI
Item 1													
Item 2													
Item 3													

EXHIBIT 4.2 Application Portfolio Example

Applications Portfolio								
Application	Unit of Work	Category	Cost ($millions)	Metric	Alignment Value	Service Level	Quality	Intensity of Use
Sales Force Automation	# Transactions	S	3	Trans/Day	25	3	1	Low
Sales Decision Support	# Transactions	S	1	Invoice Days	42	5	4	Low
Sales/Marketing Database	# Payments	S	3	$ In Process	12	1	2	High
Accounts Payable	# Invoices	B	5	Call Wait	39	1	2	Med
Financial Consolidations	# E-Inquiries	B	3	Billing Days	16	4	2	High
Five-Year Customer History	# Clients	S	1	Client Proc Qual	43	2	2	Med
Marketing Geographic Planning	# Sales	S	3	Inquiries	11	1	1	High
Human Resources Planning	# Retained	B	1	Retention Rate	15	1	2	Med
General Ledger	# Accounts	B	1	Customer Sat.	32	2	4	Low
Customer Information	# Account Inquiries	S	4	Percent Online Data	15	2	3	Med

Exhibit 4.2, a manager can correlate the cost of the application (column 4) with its Service Level and Quality (columns 7 and 8). In this example, the highest-cost application (Accounts Payable) is also almost the lowest quality and service. The manager could ask why is the company spending so much to use a resource (the application) that performs so poorly?

This example, however, does not demonstrate the real power of portfolio analysis. Rather than examine an individual case, a portfolio enables management to look at the entire portfolio holistically and identify the *set* of resources that are poorest performing, or weakest in quality, and so forth.

Exhibit 4.3 captures the intent of this analysis. The exhibit lists a portfolio of applications, ordered in "business impact" sequence. The items at the top are those that have the highest business impact.

EXHIBIT 4.3 Portfolio Management Objectives: Improve Performance of the Portfolio

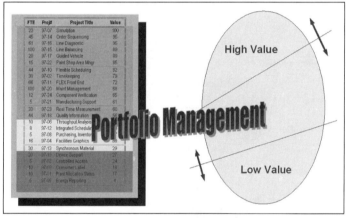

In this example, the purpose of portfolio management is to *reduce the number of low-impact applications.* By examining the entire set of lowest-value applications, management can determine which should be abandoned or replaced. Further, combining business impact information with cost information could focus on the major targets of opportunity for improvement, which would be those low-impact applications that have high cost.

ORIGINS OF PORTFOLIO MANAGEMENT

Portfolio management originated as a general approach to managing a set of financial resources.

The term "portfolio management" originated in financial asset management. Fifty years ago, the economist Harry Markowitz introduced the idea (and won the Nobel Prize in 1990) as a way to manage a set of financial investments. His conception included the mathematics to evaluate each individual investment in a consistent way, evaluating returns and risks.[3]

Today, most people are familiar with portfolios as an ingredient of personal financial management. Exhibit 4.4 shows a typical portfolio presentation for an individual's investments. The presentation gives the individual an idea of the present allocation of resources to different types of investments. The underlying idea is that the individual may wish to manage the investments by setting target percentages for each type of investment; the target percentage may change with different investors and different investment objectives.

EXHIBIT 4.4   Example of Simple Portfolio Management in Personal Finance

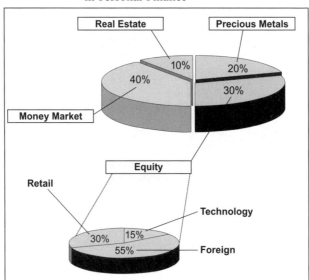

The idea of portfolio management has since been applied in many business functions. In a strategic planning context, the Boston Consulting Group applied the idea of portfolios as a way to manage and assess the lines of business (or strategic business units) that a corporation may hold. As a result of their work, the terms "star," "cash cow," and "dog" became parts of a common jargon for defining the potential a line of business may have. Other business functions also adopted this idea. Many marketing departments, for example, use portfolio management to manage and assess marketing campaigns and products. Some product development activities use it to manage and assess their portfolios of product development projects.

In IT management, managing information technology resources as a set of portfolios is an idea that has been emerging for 30 years. The idea originated in the 1970s, with the work of Warren McFarlan[4] and others, who wrote extensively about the idea, applying it to application development portfolios. More recently, the federal government has promoted the idea of portfolio management as a senior management tool for prioritizing and managing application development projects.[5]

IT PORTFOLIO MANAGEMENT IN PRIORITIZATION

In the mid-1980s, we applied portfolios and portfolio management ideas to IE Prioritization.[6] Essentially, Prioritization works on the individual items that make up a portfolio: Which are the highest priority projects, and which should we invest in?

One problem we faced was that application development really isn't a single thing, subject to a single set of rules. Some application development projects represent new strategic development, while other projects only enhance the capabilities of existing applications. Still other projects exist simply for the maintenance and support of existing applications. Strategic and enhancement projects are typically mid-size to large projects. They usually result from planning and should be connected to business strategy. Maintenance projects are typically very small; they are usually not the result of planning but rather responses to needs that pop up as an application matures, typically not in support of a business strategy but rather in support of an application and the business process it supports. In the context of Prioritization, these differences cause problems if we attempt to apply the same rules and processes. See Exhibit 4.5.

EXHIBIT 4.5   Early Portfolio Management in *Information Economics*—Separate Pools of Application Development

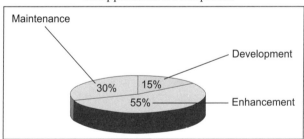

The practical problem for many companies is that the dollars spent on maintenance projects are much larger than the development projects costs and often are not easily prioritized by business impact. Whereas development projects can be prioritized effectively by looking at the strategic intentions of the company, maintenance projects are oriented more toward keeping the doors open and the lights on. Many were necessary simply to keep key applications up and running.

As a result, in *Information Economics* we developed the concept of "pools" to give management an understanding of their investment patterns. Pools are defined according to the specific requirements of the company, but most typically have been *development, enhancement,* and *maintenance.* (What constitutes maintenance compared to enhancement is one of those historical discussions that may never be finally settled. Most companies use some kind of project size, such as 30 days or less, for maintenance.) These pools, of course, were portfolios, as shown in Exhibit 4.5.

To manage these portfolios, management first decides on the *size* of each pool (e.g., in dollars or in development staff count), and then prioritizes projects *within* each pool. For each pool, or portfolio, the same Prioritization rules (e.g., risk assessments, decision factors, and valuation techniques) are applied to all members of the portfolio. Having multiple portfolios allows different rules for each portfolio. Within a given portfolio, however, the same rules are applied.

From this early development of portfolio ideas, *Information Economics* and the NIE Prioritization practice have further evolved the application of portfolios and portfolio management to address several difficult problems. For example, companies with multiple lines of business (LOB), or strategic business units (SBU), can have difficulty in prioritizing projects across LOBs or SBUs, particularly if project implementation occurs by separate IT units within those LOBs or SBUs. Using separate portfolios for LOBs makes it possible to prioritize and allocate resources separately. Similarly, companies can find it difficult to prioritize IT infrastructure projects together with strategic business projects. Again, using separate portfolios for applications and infrastructure can make prioritizing possible. Similarly, mixing back-office applications with front-office strategic applications can be troublesome in planning and in prioritization. Portfolio management offers a way to prioritize these applications in two separate portfolios.

In the next sections, we discuss how the solutions to these difficult problems have evolved into a complete portfolio management approach to IT resources and investments as implemented in NIE practices.

PORTFOLIOS IN NIE PRACTICES

Portfolios are the foundation for NIE practices.

We stated in Chapter 1 that our goal is to translate the company's business strategies and goals into the right IT actions to produce the right bottom-line impact. This is done by effective planning, appropriate resource decisions, and workable budgets and operational plans. The tools of portfolio management, implemented through the NIE practices, make this possible.

Development/enhancement and lights-on portfolios support NIE Planning, Innovation, Prioritization, Alignment, and Performance Measurement practices with consistent and complete information about IT resources. The information includes specifics such as how many applications there are and where they are being used, quality and service levels, and information about the business impact. See Exhibit 4.6.

EXHIBIT 4.6 Portfolios in NIE Practices

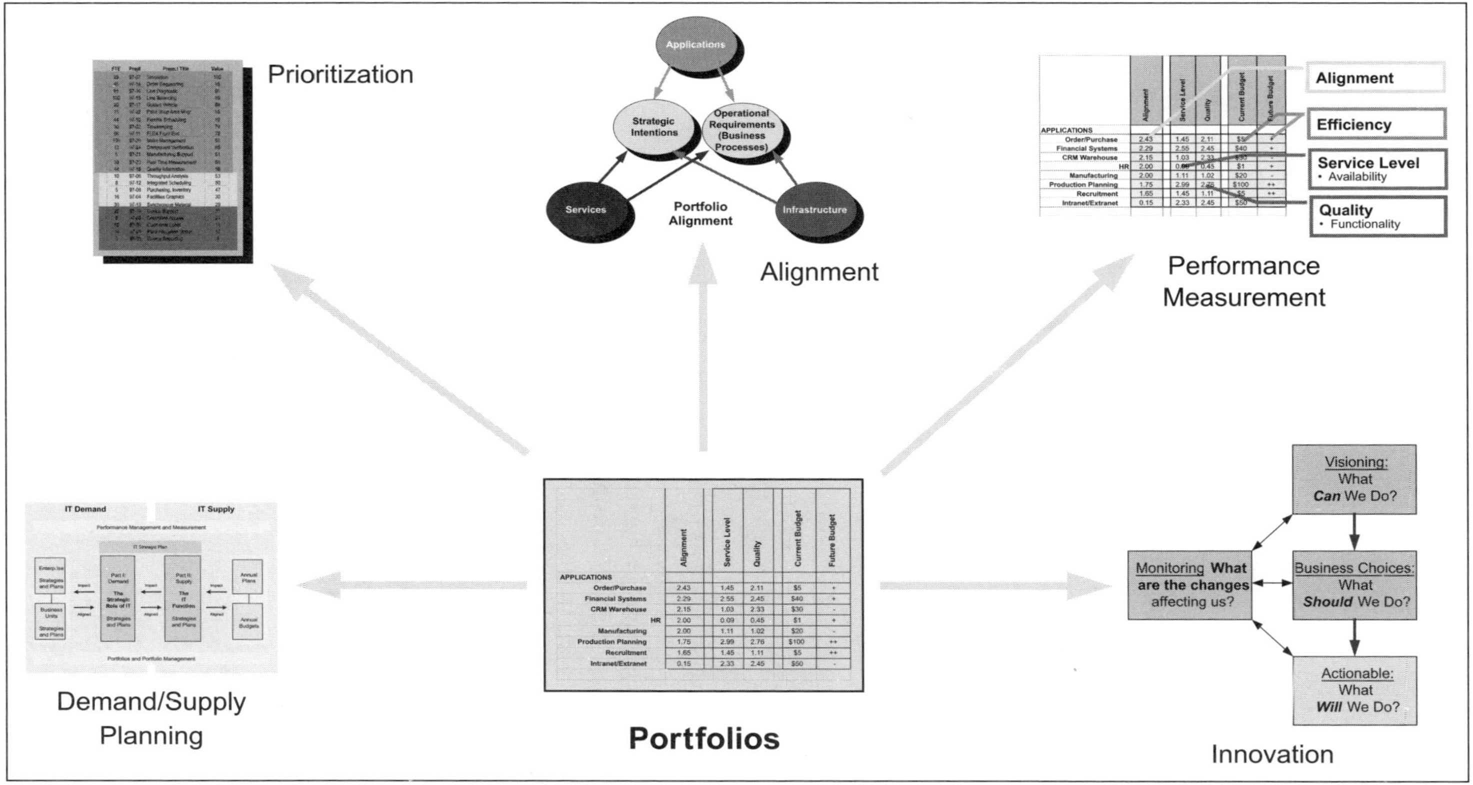

Each NIE practice makes extensive use of portfolio information. For example, the planning practice uses the assessments of quality and service, and the bottom-line impact of the lights-on applications portfolio, to develop the IT strategic plan. Portfolio management also, and perhaps equally as importantly, connects the NIE practice outcomes to the annual planning and budgeting processes of the company.

This is a core part of NIE. We believe that the outcomes of NIE practices must affect the behavior of the IT organization and the company; this can only be done if budgets and annual plans are directly affected. Portfolios and portfolio management make this possible.[7]

Applying Portfolio Information in NIE Practices

By using portfolio information, applying NIE tools such as Prioritization, Alignment, and Performance Measurement, management can make effective investment decisions.

Portfolio information can be used to give management understanding of IT investments and enable decisions about the investments. In this way, the NIE practice for the use of portfolios most closely mimics the financial investment origins of portfolio management.

Putting IT resources into portfolios permits management to analyze the line items within the portfolios using the portfolio management tools in Right Decisions/Right Results. For example, by characterizing line items in the application portfolio (in the lights-on budget) by quality and service levels, management can determine the highest and lowest quality and service level applications. This provides the input to management decision-making about renewing or abandoning applications.

Portfolio information enables management to:

- Prioritize new investments.

- Understand the allocation of resources in both new investments and in ongoing lights-on expenses.

- Set targets for resources in the lights-on budget, in terms of service and quality and in terms of cost and cost reduction.

- Evaluate the performance of portfolio elements.

- Cull the lights-on portfolios of low-quality or poorly performing or overly costly elements.

- Establish strategy for the renewal of lights-on portfolio elements.

By doing these things with portfolios, managers avoid case-by-case assessments by using the same rules for all elements. By using IT portfolios and NIE practices (as described in the next chapters), management can determine whether:

- The IT resources applied are at the right level.

- Any applications, services, or infrastructure elements need renewal or elimination.

- The set of investments in IT match the current needs of the business.

- The set of investments serve its long-term strategic intentions.

- The mix of investments in the portfolios are reasonably balanced with regard to service and quality.

- Some IT resources are underperforming.

Portfolios and Resource Pools in the Complete IT Spend

We want to be clear in our vocabulary and usage of "portfolios" and "resource pools." (This vocabulary and usage is described in detail in the "Four IT Portfolio Concepts" below.)

In the NIE context, a "portfolio" is a collection of similar items, grouped together for reporting purposes. The portfolio is a convenient and powerful way to categorize IT resources so that management can see an holistic picture of all of the resources focused in a particular area of IT.

The complete IT spend consists of development/enhancement projects and the ongoing lights-on expenses. We place the development/enhancement projects in one portfolio, and then may classify individual line items within the overall project portfolio for reporting purposes. These categories can use terms like "strategic" and "business infrastructure." These portfolios are subsets of the overall development/enhancement project portfolio.

We place the ongoing lights-on IT resources in four basic portfolios of applications, infrastructures, services, and management. Added together, these four portfolios equal the total lights-on budget. We perform alignment, technical, service-level, quality, and intensity-of-use assessments on each portfolio. As in the project portfolio, we may also classify individual line items within those four portfolios using terms like "strategic" or "business infrastructure." (Website Note 17 on this book's website suggests a number of alternatives for these line-item portfolio classifications.) These reporting portfolios are subsets of the overall four lights-on portfolios.

When we talk about "resource pools," we are referring to the set of IT resources that are dedicated to supporting each of the portfolios. Whereas the portfolio is a classification and reporting tool, the resource pool is the element on which analysis is done. For example, how much of the application resource pool is focused on the least valuable applications? How much money is being spent on the applications resource pool? Can we move resources into higher-value activities?

In summary, the portfolio is a reporting tool for similar line items, while the resource pool supports the portfolio line items.

FOUR IT PORTFOLIO CONCEPTS

Four concepts describe the application of portfolios to IT: (1) Portfolio management applies to the entire set of IT resources; (2) IT resources are divided into new investment and lights-on portfolios; (3) lights-on expenditures are classified from an IT perspective, in portfolios related to technology management; and (4) the New Investment portfolios are classified from a business perspective, similar to financial investments.

◆

Concept 1: *Portfolio Management applies to the entire set of IT resources.*

---

100 percent of the IT resources, including operating and capital budgets, are included in IT portfolios. IT Portfolio Management applies to all IT, not just application development.

Most current industry practices limit the role of portfolio management to the new application development and infrastructure development projects for the company. This, however, is often a small percentage of the total resources devoted to IT. While this is useful for new projects, it limits the power of portfolio management to a small portion of the total IT spend.

For the five practices used for Right Decisions/Right Results, IT portfolios represent all IT activities within the company. Portfolios for applications, infrastructure, services (such as help-desk), and management provide the framework for Planning, Innovation, Prioritization, Alignment, and Performance Measurement.

There are, however, some practical problems to consider when using portfolio management for the entire IT spend. First, for companies with both corporate IT and line-of-business IT, does portfolio management cover the decentralized IT as well? Ideally, yes, but the practical problem of governance, organizational relationships, and so forth complicate this. Second, what about decentralized IT spend at the level of workstations, locally-developed applications, and so forth? Whereas portfolio management offers tools for insights into the pattern of IT expenditures company-wide by capturing information from decentralized as well as centralized IT activities, the culture and organizational relationships may complicate this. Third, does outsourcing become a part of the portfolios? The answer, ideally, is yes.

In all these cases, portfolio management can be a very powerful tool for maintaining information about applications and infrastructures throughout the enterprise, without respect to the varying organizational and governance issues. Whether this is practical and/or possible is dependent on the specific company circumstances.

◆

Concept 2: *IT resources are divided into* new investment *and* lights-on *expenditures.*

The new investment category is projects, including both capital and expense budgets. The funds are to be invested in terms of projects or new hardware/software acquisitions.

The lights-on expenditures category is the existing set of applications, infrastructure, services, and management activities. From a budget perspective, these can be thought of as the "Base" budget.

This separation permits differing kinds of analysis. For the lights-on category, for example, the analysis focuses on the service, quality, and connection to business strategies. For the lights-on application portfolio, the analysis asks about the current condition of the application (is it obsolete, does it continue to support the current business strategies, is the company continuing to get value from it?). Just like a financial investment portfolio, we're interested in whether each resource should be kept, disposed of, or renewed. See Exhibit 4.7.

For the new investment category, the analysis focuses on the connection to business strategies and the bottom-line impact of the investment. For example, does the proposed new application directly support the business strategy? Will the business return be sufficient to justify its investment? Like a prospective financial investment, we're interested in how each proposed investment

EXHIBIT 4.7   Total IT Resources Divided into Portfolios

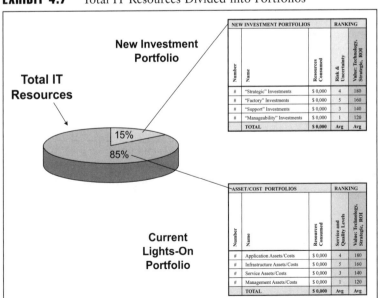

measures up compared to the alternatives to which the resources could be devoted. We are asking: Is this the most valuable possible investment?

To summarize: for the new investment portfolios, the important concern is prioritization and allocating resources to the respective portfolios; for the lights-on portfolios, the important concern is the *alignment* of the resources to the business, and the *performance* of those resources, in terms of service and quality, and technology obsolescence.[8]

◆

Concept 3: *Lights-on expenditures are classified from an IT perspective, in portfolios related to technology management.*

All IT lights-on resources and expenditures are classified into (1) applications, (2) infrastructure, (3) services, and (4) management portfolios (resource pools).

Applications are operated and supported for the use of business organizations; *infrastructure* is provided to support applications and services, and *services* are extended to business organizations. All of these can be assessed as to service, quality, technical quality, and so forth. Both ongoing lights-on expenses and new investments in lights-on categories, such as application, enhancements and infrastructure upgrades, are classified into the four portfolios' categories. By adopting a portfolio view of the management resources and services associated with IT, we clearly identify what is being managed in IT and, more importantly, what is being supplied to the business through IT. See Exhibit 4.8.

There can be practical problems in defining exactly what should appear in each portfolio. In *services,* this typically includes help desks, workstation installation and repair, and consulting. In *applications,* the full set of developed and acquired applications is included, although the dividing line between infrastructure and applications can be blurred. (For example, e-mail may be included in infrastructure, but functions delivered through e-mail or groupware, such as time reporting, may be considered an application. In fact, it doesn't matter too much whether e-mail is classified as an application or as infrastructure. What does matter is that e-mail is included in one of the portfolios and, therefore, subjected to the analysis and management scrutiny that portfolio management and NIE affords.) Infrastructure is the communications, platforms, and software needed to support applications and services. *Management* is the set of activities—such as planning, budgeting, and HR—for the IT activities.

We should not lose sight of the objectives. First, we want to account for 100 percent of the IT activity. Second, we want to group similar items into suitable portfolios in order to permit management analysis of the line items and the portfolio as a whole. Above all, we want the portfolios to be meaningful to management. Overall, the purpose is to afford management a way to easily understand and analyze the current expenditures and future investments in IT. Categorizing them into applications, infrastructures, services, and management is a proven way to accomplish this.

EXHIBIT 4.8   Four Lights-On Portfolios

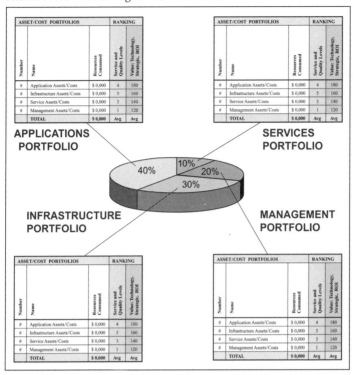

APPLICATIONS PORTFOLIO

SERVICES PORTFOLIO

INFRASTRUCTURE PORTFOLIO

MANAGEMENT PORTFOLIO

◆

Concept 4: *The New Investment portfolios are classified from a business perspective, similar to financial investments.*

New investments are also classified into strategic, factory, mandated, and future strategic portfolios.

Portfolios that classify resources and expenditures, and new investments, into functional categories (applications, infrastructures, services, and management), represent an IT management perspective. We also need to take a business perspective in portfolio classification, particularly for new investments. See Exhibit 4.9.

Our purpose here is to classify prospective IT investments in ways that are meaningful to management, similarly to how financial investments are classified. The objective is to increase management's understanding about the nature of the investments but, more important, to enable management to "balance" the investments it makes among the investment categories. Just as in financial investments, where the objective is to balance risk and returns (e.g., stocks versus bonds, cash versus real estate, and so forth), here we want to balance not only

EXHIBIT 4.9 Separating New Application Investment into Four Portfolios for Balancing and Decision Making

Portfolios from IT Perspective	Applications	Infrastructure	Services	Management
Existing Portfolios	Application Portfolio(s)	Infrastructure Portfolio(s)	Services Portfolio(s)	Management Portfolio(s)
Added Investment to Portfolios	Application Development Portfolio(s)	Infrastructure Development Portfolio(s)	Services Development Portfolio(s)	Management Development Portfolio(s)

Portfolios from Business Perspective		Strategic	Factory	Mandated	New Strat
	Investment	Applications Infrastructure Services Management	Applications Infrastructure Services Management	Applications Infrastructure Services Management	Applications Infrastructure Services Management

the risk and return of the company's investments in IT, but also what the company is capable of doing.

Two issues must be considered when balancing IT investments. The first is the distinction between discretionary and nondiscretionary funds. Often, IT investment is made necessary because of legal or ownership mandates, irrespective of the business value of the investment. Second, differing kinds of IT investments have different kinds of risks and returns. For example, the risks associated with existing applications that have ongoing support requirements are different than the risks carried by a brand new technology or an enterprise-wide process change. See Exhibit 4.10.

Twenty-five years ago, McFarlan[9] proposed a way to view the IT activities of a company. He proposed two basic considerations: the degree to which IT

EXHIBIT 4.10 Four Portfolio Categories

Current Importance of IT to Enterprise Operations			
	HIGH	**FACTORY**	**STRATEGIC**
	LOW	**MANDATED** (Nondiscretionary)	**FUTURE STRATEGIC**
		LOW	HIGH

Importance of IT in the Future Competitive and Business Capabilities of the Enterprise activities are currently important to the operations of the company, and the degree to which the IT activities will be important to future competitiveness. We adapt their classifications into those shown in Exhibit 4.11, which take into account different risks/returns and the distinction between discretionary versus nondiscretionary investments.

EXHIBIT 4.11   Four Portfolio Category Descriptions for Development Portfolios

NIE Portfolio Categories	Description	Typical Value/ Justification	Typical Risks
Strategic	Investments that directly impact the competitive performance of the company. This can be as simple as new revenue generation, or as complex as reengineering basic processes or maintaining barriers to competitive entry, and so forth.	Revenue Market share Innovation Flexibility	High
Factory	Investments that keep the company running. These typically are thought of as "back office" investments. The company depends on the underlying applications to "keep the lights on" as well as perform the company's basic functions.	Reduced costs Increased throughput Reduced time Individual productivity	Low
Future Strategic	Investments that will impact the future performance of the company, typically new businesses, new products/services, and so forth.	Same as Strategic	High
Mandated	Legally or board-mandated investments.	None, or same as Factory	Low

The desired outcome is to allow management to determine the relative percentage of resources to be put into each portfolio category, based on risk/return, discretionary versus nondiscretionary, and the outcomes of Planning, Innovation, Prioritization, Alignment, and Performance Measurement analysis.

Some companies, however, may be more comfortable with just two basic classifications: Strategic (all those with competitive implications), and Operational (all those that keep the doors open in the company). Still others may prefer a single portfolio classification and, consequently, perform all portfolio analysis with all current resources or all investments. See Exhibit 4.12.

At the highest level, the management decision is on the balance of investment among classifications. One company may be comfortable with 50 percent Strategic, 20 percent Factory, 20 percent New Strategic, and 10 percent Mandatory. Another company's balance may be entirely Factory.

EXHIBIT 4.12   Example Balance of IT Portfolios

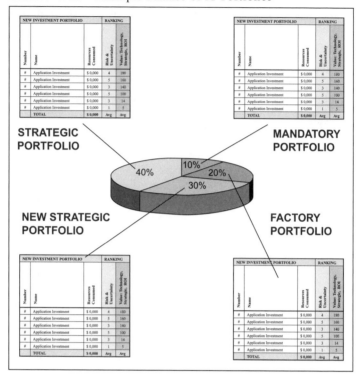

Portfolio Management Integrates the NIE Practices

A common Portfolio Management template coordinates the information across NIE practices and provides the linkage to other management processes such as annual planning and budgeting.

Exhibit 4.13 shows the relationship of individual NIE practices and the portfolio management template. Briefly, each NIE practice description found elsewhere in this book, defines the information needed and the analysis that is done. Alignment, for example, operates on the connection between applications and the company's strategic intentions. It also considers the technology assessment for the application, whether obsolete, requiring renewal, and so forth. Similarly, prioritization defines the connection between a project and the company's strategic intentions.

PRACTICAL PROBLEMS IN APPLYING PORTFOLIO MANAGEMENT

The most critical practical issues have to do with the definition of the contents of the portfolios. For example, for applications this would seem simple: the

EXHIBIT 4.13   Portfolios Used in NIE Practices

Basic Information	Service and Quality				Risk and Uncertainty				Value/State		
This table shows how each NIE practice provides and uses information from Portfolio Management	Functionality	Accuracy	Availability	Responsiveness	Business	Technology	Organizational	Project	Technical Assessment	Strategic Alignment	ROI
Demand/Supply Planning	X	X	X	X	X				X	X	
Innovation					X				X	X	
Prioritization					X	X	X	X		X	X
Alignment									X	X	
Performance Measurement	X	X	X	X					X	X	

lights-on applications portfolio consists of all the applications. One key issue, however, is the level of detail, or granularity. Most companies could, if the level of detail were at a low level, have 500 applications. This is not workable or meaningful. Similarly, for applications, should the portfolio contain applications supported by others than the IT organization (e.g., by the individual business units) or by individuals (e.g., local applications.) The problem, then, is to decide what the appropriate level and coverage is for each portfolio.

Practical Problem in Lights-On: Choosing the Portfolios and Line Items

For most companies, the lights-on portfolios consist of four basic areas:

Applications   The complete set of user applications maintained and operated by the IT organization. The costs assigned to the portfolio include the management and staff devoted to applications.

Infrastructure   The hardware and software platforms that provide services to users. Includes all processors, peripherals, communications, operating software, as well as facilities. The costs assigned to the portfolio include the management and staff devoted to infrastructure.

Services   Services and support provided to users, such as help desks and PC repair. This portfolio excludes services to support the IT organization itself. These services can be available at the request of a user, or be a regularly provided and scheduled service available to all users. The costs assigned to the portfolio include the management and staff devoted to services.

Management   The management and service activities that support the IT organization in its provision of services, infrastructure, and applications to users.

The key is to include 100 percent of the lights-on costs. All of the operating budget, excluding projects, should be accounted for in the portfolios. Examples of line items that might be included in portfolios are shown in Exhibit 4.14. The data contents for the portfolios were described in previous sections of this chapter, with the Portfolio Templates.

EXHIBIT 4.14   Examples of Line Items

Portfolio	Category of Line Items	Example of Line Items
Applications	Centrally managed applications	Payroll
	Business unit managed applications	Sales information
	Individual user managed applications	Financial analysis
Infrastructure	Application Development Support	Application development environment and tools
	Infrastructure-delivered service	E-mail
	Data management	Warehouse
	Networking	Network facilities
	Infrastructure Management	Management tools, information
	Platform	Hardware and software
Services	Services provided to users (does not include services internally consumed within the IT organization)	Data administration
		Help Desk
		Break/Fix
		Trouble Ticket Management
		Network Monitoring
		Training
Management	Services or activities consumed within the IT organization	Budgeting/Finance
		Enterprise Architecture
		Planning
		Procurement
		Employee development

Practical Problem: Working with Portfolio Information to Make the Right Decisions

The five NIE practices apply the portfolio information. However, the practical problem is what to do with the information. Although this is also tied up in applying the NIE practices, the problem is common to all of them. The issue is: Will having the information support management decisions, and will those management decisions "take hold" with respect to the use of IT in the enterprise? Our purpose, again, is to control IT spending and improve IT's bottom-line impact. Practices such as Prioritization produce rank-ordered project portfolios; practices such as alignment produce rank-ordered applications, infrastructures, and services, including assessments of quality and service levels. But managers may still ask "So what? What does all of this information mean to me?"

This is a critical connection issue. Will the use of portfolio information, that supports decisions, actually penetrate to budgets, and to IT management practices, and to IT user expectations? We pose this connection issue as the basis of the Strategy-to-Bottom-Line Value Chain. Decisions enabled by portfolio information in strategic planning, or in annual project planning, or in budgets, *must* connect to the right actions, in order to effectively control IT spending and to improve IT's bottom-line impact. These actions include budget decisions, application abandonment or renewal decisions, project selection or abandonment/deferral, and the like. Making this happen is the key challenge, which will be raised consistently in each of the subsequent chapters.

For example, consider the lights-on applications portfolio for a financial services company. Through the Alignment Assessment practice (see Chapter 8), the applications are assessed according to "dependency" (Are the applications actually used?) and quality (Is the information the applications provides accurate? Is the application available when needed? and so forth). Through the application portfolio, personnel costs required for operations and support, and the computer processing costs are assigned to each application. With this assessment, a management team can consider investment strategies, as shown in Exhibit 4.15. (Details of the scoring are described in Chapter 8.)

As a result of the analysis, the portfolio can be portrayed as shown in Exhibit 4.16, including the cost of the applications. Portfolio analysis identifies the applications for which management action is possible. By identifying the applications (in this example, in the "crisis" category $8 million is the annual operating cost for support personnel and computer costs; six applications are included in this category), management can take action to abandon or invest in improvement. By doing so, the business processes that use the application will benefit, and the impact on the bottom line will increase.[10]

But, and this is a large but, if management does not take action, then the analysis of the lights-on application portfolio is useless. Getting management to see the opportunities and take the required action is the key problem. (Some of the issues involved in generating management action will be considered within the specifics of the NIE practices, in Chapters 8, 9, and 10. Chapter 13, in describing IT Impact Management, offers methods for responding to the problems.)

EXHIBIT 4.15   Sample Investment Strategy

Category	Investment Strategy
Abandon: Dependency is low	Applications should be abandoned.

Crisis:
    Dependency is high (4,5)
    and Quality is 2 or less
	Applications are candidates for investment to improve quality, especially with high dependence.

Noncritical, Stabilize: Dependency is moderate (3)	Dependence is moderate. Spend as little money on maintenance and enhancement as possible.

Improve Only as Needed
    Dependency is high (4,5)
    and Quality is moderate (3)
	Although dependence is high, quality is adequate. Spend money only in emergency or as resources are left over.

Excellent, Monitor
    Both Dependency *and*
    Quality are 4 or 5
	Monitor applications for quality issues. Spend money to maintain quality levels, but new investment is likely not needed.

EXHIBIT 4.16   Investment Decisions within Portfolio

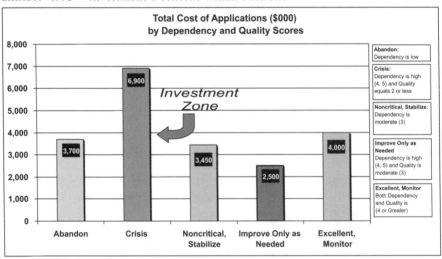

Practical Problem: Maintenance of the Portfolio Information

Most companies spent considerable time and energy constructing application and infrastructure portfolios as part of the Y2K effort. Often this was the first time that company management saw the holistic listing of everything that IT managed. The outcome was a successful transition to 2000. However, almost all companies then put aside the portfolio information so arduously completed, with the result that the portfolios are no longer accurate or useful.

Adopting portfolio and portfolio management as a component of the Strategy-to-Bottom-Line Value Chain, and as applied in the NIE practices, is a commitment to continue portfolio maintenance. This is a management commitment and a process development problem. For example, in many ways, the "asset management" which companies undertake to control the proliferation of hardware/software in the company is a form of infrastructure portfolio. Companies rapidly learn how difficult it can be to maintain the information, given the pace of acquisition of new hardware (e.g., PCs) and the retirement of old hardware.

SUMMING UP PORTFOLIOS AND PORTFOLIO MANAGEMENT IN INFORMATION TECHNOLOGY

We made the point earlier that the use of portfolios integrates the five NIE practices and applies to the entire IT spend rather than just the application development portfolio. We also noted that current industry practice relegates portfolio management to prioritization of the application development projects. See Exhibit 4.17.

EXHIBIT 4.17   Portfolio Analysis for Decision Making

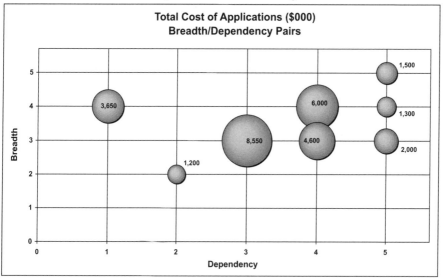

The use of portfolios is more than Prioritization.

The use of portfolios is much more. It is the foundation for managing IT in the company. Including risk and uncertainty in project assessment and including service and quality in base resource assessment permits management to understand and take appropriate action about these portfolio elements.

Using IT Portfolio Management to Control IT Costs

A pervasive problem facing most companies is cost containment, particularly in difficult economic times. By defining exactly how much resource is devoted to each portfolio category and line item, and by providing information about service and quality and strategic alignment, management can identify the least valuable (in business impact terms), and the least well performing, element of each portfolio. This allows cost-containment actions based on bottom-line impact and performance. Again, the key point is that portfolios represent 100 percent of IT costs.

The power of portfolios applied to the lights-on budget is that it enables management review of 100 percent of the IT spend, rather than the "add-on" entitlement mentality that pervades most organizations. As we've noted, management has tended to spend most time on the project/development budget, which is normally around 20 percent of the whole spend. By understanding where costs are, and by applying NIE practice tools such as alignment to the portfolios, management can assess the 80 percent, with the likely outcome of identifying poorly performing resources, and poorly performing or poorly aligned activities, with a view to reallocating those resources to higher performing opportunities or, even more valuably, to additional new projects.

For example, consider the application portfolio for a financial services company that is assessed (using the Alignment Assessment practice described in Chapter 8). These applications have been assessed for the "breadth" of use (whether the application is used by just a few individuals, or a business function or department, or company-wide) and for dependency (how important is it to the functioning of the individual or department or company). The size of the bubble is application cost (annual support personnel and computer processing). In this example, management should consider the cost of the applications that are not used widely *and* are not depended upon. In this case, this is the applications represented by the lower left-hand bubble. The management question is: Why are we spending money on this? Are there opportunities for cost reduction here?[11]

CHAPTER SUMMARY

Portfolios allow management to classify costs and resources into useful groupings for asking the important Affordability and Impact Questions. Portfolio Management allows management to understand the full IT spend, make resource investment tradeoff decisions, and improve the bottom-line impact of its IT investment decisions.

Portfolio Outcomes in NIE Practices

Portfolios are applied in each of the five NIE practices. By doing so, a number of outcomes can be expected:

Overall

- Provide visibility to 100 percent of IT spend
- Establish a framework for planning through budgeting (supporting the Strategy-to-Bottom-Line Value Chain)

Strategic Demand/Supply Planning and Innovation NIE Practice

- Link as-is and to-be resources to the company strategic intentions
- Establish the foundation for assessing the as-is portfolios and defining the strategic to-be portfolios
- Establish a consistent vocabulary for IT and the business
- Describe where IT resources are applied and connect them to company budget and planning processes
- Provide a framework for defining IT requirements, including renewal and growth
- Establish connections to performance measurement

Prioritization NIE Practice

- Establish strategic-intention basis for resource allocation and prioritization
- Provide perspective for future investment requirements
- Provide basis for assessing project risk and benefits

Alignment NIE Practice

- Establish basis for service, quality, reliability, and risk assessments
- Establish multiyear information for alignment
- Address 100 percent of the IT spend and connect the IT spend to business strategic intentions

Performance Measurement NIE Practice

- Provide a framework for performance measurement of 100 percent of the IT spend
- Connect performance measurement to strategic planning
- Connect to the business performance affected by IT portfolios

UNDERSTAND COSTS AND RESOURCES: MANAGEMENT AGENDA

The following is a self-examination for the critical success factors for Right Decisions/Right Actions, in the use of portfolios.

Management Question	Yes or No?	If No, What Is Our Plan for Correcting This?
Do we manage our development and enhancement projects as a portfolio of projects?		
Do we analyze our lights-on expenditures from a portfolio point of view?		
Do we assess lights-on activities by strategic alignment?		
Do we assess lights-on activities by quality or services levels?		
Do we know how much we are spending for IT services? For IT management?		
Do we have an investment strategy for our lights-on expenditures?		
Do we have an investment strategy for existing applications?		
If we are doing portfolios now, are we able to maintain the information accurately?		

The balance of this book provides answers to the "What is our plan for correcting this?" statements.

ADDITIONAL READING

The book's website contains additional information:

Website Note 5: Modern Portfolio Management

Website Note 6: One Company's View of Portfolio Management

Website Note 7: Constructing Portfolios

Website Note 17: Other Portfolio Classifications

The appendices also contain related information for Chapter 4:

Appendix C: The Development of Strategic Intentions, with Examples

NOTES

1. F. Warren McFarlan, "Portfolio Approach to Information Systems," *Harvard Business Review,* September–October 1981, pp. 142–150.
2. The template shown in Exhibit 4.1 is adapted from Parker and Benson, with Trainor, *Information Economics* (Englewood Cliffs, NJ: Prentice-Hall, 1988), p. 145.

3. See Website Note 5, "Modern Portfolio Management," for the history of portfolio management.

4. See, for example, F. Warren McFarlan, "Portfolio Approach to Information Systems," *Harvard Business Review,* September–October, 1981, pp. 142–150.

5. "Information Technology Investment Management: An Overview of GAO's Assessment Framework" (GAO/AIMD-00-155, May 2000), *http://www.gao. gov/special.pubs/a10123.pdf.*

6. See Parker and Benson, with Trainor, *Information Economics: Linking Business Performance to Information Technology* (Englewood Cliffs, NJ: Prentice-Hall, 1988).

7. See Website Note 6 for a perspective on the use of portfolios to manage IT.

8. See Website Note 7, "Constructing Portfolios," about the issues in establishing portfolio information.

9. Warren McFarlan, "IT Changes the Way You Compete," *Harvard Business Review,* May–June, 1984, pp. 98–103.

10. The specific analysis shown here is tailored to the specific company. The example is included to show the kind of analysis possible, not to limit or define the only possible analysis.

11. The examples shown here are based on specific company situations. They are included to illustrate the point made in the text, not to limit the kind of analysis that can be done. Each company situation and, consequently, the application of the NIE practice, is different and tailored to the specific needs of the company.

CHAPTER 5

Focus on the Right Things

In Chapter 2, we introduced seven basic questions that management teams should answer. Four questions are about the alignment of IT activities to what is important to the company. Three questions are about the affordability of IT expenses to the company. The questions:

Impact Questions

1. Are we investing IT resources in the right places?

2. Do our business strategies drive our IT actions and produce bottom-line impact?

3. Are we getting bottom-line impact from our lights-on resources?

4. Are we balancing our strategic and tactical investments?

Affordability Questions

1. What can we afford to spend on IT?

2. Can we reduce unnecessary IT costs?

3. Can we redeploy expenses to support needed projects?

Control Spending and Maximize Impact on the Bottom Line
1   Define the Goals
2   Ask the Right Questions
3   Connect to the Bottom Line
4   Understand Costs and Resources
5   Focus on the Right Things
6   Adopt Effective Process to Produce Action
7   Tackle the Practical Problems
8   Make the Right Decisions
9   Plan for the Right Results
10   Keep Score
11   Deal with Culture
12   Chart the Path to Implementation
13   Define What's Next
14   Answer the "So What?" Question

We also introduced basic concepts of portfolio management (Chapter 4) and shareholder value (Chapter 3) as foundations for answering the seven questions.

Our intent now is to introduce and formalize the detailed description of the Strategy-to-Bottom-Line Value Chain and the five management practices that enable the management team to answer the seven basic questions, and thereby control IT spending and improve IT's impact on the bottom line.

We do so in four steps:

- Step 1: The goals and principles that best characterize what the Strategy-to-Bottom-Line Value Chain and the five practices require (Chapter 5).
- Step 2: The Strategy-to-Bottom-Line Value Chain (Chapter 6).
- Step 3: The practical issues that must be solved (Chapter 7).
- Step 4: The five New Information Economics practices (Chapters 8–10).

We conclude with chapters on management culture and the Business Value Maturity Model™, both intended to help management teams introduce the goals, principles, and practices described here.

THE GOALS AND PRINCIPLES FOR RIGHT DECISIONS/RIGHT RESULTS

We recommend that management teams adopt five Right Decisions/Right Results goals for taking business strategy and IT action to the bottom line.

- Translate enterprise mission and strategy into *actionable, commonly understood strategic intentions.*
- Get the *right bottom-line results from all current and future IT spending* by evaluating the impact on strategic intentions.
- *Manage the culture and define management roles* regarding the use of IT to achieve business strategic intentions.
- Manage IT as a set of *resource and process portfolios.*
- Produce the *right actions and bottom-line results* and use budgets, projects, and performance measurement to achieve them.

Each goal is described with several basic principles. Together, the goals and principles underscore the fundamentals and philosophies of Right Decisions/ Right Results. By focusing on these goals and their related principles, management teams will control IT spending and improve IT's bottom-line impact.

GOAL 1: ACTIONABLE, COMMONLY UNDERSTOOD STRATEGIC INTENTIONS[1]

Translate enterprise mission and strategy into actionable, commonly understood strategic intentions.

We introduced "strategic intentions" in Chapter 3, where we said, "Management's strategies and plans to improve strategic and operational effectiveness are its strategic intentions."[2]

We believe company leaders need to translate their mission, goal, and strategy statements into statements of *strategic intentions:* statements that tell everyone in the organization how the company will make progress in its business. IT, as well as other parts of the company, needs high-level direction on *how* an enterprise intends to achieve its objectives, as well as clear direction on *what* the objectives are. The litmus test is simple: If a manager in an enterprise looks at the strategic intentions, the manager should be able to describe in specific terms what will be done differently tomorrow to help achieve the objectives and how the functional area can contribute to moving the enterprise forward.

Unfortunately, high-level statements of strategy and intention (if made or documented at all) are open to interpretation and will invariably be understood differently across the company. Any process that intends to translate strategy into effective actions must ensure that there is common understanding, across the organization and at all levels of management, of what the strategic intentions really mean.[3] The process must explicitly include methods to refine and communicate strategic intentions such that a common understanding emerges at all levels across the company. This is not just a static process but an ongoing and dynamic process. Jack Welch makes the point that every chance he had, he would preach the current GE strategy to any employee that would listen. Strategic Intentions are not set in concrete; they change with the business, and their relative importance one to another changes as markets and society change. But they need to be known and acted on.[4] As opposed to being merely the designers of strategy, managers take on the role of establishing a sense of purpose within the company.[5]

◆

The result: An actionable set of strategic intentions, commonly understood across the enterprise, is the foundation for producing action and the improved bottom-line impact from IT.

Principle 1.1: Actionable Strategic Intentions

Enterprise planning and management processes should produce explicit and actionable strategic intentions that will lead to the business and IT initiatives that will achieve them.

Managers find it difficult to know what to do to support a company's strategy when the leadership team does not provide effective strategic direction. "Our strategy is to be the low-cost producer" is less helpful than "our strategy is to drive cost out of our supply chain," because (among other things) the first statement gives no sense of how. Regardless of how the leadership team does its planning and management, a good starting point is to establish strategic objectives and strategic intentions. The result is a clear strategic direction for the rest of the company and, in broad terms, how the company intends to get there. By extension, managers can then determine the role they may play in supporting the strategy.

Some companies already have clear expressions of actionable strategic intentions in place, which can be used without change throughout the planning and management processes that lead to IT action. For other companies, strategic intentions can be found in, and developed from, company mission, vision, high-level strategies, and the operationalizing statements used in annual planning. In these cases, the strategic intentions need to be clearly stated and then validated against what the management team believes is important. For example, one way is to compare the strategic intentions to the actual priorities of the management team as expressed by how its members devote their own time and attention. Companies that do not have clear strategic intentions need to develop and validate them.

However, even with clearly stated strategic intentions, managers probably will not pay attention to them when the management culture is otherwise. For example, a culture that focuses exclusively on achieving operational or tactical goals rather than strategic intentions probably prevents the company from achieving its strategies, because managers will devote their full attention to those tactical goals. Cultures that focus solely on financial performance especially highlight this problem of culture leading to organization and planning disconnects. Companies that lack clear strategies, in addition to establishing them, face the additional difficulty of dealing with the cultural impediments.

For example, if the business strategic plan states, "Our strategy is to achieve world-class performance by attaining a strong competitive position in target markets," it is quite difficult for the IT organization (or any business unit) to establish specific initiatives connected to the statement. The reason is that the strategy does not say anything about *how* the company plans to attain that strong competitive position. Is it based on lowest cost? Product capabilities? Customer services? Customer relationships? Supply chain innovations? The point is that the strategy statement offers no guidance as to the underlying actions or initiatives to be taken. Consequently, it has little power to guide either business management or IT management in the development of IT strategies or actions.

Now, consider a business strategy that states, "Our strategy is to attain a strong competitive position by improving customer service by placing up-to-date customer and product information in the hands of every account executive." This statement provides guidance to everyone as to exactly what the company means and what needs to be done. Although many strategy statements are somewhere in the middle of the two examples, our experience is that most companies err on the side of generality, thus producing strategy statements that are not actionable.[6]

Process and culture go hand in hand. A process that produces and applies actionable strategic intentions runs up against culture but, at the same time, has a role in changing that culture. Doing both process and culture change demands clear management support and a consistent approach reflected in all related management processes.

The result of *actionable strategic intentions* is the clear expression of how management intends to drive the business forward. This clear expression establishes the starting point for business unit planning and activities directed towards the achievement of the intentions. Applied to IT, the clear expression of strategic intention is used to establish business priorities, to prioritize initiatives and projects, allocate IT resources, assess the alignment of all IT activities and resources, establish the bases of performance measurement, and provide the context for innovation.

This sounds mechanical. "Just change culture and then implement processes, based on our practices of planning, prioritization, and so forth." Or alternatively, "Just implement the processes, and this will change the culture." But what about details like politics, company history, industry practices, and so forth? It cannot be mechanical. We have to deal with politics and existing practices in achieving necessary changes.

Principle 1.2: Actions Tied to Strategy

All IT actions and spending should be driven by business strategic intentions.

Business and IT planning activities often occur separately, with disconnected results that do not let managers connect their actions to the other side. In some companies, strategic planning often is ineffective, producing strategy statements that do not easily translate into actions that people can take.

An organization needs integrated business and IT planning, and effective planning that lets managers know what they should be doing tomorrow. In Chapter 9, we explain and expand on two related concepts. The first is a framework that can be used to clearly express business strategies, objectives, and initiatives in ways that let everyone understand exactly what the business intends. The second is a straightforward process that provides for integrated planning results that combine consensus, clarity, and clear direction. An extra bonus is the ease of connecting performance measurement and management to this framework.

A special challenge is infrastructure, both technical and business. We run into this problem with administrative systems, with back-office systems, with utility systems, and with run-the-business systems. Their connection to business strategic intentions can seem to be less direct than systems that face the customer. As we discuss in the next section and then in Chapter 8, this challenge is addressed through appropriate statements of strategic intentions and through portfolio presentations of alignment and prioritization.

Principle 1.3: Common Understanding and Commitment

Managers across all functional areas should have a common understanding of, and commitment to, enterprise strategic intentions. Each organizational unit, including IT, should understand how current and future activities in all functional areas support the enterprise strategic intentions.

This principle focuses on a company's ability to operationalize and communicate its actionable strategic intentions. It does no good to have strategic intentions if no one knows what they are and what they mean. The key objective is establishing a common understanding across functional areas of the strategic intentions and what needs to be done, or is being done, by other parts of the business, to achieve them. This is a direct assault on the silos of a company, which can be as simple as silos reflecting business vs. IT organizations, or as complex as silos in multiple functional areas and business units.

Anything that prevents agreement on strategies across the silos of the company is a serious disconnect. We expect IT to be well connected to business strategies and plans. We expect IT to connect its technical strategies and plans to the business strategies and plans. But what, exactly, should IT connect to? The problem in many companies is there is little awareness of exactly what the company's strategies are. It is surprising how often we find that company leadership teams do not agree on the details of the strategies they are pursuing. It is not that the company has no mission or high-level strategy statement. It is that the individual members of the team do not have a common understanding of the strategies they are using to reach the company mission and high-level strategies.

The cultural implications can be quite large. Many companies exhibit strong functional organizations, with long-standing traditions of operational independence, particularly when it comes to management planning and internal strategies. Yet the new reality of information technology is that it is increasingly cross-functional and cross-organizational. Some things like e-mail and connectivity and collaboration are obvious. Others are business process-based. Companies that already have a strong commitment to process management have made inroads against functional silos. But even in a process-focused company, the issue of common understanding of strategic intentions and their implementation can be difficult across functions and among geographies.

The management practices of planning, prioritization, alignment, innovation, and performance management can be equally cross-functional. Doing them,

Outcomes from Goal 1

Goal Title	Statement of Goal	Desired Outcomes
Actionable, commonly understood strategic intentions	Translate enterprise mission and strategy into *actionable, commonly understood strategic intentions.*	The business has a set of stated strategic goals that clearly identify how the business will achieve its competitive and operational objectives. Management has established explicit and actionable strategic intentions that describe the strategies/goals for the business and that lead to the business and IT initiatives that achieve them. Business and IT managers have a common understanding of, and commitment to, enterprise strategic intentions. Each organizational unit, including understands how current and future activities in all functional areas support the enterprise strategic intentions.

as described in the prior section, may encounter cultural barriers, but doing them may also help in re-directing the culture by engaging managers in new and different roles with respect to IT.

GOAL 2: THE RIGHT BOTTOM-LINE RESULTS FROM IT

Get the right bottom-line results from all current and future IT activities by evaluating their impact on strategic intentions.

Strategic intentions tell us what management intends to do to improve strategic and operational performance, in order to improve financial performance. Therefore, we assess the bottom-line impact of plans, initiatives, and current resources based on their impact on those strategic intentions. This is accomplished through formal and consistent practices that identify and assess the cause-and-effect links between plans, initiatives, and resources, and the enterprise strategic intentions. The goal is for all plans, initiatives, and resources to be connected to achieving enterprise strategic intentions.

◆

The result: Enterprise IT investments and resources will directly support enterprise strategic intentions; the business bottom-line impact of IT will be improved. The company gets the right results from IT.

Principle 2.1: Business-Focused Outcomes

IT's business impact should be determined by cause-and-effect linkages with business outcomes. Activities and resources should be planned, prioritized, executed, and measured based on their connection and contribution to bottom-line outcomes.

As stated earlier, our basic theme is that IT resources should be allocated to activities that bring success to management's strategic intentions. This is what we mean by *impact-based resource allocation.* The success of management's strategic intentions is determined by actual business outcomes, such as bottom-line performance in the case of for-profit companies or achieving mission goals in the case of government and nonprofits.

The key is *cause-and-effect.* The test for connecting IT to business, for determining contribution to business outcomes, is how well IT impacts those outcomes. We understand that IT does not stand alone in this. Impact on operational or strategic effectiveness, and impact on management strategic intentions, are ultimately achieved by the organizations, managers, and people that apply IT in their areas of responsibilities. IT is an enabler, a partner, a component of the activities leading to business outcomes. It is in this context that we search for IT's cause-and-effect connection. How planning, prioritization, execution, and measurement is done, is based on determining how IT will enable the specific activities that lead to improved business performance.

Principle 2.2: Impact-Based Resource Allocation

IT resources for both lights-on expenses and new investments should be allocated and budgeted based on explicit connection to strategic intentions.

A manager's job is to assure that scarce resources are directed to the most important areas of the business. IT, like any business resource, is finite. In IT's case, the finite characteristic could be based on the money available to spend on IT, management time available to manage IT, or people available with the necessary IT talents. Companies must allocate finite IT resources to their most important problems and opportunities. IT is no different from any other resource.

The way to determine "what is most important" can be tricky. Business journal articles as early as the 1960s bemoaned the difficulty of effectively applying data processing to the right business problems.[7] During that period, the recommended approach was careful cost-benefit analysis and financial business cases, to be done for all proposed data processing projects. Doing ROI, or EVA, or some other financial analysis has become one popular method for determining the most important projects. The greater the projected ROI, the more important the project would be. This makes sense given that a company's goal is bottom-line performance.[8]

The issue that the original *Information Economics* books[9] addressed was the difficulty of applying ROI to strategic IT projects as well as to projects that produce so-called *intangible benefits. Information Economics* described six classes of benefits, only one of which was economic impact such as ROI. The others were strategic match, competitive advantage, management information, competitive response, and strategic IT architecture. *Information Economics* presented a specific evaluation methodology using the six classes of benefits, and used the term *value* rather than benefit to describe them. As will be established in the following sections, a better interpretation is that the six value-based benefits are part of *operational effectiveness* and *strategic effectiveness*, elements of management and financial principles used in such disciplines as shareholder value and balanced scorecard.

We operationalize these ideas by defining the concept of *strategic intention* to represent management's goals and strategies to improve the financial performance of the business.[10] Impact is defined as the contributions IT has made towards achieving management's strategic intentions. This includes strategic intentions to reduce cost and increase revenue, and consequently ROI, of course. But strategic intention also includes management's intentions about the other *Information Economics* benefits such as competitive advantage. Taken together, costs, revenues, competitive advantage, and so forth, are reflected in management's strategic intentions to improve operational and strategic effectiveness of the business, and thereby improve its overall financial performance.

Our basic theme is that IT resources should be allocated to activities that bring success to management's strategic intentions. This is what we mean by *impact-based resource allocation.* Whereas the original *Information Economics* focused on new IT investments, Right Decisions/Right Results applies impact-based resource allocation to the entire IT spend. Most companies spend only a small fraction of their overall IT resources on new development. The bulk of a company's IT expenditures are in maintenance, operations, and supporting existing applications and infrastructure.

Further, there is a tendency for managers to think of new IT projects in strictly capital budgeting terms, focusing on spending new resources rather than spending ongoing budget resources. For example, maintenance budgets typically are larger than many new development projects, and often business units have budgets for small projects as large as maintenance or development budgets. Managers may not think of these budgets are part of the resource-allocation opportunities, but they are certainly part of the company's IT spend.

Impact-based resource allocation applies to the entire IT spend, and to the annual budget process as well as capital or new resource processes. We expect to improve the company's overall performance by improving the allocation of IT resources, for development as well as lights-on, in operating budgets as well as capital budgeting. This puts the IT budget under significant business-based scrutiny, which can affect the management culture as well.

Outcomes from Goal 2

Title	Statement of Goal	Desired Outcomes
Right Bottom-Line Results from IT	Assess the impact, and get the right results, from all current and future IT activities by *evaluating their impact on strategic intentions.*	IT resources, both lights-on and future investments, are evaluated according to their impact on the achieving the businessís strategic intentions.
		Resources, both lights-on expenses and new investments, are allocated and budgeted based on explicit connection to strategic intentions.
		Activities and resources are planned, prioritized, and measured based on their cause-and-effect connection and contribution to business operational and strategic effectiveness.

GOAL 3: THE RIGHT MANAGEMENT CULTURE AND MANAGEMENT ROLES

Manage the culture and define management roles regarding the use of IT to achieve business strategic intentions.

Business managers generally know what IT is doing for them in their functional area because of their tactical, day-to-day dependence on IT in their operations, but are largely unaware of what IT accomplishes elsewhere in the enterprise. To successfully link business strategy with IT action, business managers must participate in IT planning and decision making, based on enterprise strategic intentions and with an enterprise point-of-view. Their role and responsibility in IT planning and decision making requires understanding the full range of IT possibilities across the enterprise, the possible IT demands from the business, and the organizational requirements for successful implementation.

The Right Decisions/Right Results framework and NIE practices define business management roles in planning initiatives, investments, and the decision-making associated with them. For IT investments especially, it is business managers, not IT, who are most suited to making connections to enterprise strategic intentions. We expect business managers who are responsible for enterprise investments to understand the full range of IT resources, activities, and investments under consideration, and their business impact. This is one example of the management culture implications of Right Decisions/Right Results. It can change the roles that managers play and alter the perspective managers have of IT.[11]

◆

The result: Business managers will understand the full range of IT activities and the overall impact of IT on enterprise performance; this understanding influences the management culture and management's roles with regard to IT.

Principle 3.1: Role-Based Culture Management

Managers' roles are clearly defined to assure proper participation and avoid disconnects created by an organization's existing culture.

Getting from business strategy to IT action requires a disciplined, formal approach to business and IT planning. This discipline requires a culture that accepts the role of IT in the business and requires an enterprise-wide view on the part of each manager. *New Information Economics* practices deal with the cultural requirements of business strategy to IT action by clearly defining the role of business and IT managers in each of the practices. Both business and IT management needs to have a common understanding of the strategic intentions of the company, and each has specific roles in creating the plans for driving IT actions. IT managers for their part are measured in business terms and are responsible for producing, with business partners, business results from IT activities. By clearly defining all of these roles and responsibilities, the cultural obstacles to effective IT actions can be overcome, and in fact over time a culture that accepts an enterprise-wide view of IT contributions emerges throughout the company.

An emphasis of this book is on management role development, with management practice development as a means to that end. This approach addresses the practical problems associated with executive participation and support. In the final analysis, it is the people and culture that will dictate success. In this way, we will help managers understand how to improve IT's contribution to company performance. This understanding focuses on the roles each leadership group needs to play. For example, the CEO understands the role of his senior leadership team. The senior leadership team members can see their role in establishing strategic direction and priorities. The IT leadership team members can see their specific leadership role and their role in setting the stage for the CEO and senior leadership team's involvement.

Outcomes from Goal 3

Title	Statement of Goal	Desired Outcomes
Culture and Management Roles	*Manage the culture and management roles* regarding the use of IT to achieve business strategic intentions.	Business and IT managers have a common, consensus view as to the role of IT to achieve the business strategic intentions. Business and IT managers have a common understanding of and commitment to enterprise strategic intentions. Managers' roles are clearly defined to assure proper participation and avoid disconnects created by an organization's existing culture.

GOAL 4: PORTFOLIOS AND PORTFOLIO MANAGEMENT

Manage IT as a set of resource and process portfolios.

It is not just investments in new IT capabilities that are important to improving a company's strategic and operational performance. Most of a company's IT expenditures are for the more mundane maintenance, operations, and infrastructure activities. To be effective at improving operational and strategic effectiveness, a company needs to manage the impact of all of its IT investments, not just new development. Portfolio Management is the foundation for increased IT impact through improved operational and strategic effectiveness.

The NIE practices of Planning, Innovation, Prioritization, Alignment, and Performance Measurement focus on all resources devoted to IT, including development, maintenance, operations, and management. By looking at IT as a set of portfolios, all of the resources can be managed for bottom-line impact.[12] The key is to look at all the resources in a consistent manner, linking them to business outcomes, and including cost, service level and quality, and technical obsolescence in the assessments.

◆

The result: The entire IT spend, the complete set of IT activities and resources, is considered in assessing business bottom-line impact, service and quality, and performance.

Principle 4.1: Impact and Portfolio-Based Resource Management

All IT activities and spending should be organized into resource and process port-folios for purposes of impact assessment, performance management, quality and service level assessment, and resource commitment.

Getting a handle on IT for the purpose of impact-based resource allocation is difficult because of its dispersion throughout the enterprise, a complex mixture of people, space, hardware, and software, and management practices in managing support, operations, and infrastructure. Development projects, of course, are not difficult. It is the rest of the IT spend that is hard.

Our goal is to examine 100 percent of the IT spend, wherever it occurs in the organization. Our objective is to *improve* the impact all expenditures have on achieving the company's strategic intentions, and consequently its financial performance.

Our approach is to apply portfolio management. *Information Economics* examined all IT development projects and ranked them according to their impact. This required looking at all projects together in a consistent fashion, determining the highest impact projects and allocating resources to them. This is a simple form of portfolio management. The key idea is that the entire portfolio is being managed as an entity rather than as a collection of individual project approval decisions.

With Right Decisions/Right Results, we apply portfolio management to the entire IT spend. This allows impact assessments of each resource portfolio and also provides the context for a larger set of management questions, such as service level and quality assessment, technology obsolescence, and other performance measurements. The result is a comprehensive IT management discipline that enables management to achieve the basic goal of maximizing the impact IT resources have on the strategies and performance of the company.

Outcomes from Goal 4

Title	Statement of Goal	Desired Outcomes
Resource and Process Portfolios	Manage IT as a set of *resource and process portfolios.*	IT activities are organized into resource and process portfolios for purposes of impact assessment, performance management, quality and service level assessment, and resource commitment. Resources—both ongoing expenses and new investments—are allocated and budgeted based on explicit connection to strategic intentions.

GOAL 5: ACTIONS AND RESULTS

Produce the right actions and bottom-line results and use budgets, project evaluations, and performance measurement to achieve them.

The consequences of portfolio management must be explicitly connected to budgets, which results in channeling resources to the activities that most support strategic intentions This is also done by tracking the performance of IT projects against strategies and, in particular, by tracking the performance of managers in terms of the budgets, portfolios, and projects they manage. This, ultimately, is how change is produced in the practices and cultures of an organization.

◆

The result: All IT resources are actively deployed on projects and in support of activities that directly support business strategies. IT produces actions and the right results.

Principle 5.1: Responsive to Change

Planning, prioritizing, and measuring should combine the support of "strategy to action" with the ability to react to unexpected events and business change.

Neither business nor IT environments remain static, especially in the time-line of one- to five-year strategic planning processes and resulting plans. New Information Economics processes drive the organization to actions that are directly related to the organization's strategic intentions. We must understand that those actions may become less relevant as the business environment changes and the company adjusts its strategic intentions to account for new opportunities or problems. The tools we use should help the organization respond quickly to these strategic changes and allow management to understand the downstream impact of the changes and adjust IT actions accordingly.

Outcomes from Goal 5

Title	Statement of Goal	Desired Outcomes
Actions and Results	*Produce the right actions and bottom-line results* and use budgets, project evaluations, and performance measurement to achieve them.	Management applies budgets, project evaluations, and performance measurement to determine the success and contribution of IT to business success. Activities and resources are planned, prioritized, and measured based on their cause-and-effect connection and contribution to business operational and strategic effectiveness. Planning, prioritizing, and measuring combine "strategy to action" with the ability to react to unexpected events and business change.

SUMMARY OF RIGHT DECISIONS/RIGHT RESULTS— GOALS AND PRINCIPLES

The table below summarizes the Goals and Principles for Right Decisions/Right Results and the five NIE practices.

Goals	Principles
Translate enterprise mission and strategy into actionable, commonly understood strategic intentions.	Enterprise planning and management processes should produce explicit and actionable strategic intentions that will lead to the business and IT initiatives that will achieve them. All IT actions and spending should be driven by business strategic intentions. Managers across all functional areas should have a common understanding of, and commitment to, enterprise strategic intentions. Each organizational unit, including IT, should understand how current and future activities in all functional areas support the enterprise strategic intentions.
Get the right bottom-line results from all current and future IT activities by evaluating the impact on strategic intentions.	IT's business impact should be determined by cause-and-effect linkages with business outcomes. Activities and resources should be planned, prioritized, executed, and measured based on their connection and contribution to business outcomes. Resources for both ongoing expenses and new investments should be allocated and budgeted based on explicit connection to strategic intentions.
Manage the culture and management roles regarding the use of IT to achieve business strategic intentions.	Managers' roles are clearly defined to assure proper participation and avoid disconnects created by an organization's existing culture.
Manage IT as a set of resource and process portfolios.	All IT activities and spending should be organized into resource and process portfolios for purposes of impact assessment, performance management, quality and service level assessment, and resource commitment.
Produce the right actions and bottom-line results and use budgets, project evaluations, and performance measurement to achieve them.	Planning, prioritizing, and measuring should combine support of "strategy to action" with the ability to react to unexpected events and business change.

GOALS AND PRINCIPLES APPLIED TO THE STRATEGY-TO-BOTTOM-LINE VALUE CHAIN AND NIE PRACTICES

The solution being presented here is more than just prioritizing activities by applying Right Decisions/Right Results frameworks, New Information Economics practices, and choosing the most valuable. It is a complete, full-process, full life-cycle view of the relationship between business units and IT, based on the principle that all of an enterprise's activities must be consistent with, and support, enterprise strategic intentions. This requires a consistent, integrated approach to planning, prioritizing, allocating resources, and managing performance of business and IT activities across the enterprise. See Exhibit 5.1.

We began by stating the five goals we seek: actionable strategic intentions, business evaluation of IT's impact on these intentions, an appropriate management culture, portfolios to manage IT resources, and action leading to business results. These goals, and desired outcomes, lead to the one important result: that the company gets the most business impact from their IT investments companies by managing and deploying their scarce IT resources most effectively.

EXHIBIT 5.1 Tying Goals to Practice Principles

Right Decisions/ Right Results Goals	New Information Economics Practice Principles
Actionable, Commonly Understood Strategic Intentions	1. Actionable Strategic Intentions
	2. Actions Tied to Strategy
	3. Common Understanding of, and Commitment to, Strategic Intentions
The Right Bottom-line Results from IT	4. Business-Focused Outcomes
	5. Impact-Based Resource Allocation
Culture and Management Roles	6. Role-Based Culture Management
Portfolios and Portfolio Management	7. Impact/Portfolio-Based Resource Management
Actions and Results	8. Responsive to Change

Summing Up: The Eight NIE Principles

Although processes are important, they are not the complete solution to the problems that we have described. We will later present the details of five practice areas to achieve our objective of maximum IT impact on company performance.

EXHIBIT 5.2 NIE Principles as Critical Success Factors

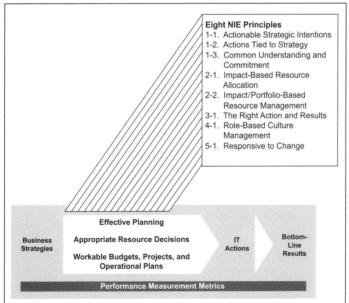

Eight NIE Principles
1-1. Actionable Strategic Intentions
1-2. Actions Tied to Strategy
1-3. Common Understanding and Commitment
2-1. Impact-Based Resource Allocation
2-2. Impact/Portfolio-Based Resource Management
3-1. The Right Action and Results
4-1. Role-Based Culture Management
5-1. Responsive to Change

Business Strategies

Effective Planning
Appropriate Resource Decisions
Workable Budgets, Projects, and Operational Plans

IT Actions

Bottom-Line Results

Performance Measurement Metrics

However, the management culture issues are equally important, not only as impediments but also as outcomes from applying the processes. We will devote considerable time to addressing the culture issues and the disconnects, as we present our five practice areas.

FOCUS ON THE RIGHT THINGS: MANAGEMENT AGENDA

Management Question	Yes or No?	If No, What Is Our Plan for Correcting This?
Do enterprise planning and management processes produce explicit and actionable strategic intentions?		
Are all IT actions and spending driven by business strategic intentions?		
Are IT activities and resources planned, prioritized, executed, and measured based on their connection and contribution to business outcomes?		
Are resources—both ongoing expenses and new investments—allocated and budgeted based on explicit connection to strategic intentions?		
Are managers' roles clearly defined to assure proper participation and avoid disconnects created by an organization's existing culture?		
Are all IT activities and spending organized into resource and process portfolios for purposes of impact assessment, performance management, quality and service level assessment, and resource commitment?		
Do planning, prioritizing, and measuring combine support of "strategy to action" with the ability to react to unexpected events and business change?		

ADDITIONAL READINGS

Additional information relating to Chapter 5 can be found in Appendix C, "The Development of Strategic Intentions, with Examples."

NOTES

1. We developed the idea of "management factors" in the original *Information Economics* work in 1987, and these evolved into strategic intentions. Our use

of strategic intention is parallel to the concept of strategic intent, described in Gary Hamel and C.K. Prahaled, "Strategic Intent," *Harvard Business Review,* May–June 1989, pp. 67–83.

2. See Chapter 3.

3. See Chapter 3 for other examples of strategic intentions. See also Appendix C, "The Development of Strategic Intentions, with Examples," for examples of strategic intentions from business and government.

4. Tichy Noel and Stratford Sherman, *Control Your Destiny or Someone Else Will* (Doubleday, 1993).

5. Sumantra Ghoshal, Christopher A. Bartlett, and Peter Moran, "A New Manifesto for Management," *Sloan Management Review,* Spring 1999, pp. 9–20.

6. See Appendix C, "The Development of Strategic Intentions, with Examples," for examples of strategic intentions from business and government.

7. See, for example, R. Swift, M. Mack, and J.M. Descarpentries, *Unlocking the Computer's Profit Potential* (New York: McKinsey, 1968). See also John Dearden, "MIS Is a Mirage," *Harvard Business Review,* January–February 1972, pp. 90–99.

8. How to do ROI other than on the basis of expense reduction for projects in nonprofit and government organizations remains problematic.

9. See Parker and Benson, with Trainor, *Information Economics* (Englewood Cliffs, NJ: Prentice-Hall, 1988) and, by the same authors, *Information Strategy and Economics* (Englewood Cliffs, NJ: Prentice-Hall, 1989).

10. The ideas and methodologies apply equally to nonprofit and government organizations.

11. See, for example, David A. Garvin, and Michael A. Roberto, "What You Don't Know about Making Decisions," *Harvard Business Review,* September 2001, pp. 108–116.

12. IT expenditures might be enterprise-wide, covering multiple IT organizations and business units. Hence, portfolio management could open important enterprise-wide coordination and management issues. In practical terms, however, the primary application of portfolio management begins within individual IT organizations and then is extended enterprise-wide.

CHAPTER 6

Adopt Effective Process to Produce Action

This book is about controlling the IT spend and maximizing IT's bottom-line impact. The goal is to move companies past their disconnected and ineffective management processes and into an area where IT can consistently make significant contributions to the business.

We make three basic points here. First, a company should formally adopt a connected set of management processes to produce the 12 elements of the Strategy-to-Bottom-Line Value Chain as displayed in Exhibit 6.3. Second, we recommend that management employ five New Information Economics (NIE) practices to be embedded in this connected set of management processes. These five practices will strengthen the deliverables and, significantly, strengthen the connections between them. Third, we encourage the management team to focus on producing action through the Value Chain and the NIE practices.

Control Spending and Maximize Impact on the Bottom Line	
1	Define the Goals
2	Ask the Right Questions
3	Connect to the Bottom Line
4	Understand Costs and Resources
5	Focus on the Right Things
6	**Adopt Effective Process to Produce Action**
7	Tackle the Practical Problems
8	Make the Right Decisions
9	Plan for the Right Results
10	Keep Score
11	Deal with Culture
12	Chart the Path to Implementation
13	Define What's Next
14	Answer the "So What?" Question

We emphasize our third recommendation because merely having good answers to the questions about IT's alignment and affordability, and using good management practices to get the answers, is no longer sufficient for most companies.

Actions, and the resulting bottom-line impacts, are what matter.

Action is vital due to the importance of IT to the company's basic business strategies. As one commentator put it: "The vast array of web applications for supply chain integration, customer relationship management, sales force automation, work group collaboration and the sale of everything from equities to automobiles should make it perfectly clear that information technology has evolved beyond the role of mere infrastructure in support of business strategy. In more and more industries today, IT *is* the business strategy."[1] Without action, however, the strategy—and IT—become meaningless.

Too many times, we have seen managers make decisions without the necessary follow-up to ensure actions take place. Even with the best of project prioritization, there is no guarantee that any of the projects will actually get done successfully or actually affect the bottom line. Decisions are not enough; successful action is required. Getting bottom-line results requires action by senior managers to implement their decisions, and action by IT and business managers to follow through on the projects and operational decisions.

In this chapter, we describe the Strategy-to-Bottom-Line Value Chain with its five NIE practices. Applying the Value Chain enables a company to move from its business strategies to the IT actions that produce the appropriate business bottom-line results. We previously introduced some of the practical problems in doing this, such as existing management culture, disconnects in management practices, and the legacy of IT applications and infrastructures. We will describe the details of the practices in Chapters 8 through 10, and how they fit into the existing management practices a company currently employs, such as capital and operational budgeting, strategic planning, and management compensation.

The five NIE practices have evolved and developed in the two decades since the original *Information Economics* book. The core concept, however, has remained as powerful as when we started in 1985: that IT has to fundamentally improve how the business[2] performs; to do this, business management must be directly involved in IT decision making. The NIE goals further elaborate this core concept, defining exactly what the business goals are, assessing and prioritizing alternatives, and implementing the right ones and measuring the results. The five practices implement the ways and means to achieve the goals.

THE STRATEGY-TO-BOTTOM-LINE VALUE CHAIN

We define the Strategy-to-Bottom-Line Value Chain as a series of connected management processes that culminate in project and operational budgets and the performance metrics to monitor action and bottom-line impact.

Exhibit 6.1 portrays at a high level the elements of planning and managing processes needed to produce the right decisions and right results for the bottom line.

- **Effective Planning**—Generates IT strategies, programs, and initiatives driven by business strategies, goals, and operational needs.

EXHIBIT 6.1   Strategy-to-Bottom-Line Value Chain

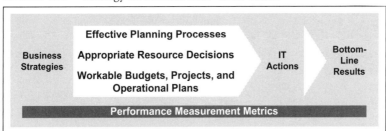

- **Appropriate Resource Decisions**—Reviews investments and prioritizes strategic programs and initiatives and projects, resulting in resources allocated to IT projects.

- **Workable Budgets, Projects, and Operational Plans**—Operationalizes and establishes the operating budget for the year and determines the schedules and goals of IT actions and projects, resulting in IT Actions that will produce the desired business results.

The Value Chain is made up of:

1. An integrated framework for the entire chain that is based on shared and consistent management roles, responsibilities, and information. The framework uses tools such as the IT portfolios described in the previous chapter as a kind of connective tissue.

2. A set of interconnected and interrelated practices that can take advantage of the overall framework and bring it to life. This requires that these practices be well-defined with consistent roles and processes.

3. A defined set of deliverables (as shown in Exhibit 6.3) that is internally consistent, carrying through from business strategic intentions to the IT projects and budgets that produce action.

This generic process model incorporates NIE practices and supporting practices such as portfolio management to provide a more integrated and effective strategy-to-bottom-line connection, as shown in Exhibit 6.2. These practices close the gaps within the strategy-to-results.

The practices, when integrated with existing company management processes such as budgeting and annual planning, will give the company a sound set of management processes that satisfy the goal of translating business strategy into IT actions that produce the right business results. The practices used in a connected set of management processes will enable management to control IT spending and improve IT's impact on the bottom line.

Unfortunately, many companies lack the integrated and connected planning processes that can produce IT plans or budgets that consistently support business strategies. Our experience has shown that companies, no matter how

EXHIBIT 6.2   NIE Practices in the Strategy-to-Bottom-Line Value Chain

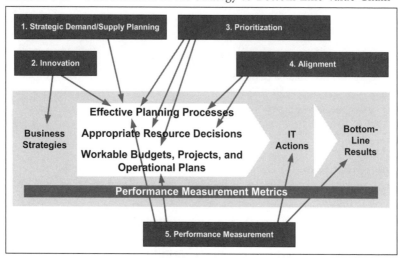

sophisticated or formal their planning processes, usually fall short of getting IT to contribute all that it can to achieving the strategic intentions. This chapter will offer specific ideas, techniques, and tools that will address that problem.

At a minimum, a company should have management processes that result in a strategic plan, IT projects, and an operating plan covering the business and IT. Many companies have processes that also produce the other deliverables as shown in Exhibit 6.3.

For companies with robust planning processes, the NIE practices are tools that can be plugged into the existing planning and management processes, and modified to meet the specific needs and circumstances of the company. Used in this way, the practices can serve to strengthen existing management and planning processes, and help the company improve IT's impact. (We do not propose that companies replace functioning planning processes with these practices. However, we do suggest that these five practices will provide new and useful data and insights that can be fed into existing processes, greatly improving their results.)

The Deliverables in the Strategy-to-Bottom-Line Value Chain

Twelve deliverables make up the Value Chain. They provide the information context within which each NIE practice operates and establish the basis for the process and information connections that lead from business strategy to the bottom-line outcomes.

Exhibit 6.3 should be looked at as a template defining the 12 deliverables. A company with well-established management processes may find they obtain the same information in different formats. However, the key points are:

EXHIBIT 6.3   Value Chain Deliverables

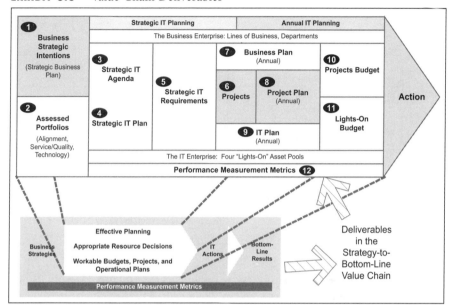

- The connection from the information on one deliverable to the creation of the next deliverable in the Value Chain.

- The connection of information from business sources (strategic intentions, business plans) to IT sources (portfolios and, within those portfolios, information from enterprise architecture and related technical planning processes).

- The connection to the budgeting business processes (and related processes of performance measurement).

For example, the information on business strategic intentions drives the creation of the strategic IT agenda, which drives strategic IT requirements, which are then turned into projects, and so forth. It is the connections that are important. The 12 deliverables are listed in Exhibit 6.4 and defined as follows.

1. **Business Strategic Intentions.** We defined these in Chapter 3. Examples are found in the Prioritization and Alignment practice descriptions in Chapter 8. As a deliverable, a chart formatted as shown in Chapter 3 defines the company's strategic intentions and, for each, goals, metrics, and weights. These are used in all five NIE practices. The content is company mission plus strategic intentions.

2. **Assessed Portfolios.** Chapter 4 introduced Portfolio Management. The portfolios of applications, infrastructures, services, and management areas

EXHIBIT 6.4   Descriptions of the 12 Deliverables

Strategy-to-Bottom-Line Value Chain			
		Deliverable Name	Deliverable Description
Strategic Planning	1	Business Strategic Intentions	Mission plus weighted Strategic Intentions
	2	Assessed Portfolios	As-is alignment, service, quality, technology, use
	3	Strategic IT Agenda for Use of IT	Strategic Intentions to Strategic Initiatives
	4	Strategic IT Plan	Strategic Intentions to Strategic Initiatives
	5	IT Strategic Requirements	Initiatives—3 to 5 years horizon—portfolio format
	6	Projects	Real, doable projects
Annual/Tactical Planning	7	Annual Project Plan	One year annual horizon—with portfolio format
	8	Annual Business Plan	Documentation according to company practices
	9	Annual IT Plan	Documentation according to company practices
	10	Annual and Capital Projects Budgets	Documentation according to company practices
	11	Annual Lights-On Budget	Documentation according to company practices
	12	Performance Measurement Metrics	Documentation according to company practices

are assessed for alignment, service, quality, technical, and intensity of use. These assessments are described in Chapter 8. The assessed portfolios are used in planning and in the development of strategic IT requirements through projects. The content is as-is alignment, service, quality, technology, and intensity of use for each line item in the portfolios.

3. **Strategic IT Agenda.** The agenda is an outcome of strategic IT planning. It defines what the business expects to do with IT to meet its strategic intentions. A further description and example is found in Chapter 9. The strategic IT agenda is used to drive strategic IT requirements and projects, as well as establish the obligations business management has to produce the expected bottom-line impact from IT spending. The content is business management's strategic intentions for the use of IT, strategic objectives for the use of IT, and the strategic initiatives with IT to achieve the company's business strategic intentions.

4. **Strategic IT Plan.** This plan is the outcome of strategic IT planning; it defines what the IT organization must do to meet the demands of the strategic IT agenda. It is used as the strategic framework for the IT lights-on budget and the technology-related projects needed to support the business projects. The content is the IT organization's strategic intentions to deliver IT to meet the business requirements defined above.

5. **Strategic IT Requirements.** This is a prioritized statement of programs and initiatives that, over the life of the strategic plan, will satisfy the requirements of the strategic IT agenda and the business strategic intentions. It is the portfolio of potential strategic initiatives, on a 3 to 5 year horizon, to meet the business requirements defined above, prioritized according to business strategic intentions.

6. **Projects.** Specific projects are defined in response to the programs and initiatives defined in strategic IT requirements. These are candidates for prioritization and inclusion in an annual project plan or budget. The content is real, do-able projects. (Not an NIE deliverable.)

7. **Annual Project Plan.** This is the annual set of projects expected to be undertaken during the current fiscal year. Of course, an "annual" perspective of projects is not timely or responsive enough for most businesses, so this deliverable is usually revisited quarterly or even more frequently for particularly dynamic businesses. The content is a portfolio of scheduled projects, with resources assigned, prioritized according to business strategic intentions.

8. **Annual Business Plan.** This is the set of annual[3] tactical and operational plans for the business units. It is the basis for establishing the annual project plan (see point 8 below) and defines what the business units will require tactically from IT. (Not an NIE deliverable.)

9. **IT Plan.** This is the set of annual tactical and operational plans for the IT organization. It is the basis for establishing the Lights-On budget for support of the business units. The content is documented according to company practices. (Not an NIE deliverable.)

10. **Projects Budget.** The budget is the aggregate investment budget for projects for the year. It is based on the "affordability" for the business units. Of course, this budget may be affected by business events during the year, and so is normally revisited quarterly or even more often depending on business dynamics. The content is documented according to company practices.

11. **Lights-On Budget.** This is the base budget for ongoing activities of the IT organization. It provides for all services and support not specifically provided in the Projects Budget. Taken together with the Projects Budget, 100 percent of the IT spend is defined. The content is documented according to company practices.

12. **Performance Measurement Metrics.** This is the set of metrics for IT and for the use of IT in the business. The content is documented according to company practices.

We recognize that the deliverable descriptions above may not apply cleanly to each company situation, due to such variables as company size, company complexity, and the ways in which IT services are delivered (e.g., outsourcing, shared service organizations). Nevertheless, they represent a framework to define the needed information in the Strategy-to-Bottom-Line Value Chain.

Moreover they represent the *connected set of information* to drive from strategy to bottom-line impact. However the company may manage its activities and processes, the information defined here is required. To the extent the information is not available, or is developed in a disconnected way, the company will have great difficulty in controlling IT spending and maximizing IT's impact on the bottom line.

ESTABLISHING THE PROCESS CONNECTIONS

The Strategy-to-Bottom-Line Value Chain, in addition to being a connected set of information represented by the deliverables, is also a connected set of processes.

Exhibit 6.5 shows a generic set of processes that deliver the 12 Value Chain deliverables. The corporate/business processes of corporate strategic planning, business unit planning, budget, procurement, capital budget, and measurement interact with the Value Chain processes by providing the basic business information and, critically, operationalizing the results through budgets and performance measurements. The IT management processes of enterprise architecture, project management, systems development, IT planning, and the administrative processes interact by providing technical direction and, ultimately, the lights-on and project budgets.

EXHIBIT 6.5   Management Processes in and around the Value Chain

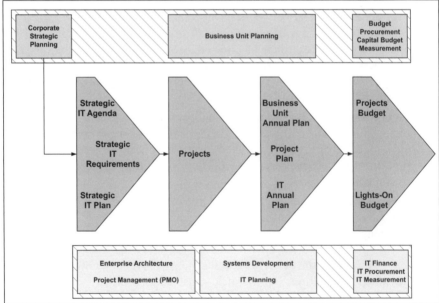

MANAGEMENT ROLES

Achieving the goals of connected information and processes, in an unbroken chain that carries on from business strategy to budgets and actions, requires that management understand the roles to be played, and then actually play them.

Management, in this case, includes the senior leadership team, one or more business leadership teams, the technology leadership team, and the manager who is responsible for conducting and coordinating the processes that produce the deliverables in the value chain.

This is so easy to say, and potentially so difficult to do. The risk is that what we describe in this chapter and the book sounds so overwhelming and intimidating that a manager interested in pursuing the ideas abandons them because the task of interacting with senior and business leadership is so daunting and may feel impossible. The potential impediments include management culture, management disinterest in the process, misunderstanding the goals and the importance of achieving them, politics, awkward organizational structures, and personalities. This is a tough list.[4]

Here, we introduce the big picture of the management roles needed, according to the Strategy-to-Bottom-Line Value Chain. Again, we understand that companies have existing processes that do produce most if not all of the deliverables. Our primary interest is in their connection and consistency, and the tool set used (e.g., prioritization with strategic intentions, etc.). See Exhibit 6.6.

The *senior leadership team* is corporate leadership, typically consisting of the CxOs. The *business leadership team* can be business unit CEOs and, in the case of multi-SBU companies, their direct reports. More typically, this team comes from the set of direct reports to the senior leadership team. The *IT leadership team* is from the IT providers; note that this can include representation from outsourcing organizations if they are in the picture. The *Value Chain Process Owner* is an awkward way of stating which individual is accountable for accomplishing parts or all of the Value Chain activities.

This description is necessarily very generic, as every company has differing management patterns. In some situations, for example, the same set of individuals fulfill more than one role. This description also flows from a "central" perspective, with the notion of one company leadership team and one IT team. This may not be the case, and possibly several sets of individual teams, and management processes, are required. It should be apparent that the specifics of the individuals and teams are highly dependent on the company situations and have to be developed uniquely for every company. Nevertheless, the table in Exhibit 6.6 gives a good perspective on what is required.

NEW INFORMATION ECONOMICS PRACTICES

The New Information Economics is a set of coordinated practices base on principles and integrated activities that effectively connect business and IT management processes and, thereby, connect the enterprise's business strategies to its IT initiatives and activities. NIE is a complete view of the required relationships between business units and IT, based on the overriding principle that all enterprise activities and resources must support the enterprise's strategies and impact its bottom line. This requires a consistent, integrated set of practices for planning, innovating, prioritizing, aligning and allocating resources, and managing

EXHIBIT 6.6   Management's Role in the Value Chain

		Deliverable Name	Senior Leadership Team	Business Leadership Team	Technology Leadership Team	Value Chain Process Owner (IT Impact Management)
Strategic Planning Cycle	1	Business Strategic Intentions	Approve and weight strategic intentions	Revise and review strategic intentions		Create initial draft strategic intentions (strawman)
	2	Assessed Portfolios	Review	Assess portfolios/ alignment, service, quality	Contribute to portfolio development Assess portfolio/ technology	Manage portfolio development Manage the assessment process
	3	Strategic IT Agenda for Use of IT	Approve	Develop IT Agenda	Participate in IT Agenda process	Create the initial drafts (strawman)
	4	Strategic IT Plan	Review	Review IT Plan	Develop IT Plan	Create the initial drafts (strawman)
	5	IT Strategic Requirements	Review	Develop Requirements Prioritization Recommend decisions	Participate in IT requirements process	Drive the process
Annual/Tactical Planning Cycle	6	Projects	Review, approve large projects	Create project requirements and business cases	Form detailed projects and technical requirements	Assure that project formation works right
	7	Annual Project Plan	Make decisions or approve funding	Prioritization Recommend funding	Establish annual project plan and schedules	Drive the process
	8	Annual Business Plan	Approve	Review IT plans Establish business unit plans	Advise	Assure this happens
	9	Annual IT Plan	Approve	Review	Develop IT plans Establish budgets	Assure this happens
	10	Annual and Capital Projects Budgets	Approve	Develop budgets	Participate in budget planning	Create initial draft (strawman)
	11	Annual Lights-On Budget	Review	Review	Develop budget Initiate plans	Create initial draft (strawman)
	12	Performance Measurement Metrics	Approve	Establish business performance metrics	Establish IT performance metrics	Assure this happens Create initial drafts (strawman)

performance across the enterprise. This also requires attention to the management culture that can inhibit the adoption of NIE practices.

In practical terms, as we noted earlier, companies have existing, though possibly disconnected, management processes that deal with IT planning and budgets. These existing processes deal with *plans, resource decisions,* and *operationalizing* those plans through budgets and metrics. We propose to connect those existing processes, define the appropriate deliverables, and make them effective in producing business impact (IT's contributions to profitability, and in the case of government and nonprofit, impact on the organization's mission). We do so by applying the five basic NIE practices, defining the information to be produced (e.g., the annual project plan), and embedding them in the company's processes.

With the right goals in mind, and mindful of the management culture needed to support the NIE practices, the result is that the company processes that deal with *plans, resources,* and *operationalizing* will produce the *outcomes* that result in the right IT actions and the right business results. Management will be able to answer the affordability and alignment questions posed in Chapter 1, leading to controlling IT spending and improving IT's bottom-line impact.

New Information Economics Practices in the Value Chain

New Information Economics is a set of five practices, shown in Exhibit 6.7, that are tools for IT and business managers to use, embedded in management processes, in translating a company's business strategies into programs and initiatives that

EXHIBIT 6.7   Practices in the Value Chain

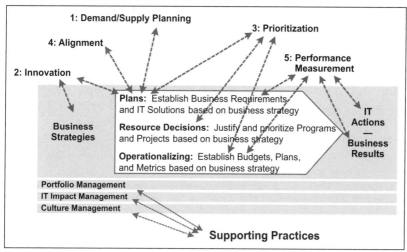

IT can implement. The table in Exhibit 6.8 shows where the five NIE practices apply with respect to the information (deliverable) in the Value Chain.

The five practices are defined briefly below.

NIE Practice 1: Strategic Demand/Supply Planning

Goal: IT planning is explicitly driven by business strategies and business requirements. It is all too easy for IT planning to focus on technology matters rather

EXHIBIT 6.8   NIE Practices in the Value Chain

		Deliverable Name	Deliverable Description	NIE Practice
Strategy-to-Bottom-Line Value Chain				
Strategic Planning	1	Business Strategic Intentions	Mission plus weighted Strategic Intentions	Demand/Supply Planning Innovation
	2	Assessed Portfolios	As-is alignment, service, quality, technology, use	Alignment Performance Measurement
	3	Strategic IT Agenda for the Use of IT	Strategic Intentions to Strategic Initiatives	Demand/Supply Planning
	4	Strategic IT Plan	Strategic Intentions to Strategic Initiatives	Demand/Supply Planning Innovation
	5	IT Strategic Requirements	Initiatives—3 to 5 years horizon—portfolio format	Demand/Supply Planning Prioritization
Annual/Tactical Planning	6	Projects	Real, doable projects	
	7	Annual Project Plan	One year annual horizon— with portfolio format	Prioritization
	8	Annual Business Plan	Documentation according to company practices	
	9	Annual IT Plan	Documentation according to company practices	
	10	Annual and Capital Projects Budgets	Documentation according to company practices	Alignment, Prioritization
	11	Annual Lights-On Budget	Documentation according to company practices	Alignment
	12	Performance Measurement Metrics	Documentation according to company practices	Performance Measurement

than strategic business matters. Planning that is not business-strategy-driven means that IT plans respond and connect to individual business unit tactical needs rather than the business strategy, and by extension, the senior management team will not believe that IT is connected to strategy. As a result, the company cannot be certain it is able to proceed from their business strategies to the necessary IT actions.

IT strategic plans are constructed with two distinct components:

1. A description of the *demand* for IT services, generated by the business strategies and goals, and articulated as strategic IT requirements,

2. A description of the future *supply* of IT services, represented by the IT strategic agenda.

In this way the strategic plan clearly separates the *requirements* for IT, driven by the business strategies, from IT's response to those requirements. Separating these components allows business management to see in specific terms the demands that their strategies are placing on IT, while allowing a clear "matching" of IT's responses to those demands. We explicitly answer the questions: What are the strategic demands on IT, and what is IT going to strategically supply?

	Management Process—Desired Outcomes	Business—Desired Outcomes
Strategic Demand/Supply Planning	IT and business planning are fully connected and integrated.	The company improves strategic and bottom-line impact from its IT investments.

NIE Practice 2: Innovation

Goal: Effectively translate new IT opportunities into competitive advantage and bottom-line results.

IT has an important role and responsibility to bring innovative opportunities to the business that can shape new products, services, and processes. In this way, IT's role includes responding to current requirements and influencing future requirements. Without a concerted effort on innovation, IT will only support existing business operational requirements, particularly those for its major user organizations. Innovation always gets squeezed when operational needs are most clearly in view.

	Management Process—Desired Outcomes	Business—Desired Outcomes
Innovation	IT-enabled innovations impact business planning and offer new strategies.	The company continually improves products, processes, and bottom-line performance through IT innovations.

NIE Practice 3: Prioritization

Goal: Spending priorities are primarily determined by business strategies. As the Prioritization Practice description in Chapter 8 discusses, in the absence of a strategy-based prioritization practice, priorities will be set by politics, the loudest voices, or historical practices. The result is that new investments will be determined not by business strategies but by tactical needs. As a result, IT resources are probably not being invested in the right places.

All programs and initiatives are prioritized based on their expected business impact. All elements of each portfolio are reviewed, and the result of program prioritization is the strategic IT agenda, which will then drive annual IT investments. Using the strategic IT agenda, business and IT develop the projects that will support the agenda. These projects are then also prioritized, providing the input for the IT annual plans and budgets.

	Management Process—Desired Outcomes	Business—Desired Outcomes
Prioritization	IT investments are prioritized against business strategy.	The company improves bottom-line impact and return on its IT investments.

NIE Practice 4: Alignment

Goal: Base IT spending for lights-on activities on what is actually needed to meet strategic and operational requirements. As discussed in the Alignment Practice section in Chapter 8, baseline budgets can typically be on a "cost plus" basis, with the result that this main part of IT expenses is not subject to strategy-based decision making. The result is that infrastructure, support, and operations spending can easily go to efforts that no longer support current business strategies. The company is not getting sufficient impact from its existing IT resources, nor can it determine whether the right amount is being spent on IT.

In many companies, these legacy activities are sacrosanct, considered by business management as an entitlement, and rarely reviewed for continued relevance to the business. However, these ongoing activities represent a large portion of IT resources and can dramatically reduce the available *supply* of IT to meet new strategic business demands. Unless they are also viewed in the context of the current business strategic intentions, the company cannot determine if they continue to provide impact and continue to warrant resources.

An important part of alignment is examining the current performance of existing IT resources. Performance is defined in service-level, quality, technology, and intensity-of-use terms. As a part of the alignment practice, the current portfolios are assessed, and produce the Assessed Portfolios deliverable in the value chain.

	Management Process—Desired Outcomes	Business—Desired Outcomes
Alignment	The entire IT spend is aligned with business strategy. The entire IT spend is assessed for quality, technology, and so forth.	The company improves returns from its IT activities in terms of bottom-line impact. The total IT spend is effectively controlled.

NIE Practice 5: Performance Measurement

Goal: Track the performance of IT investments in the business. As Chapter 10 points out, performance measurement is critical to determining whether strategy and operational goals are being met, and whether the IT resources are performing as well as possible. Without performance measurement, there is no way to assure that resources are performing, or that goals are being met. The result is that the company cannot determine if it is getting sufficient impact from IT resources or even that the right amount is being spent on IT.

A performance measurement process is included in the strategy-to-bottom-line chain. It is critical for IT to monitor its performance with metrics that the business understands, not just internal IT operational performance metrics that do not clearly relate to the business bottom line. By adding business performance metrics to the chain, we close the loop and insure that IT is focused on producing business results. It is the combination of performance metrics with strategy-driven IT plans that produces IT action. Without performance measurement programs, business will not know how well IT is performing and what impact IT is having on the business.

	Management Process—Desired Outcomes	Business—Desired Outcomes
Performance Measurement	IT business and technical performance is tracked.	Performance measures lead to improved IT and business performance.

We also employ basic concepts of IT impact, portfolio, and culture management in the five practices.

IT Impact Management

Goal: Implement NIE practices successfully and achieve the affordability and alignment goals of controlling IT spending and improving IT's bottom-line impact.

Using the NIE practices effectively requires planning and coordination. The connections with corporate and IT processes, and the assurance that the results of the practices appear in budgets and performance measurement all require constant and persistent management attention.

Treating the Strategy-to-Bottom-Line Value Chain and the NIE practices as a significant management initiative is critical to success. That means, among other things, assigning management responsibilities on an ongoing basis, and establishing long-term strategies goals and short-term tactics for the Value Chain and the Practices. We bundle all of this under the heading IT Impact Management, and devote Chapter 13 to its discussion. We also highlight IT Impact Management solutions to several practical problems that we discuss in Chapter 7.

Note that we emphatically do not recommend that a company adopt the entire Value Chain template or apply all NIE practices at once. The particular situation of a given company and its management objectives dictate how to approach improving the processes that influence IT spend and IT's bottom-line impact. Nevertheless, doing any of this does affect management roles, culture, existing practices, and does require appropriate management attention. Thus, the need for *IT Impact Management.*

	Management Process—Desired Outcomes	Business—Desired Outcomes
IT Impact Management	Business and IT management teams execute the processes that improve IT's contribution to business performance.	The total IT spend is effectively controlled. IT's contribution to bottom-line impact is improved.

Portfolios and Portfolio Management

Goal: All the IT resources (infrastructures and legacy applications as well as new development projects) are directed at business strategies. Is management paying attention to the proper allocation of ongoing IT expenses as well as new application investments? Without looking at the entire IT spend from the perspective of business strategy, resources will be wasted.

	Management Process—Desired Outcomes	Business—Desired Outcomes
Portfolio Management	Planning and management processes focus on the entire IT investment.	All IT investments and resources contribute to bottom-line impact.

Culture Management

Goal: The management team understands the impact of IT, and manages the business to achieve it. A company's culture can have many facets that inhibit effective use of IT resources, including agreement on what is important, what planning and management behavior is to be encouraged, the value of working together across silos and between IT and business, and so forth. IT is inherently cross-silo and integrating; the culture can make this most difficult. The result is that the company may not be getting full impact from IT.

Business Value Maturity Model™

Goal: Overcome company management culture hurdles and limitations on the company's ability to execute NIE practices. The Business Value Maturity Model™ describes desired business outcomes for each NIE practice area, and we use "maturity" as the measure of whether the company can produce the outcomes based on a combination of culture barriers and company capability to act on the results.

	Management Process—Desired Outcomes	Business—Desired Outcomes
Culture Management and the Maturity Model	IT and business managers participate effectively in all NIE-enabled processes.	IT's contribution to bottom-line impact is improved through effective business and IT manager participation in NIE processes.

SUMMING UP NEW INFORMATION ECONOMICS PRACTICES

The five NIE practices, together with the three supporting areas of IT Impact, Portfolio, and Culture Management, work in concert with the company's management processes that deal with IT's plans and budgets. By embedding the NIE practices into company processes, business and process outcomes are produced, all of which are part of successfully getting from *strategy* to the right *IT Action* and the right *Business Results,* thereby controlling IT spending and improving IT's bottom-line impact.

These practice outcomes are in two categories as shown in Exhibit 6.9. *Management Process—Desired Outcomes* are those that change, and strengthen, the existing company processes that deal with IT plans and budgets. These process outcomes affect how the company management teams conduct the management processes, and changes the roles management plays. *Business—Desired Outcomes* directly affect bottom-line impact and, for government and nonprofits, impact on mission performance.

EXHIBIT 6.9   Management and Business—Desired Outcomes

NIE Practices and Support Practices	Management Process—Desired Outcomes	Business—Desired Outcomes
Strategic Demand/Supply Planning	IT and business planning are fully connected and integrated.	The company improves strategic and bottom-line impact from its IT investments.
Innovation	IT-enabled innovations impact business planning and offer new strategies.	The company continually improves products, processes, and bottom-line performance through IT innovations.
Prioritization	IT investments are prioritized against business strategy.	The company improves bottom-line impact and return on its IT investments.
Alignment	The entire IT spend is aligned with business strategy.	The company improves returns from its IT activities in terms of bottom-line impact. The total IT spend is effectively controlled.
Performance Measurement	IT business and technical performance is tracked.	Performance measures lead to improved IT and business performance.
IT Impact Management	Business and IT management teams execute the processes that improve IT's contribution to business performance.	The total IT spend is effectively controlled. IT's contribution to bottom-line impact is improved.
Portfolio Management	Planning and management processes focus on the entire IT investment.	All IT investments and resources—development and lights-on—contribute to bottom-line impact.
Culture Management and Maturity Model	IT and business managers participate effectively in all NIE-enabled processes.	IT's contribution to bottom-line impact is improved through effective business and IT manager participation in NIE processes.

SUMMING UP: ADOPT EFFECTIVE PROCESS TO PRODUCE ACTION

At the outset of this chapter, we made three recommendations.

1.   A company should formally adopt a connected set of management processes to produce the 12 deliverables of the Strategy-to-Bottom-Line Value Chain, as displayed in Exhibit 6.3.

2. Management should employ five NIE practices to be embedded in this connected set of management processes. These five practices will strengthen the deliverables and strengthen the connections between them.

3. The management team should focus on producing action through the Value Chain and the NIE practices.

We have described the Value Chain and the NIE practices, along with an implementation management program we call *IT Impact Management.*

Putting the five practices together, Exhibit 6.10 states the results:

EXHIBIT 6.10   NIE Practice Outcomes

Statement of Right Decisions/Right Results Goal	NIE Practices Outcomes as Applied in the Strategy-to-Bottom-Line Value Chain
Translate enterprise mission and strategy into actionable, commonly understood strategic intentions.	The business strategic intentions are used in all five NIE practices. All IT actions and spending are driven by business strategic intentions, through Prioritization and Alignment practices. Managers across all functional areas understand strategic intentions and IT's role in achieving them, through participation in the NIE practices of Planning, Prioritization, and Alignment.
Assess the impact and get the right bottom-line results from all current and future IT spending by evaluating the impact on strategic intentions.	IT activities and resources are planned, prioritized, executed, and measured based on their connection and contribution to business outcomes and strategic intentions. IT's business impact is assessed through its cause-and-effect linkages with strategic intentions leading to bottom-line outcomes. IT Activities and resources are planned, prioritized, executed, and measured based on their connection and contribution to strategic intentions which lead to bottom-line business outcomes. Resources—both lights-on expenses and new investments—are allocated and budgeted based on explicit connection to strategic intentions.
Manage the culture and management roles regarding the use of IT for achieving business strategic intentions.	Managers' roles are clearly defined to assure proper participation and avoid disconnects created by an organization's existing culture. Managers, through participating in NIE practices, understand IT's role and connection to strategic intentions.
Manage IT as a set of resource and process portfolios.	All IT activities and spending are organized into resource and process portfolios for purposes of impact assessment, performance management, quality and service level assessment, and resource commitment.
Produce the right actions and bottom-line results and use budgets, projects, and performance measurement to achieve them.	Planning, prioritizing, and measuring combine support of "strategy to bottom line" with the ability to react to unexpected events and business change.

ADOPT EFFECTIVE PROCESS TO PRODUCE ACTION: MANAGEMENT AGENDA

The following is a self-examination for the critical success factors for Right Decisions/Right Results.

Management Question	Yes or No?	If No, What Is Our Plan for Correcting This?
Demand/Supply Planning—Does the company improve strategic and operational impact from its IT investments?		
Innovation—Does the company excel in innovating through IT, in products, processes, and performance?		
Prioritization—Does the company choose the most valuable IT investments?		
Alignment—Does the company improve returns from its IT activities?		
Performance Measurement—Does the use of performance measures lead to improved IT and business performance?		
Culture Management—Is management able to optimize IT's contribution to business performance?		
Portfolio Management—Do all IT investments and resources contribute to business performance?		
IT Impact Management—Does the effective application of NIE practices in all areas of the business improve IT's return?		

Chapters 8 through 10 explain the practices needed to answer the "What Is Our Plan for Correcting This?" question.

ADDITIONAL READING

The book's website contains additional information related to Chapter 6:

Website Note 4: Tests for Connected Business and IT

The appendices at the back of the book also contain information related to Chapter 6:

Appendix A: The Role of Enterprise Architecture in Right Decisions/Right Results

NOTES

1. Michael J. Earl and David Feeny, "How to Be a CEO for the Information Age," *Sloan Management Review,* Winter 2000, pp. 11–23.

2. While the terminology here and throughout the book is in "business" terms, the concepts and practices apply with equal force to government and nonprofit organizations. While business is concerned with competitive strategy and financial outcomes, government is just as concerned with strategy and performance to organizational mission.

3. We use the term "annual" in the description of Value Chain deliverables. However, some organizations do tactical planning in different time frames, such as quarterly or bi-annually. We are not specifying that "annual" is the only appropriate timeframe.

4. We address management role and the related problems of culture directly in Chapter 7, "Tackle the Practical Problems"; in Chapter 11, "Deal with Culture"; and in Chapter 14, "Answer the 'So What?' Question." In Chapter 13, we establish a supporting IT Impact Management practice that provides tools and directions for moving forward. In particular, we outline an incremental process for going forward.

CHAPTER 7

Tackle the Practical Problems

In Chapter 6, we made three basic points: (1) a company should adopt a connected set of management processes to produce the deliverables represented by the Strategy-to-Bottom-Line Value Chain; (2) a company should employ one or more of the NIE practices (e.g., Prioritization, Alignment) as part of those processes, and (3) a management team should focus on getting the right action to produce bottom-line impact. The three points make up what is required to control IT spending and improve IT's bottom-line impact.

The question now is: What does it take for a company to follow these three recommendations? What are the practical problems involved?

Control Spending and Maximize Impact on the Bottom Line	
1	Define the Goals
2	Ask the Right Questions
3	Connect to the Bottom Line
4	Understand Costs and Resources
5	Focus on the Right Things
6	Adopt Effective Process to Produce Action
7	**Tackle the Practical Problems**
8	Make the Right Decisions
9	Plan for the Right Results
10	Keep Score
11	Deal with Culture
12	Chart the Path to Implementation
13	Define What's Next
14	Answer the "So What?" Question

A PRACTICAL PERSPECTIVE

We need to put these issues of disconnects, management roles, and the Value Chain in some practical perspective. There is a risk that it sounds like a very large undertaking to accomplish anything practical and worthwhile. For many company situations we may overemphasize the issues of process connection and the Strategy-to-Bottom-Line Value Chain, and the "global" view of management roles. However, much of the value is contained in the individual NIE practices—in particular, prioritization and alignment. These are things that can be done well *by themselves* and, in fact, are appropriate places for a company to begin. In the right circumstances, a company can adopt an NIE practice, or parts of a practice, to good effect. That, by itself, can begin to address culture and role questions.

The reason we say so much about connection, consistency, roles, and so forth, is that they so greatly influence the long-term value of adopting a business-strategy-based focus on IT spending and IT's bottom-line impact. This is because it is, fundamentally, a systemic set of problems and solutions. As we have repeatedly said, unless the outcomes of things such as decision making in prioritization get directly reflected in budgets, nothing will happen. In order to effectively and continuously control IT spending and improve IT's bottom-line impact, the issue of connection, and related issues, really do have to be addressed.

In the meantime, if a company is interested in getting started, then we can apply one or more NIE practices and make progress. This is a good start, but it won't produce lasting changes.

THE PRACTICAL PROBLEMS REVOLVE AROUND PEOPLE

Good management processes alone are not sufficient.

The best planning and prioritization practices will fail when senior management does not accept the results, or act on them. The best alignment and performance measurement practices will fail when line management does not understand the results or does not consider them important enough to affect their areas of responsibilities. The best innovation practices will fail to generate new ideas and business opportunities when the management culture does not accept them. In proposing the kind of management processes necessary to improve IT's bottom-line impact, we treat management culture and disconnects as a critical element, and propose methods for addressing these issues.

A company cannot successfully adopt the Value Chain and NIE practices without the proper culture and without management taking necessary actions. Therefore, we explicitly describe the relationship between having good "mechanical" processes and the related cultural and management behavior requirements. The distinction is between simply executing step-by-step processes and the commitment necessary to transform the management processes to produce results consistent with the values and necessary outcomes. These are the cultures and behaviors necessary to transform mechanical *process* into an effective set of management *values* applied in *decision making,* producing decisions in which management believes and is willing to invest time and resources.

We have all experienced the real impediments, such as politics and culture: "doing things the way we've always done them." Encouraging individual managers to do what is necessary can be difficult, particularly when the actions involve many organizations across many silos. IT, often, is exactly in this situation. Getting the right results comes down to getting individual managers to do the right things. (For that matter, the same impediments occur when trying to get the right decisions from management teams.)

This chapter is as much about the questions leading to decisions as it is about the actions that may result. We want to lay the groundwork for making the right decisions, and then guide and motivate all concerned to take the right actions. None of this matters unless things actually happen.

ADDRESSING PRACTICAL PROBLEMS: IT IMPACT MANAGEMENT

In this chapter,[1] we explore several practical problems and our strategy for solving them. We adopt a program management approach, called *IT Impact Management,* to the planning and implementation of the Right Decisions/Right Results frameworks and processes. This approach is based on addressing each of the practical problems. The focus is on affecting the way the company and its managers make decisions and allocate resources.

PRACTICAL PROBLEMS GETTING FROM STRATEGY TO BOTTOM-LINE IMPACT

The fundamental challenge is to translate the company's business strategies and goals into the right IT actions to produce the right bottom-line impact. This is done by effective planning, appropriate resource decisions, and workable budgets and operational plans. The objective is to control IT spending and improve IT's bottom-line impact. But serious practical problems face the management team committed to doing this. See Exhibit 7.1.

1. *Process Disconnects.* Management is unable to consistently carry through from business planning to IT action to bottom-line results.

2. *Legacy and Entitlement Mentality.* The company's existing IT applications, infrastructures, and project backlogs are the legacy of the existing strategy-to-results management practices, and prevent starting with a clean slate. Managers feel entitled to "their" systems and support.

3. *Management Roles.* The company's management culture prevents business and IT management from playing the roles needed to effectively direct and apply IT resources to achieve improved bottom-line impact.

EXHIBIT 7.1   Strategy to Bottom-Line Impact: Business Results

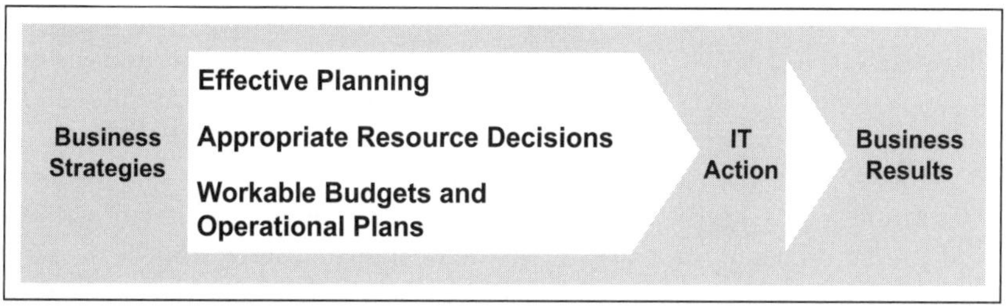

Business Strategies → Effective Planning / Appropriate Resource Decisions / Workable Budgets and Operational Plans → IT Action → Business Results

4. *Company Processes.* The new or changed management practices that connect business and IT will have to coexist and work with many other existing company management practices (e.g., capital budgets, HR, management performance/compensation, corporate budgets, purchasing, and so forth).

5. *Management Expectations.* Senior company managers only expect financial return from IT and simple measurement of its alignment and affordability.

6. *It Ain't Broke.* . . . Individual managers get what they need with the processes they currently use.

7. *Multiple Perspectives.* The company does not speak with one voice.

Our solution is IT Impact Management, a program of management initiatives that address the practical issues result in effectively controlling IT spend and improving IT's bottom-line impact.

Practical Problem 1: Process Disconnects

Existing management processes are unable to consistently carry through from business planning to IT action to bottom-line results.

Most companies already carry on planning activities; they have some means of making resource decisions, and they do have operating budgets and operating plans. Most often, however, these basic management activities are disconnected and fail to consistently carry through from business strategy to IT action. Business planning does not effectively connect to IT planning, which does not directly influence the annual budget process and which is not reflected in the performance measurement practice that governs management behavior. Management's goal should be to produce IT actions that, together with the business organization's initiatives, directly carry out the business strategies to get the right bottom-line impact.

Every organization has its own distinct planning culture that is reflected in its specific strategic and tactical planning processes (both for business and IT). Our experience has been that in most organizations, the various planning activities are loosely coordinated and not well integrated. Moving from business strategy to IT action in these cases mimics the old parlor game of passing a statement serially around a group of people: By the time business strategies eventually become IT actions, much of the original meaning of the strategy has been lost.

There can be a considerable gap between management's planning process and how something actually happens in IT (see Exhibit 7.2). In some cases, the planning process itself gets in the way (poor timing, ineffective communication, or ineffective goal setting and goal articulation), or there is no follow-up to planning to be sure that the actions taken reflect the company's intentions. The existing processes typically are not coordinated or integrated, so annual budgets and project plans are not driven by the business strategies but reflect a different set of priorities, often tactical and tied to individual managers' wants.

EXHIBIT 7.2   Process Disconnects in the Value Chain

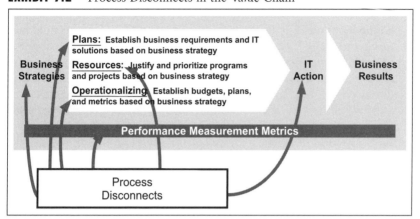

Regardless of the cause, few companies are making the best use of their IT investments and resources.

A second reason is that the people who perform each management practice are in different parts of the company's organization and do not routinely work together. Those who prepare company budgets and company management performance systems are not the same people who conduct strategic planning, who are different yet from those who make resource prioritization decisions. Without explicit connections built into consistently applied management practices, business strategies are not reflected in IT plans, resource decisions, and budgets. The result is that senior managers do not understand what the company gets from its IT investments and do not understand IT's alignment and affordability.

A third reason is the business and functional silos that exist in almost every company. The silos can be business units, such as the life insurance business in an insurance company, or they can be functional areas, such as finance or marketing or even IT. Silos can get in the way of common business strategies and, in particular, impede cross-silo IT solutions, making connecting IT action to business strategy very difficult.

A fourth reason is that significant disconnects occur in the way business and IT management work together in planning, innovation, prioritization, alignment, and performance measurement. Additionally, management culture, in both IT and business, presents significant hurdles to overcoming the disconnects. In many cases, culture reinforces the disconnect between business and IT management.

For example, in one large commercial bank, the CEO saw the operational and strategic importance of IT. He encouraged new investments to enhance the bank's infrastructure and applications for strategic and competitive objectives. Unfortunately, the existing management culture did not acknowledge the strategic importance of IT in the bank's business. IT was important to the leadership operationally, but the leadership did not see that new IT initiatives were potentially important to the bank. The bank's CEO became frustrated by his inability to get the leadership team to adopt IT as a major contributor to their individual annual plans and strategies. In spite of evangelistic leadership on his part and the focus on IT in the strategic planning cycle, he simply could not get his managers to take IT action driven from the business strategy.

The problem was not CEO leadership or attention. It was the disconnects that lay between the vision of applying IT and the individual manager's actions needed to accomplish it. These disconnects were in the culture, which encouraged existing business practices and immediate bottom-line performance, and in the processes, where nothing in the annual planning or budgeting practices required connection to the strategy statements. Without a process, the culture could not change. Without culture change, there was no incentive to put IT in the business plans.

This is a problem facing companies whether or not the context is IT growth or IT cost control. Even though the strategy statements may be direct and simple, getting business leadership to include strategy-driven IT initiatives in its annual plans and budgets, and getting IT management to connect its IT strategies and plans to those strategies, is hugely problematic. As with the bank, no one disagreed that IT was operationally important or that budgets and plans for the operational activities should be adopted. The management disconnect was about the IT's *business* importance and opportunities, including new budgets, initiatives, and actions associated with supporting business strategy.

IT Impact Management's Approach to "Process Disconnects"

A practical solution has three elements:

1. Connect and coordinate with existing non-IT company practices such as business planning and the annual budget practice.

2. Connect and coordinate the people and organizations that perform these practices.

3. Engage managers across the company in the execution of the integrated and connected NIE practices.

We discussed the first two in Chapter 6, where we identified the process connections between corporate processes and the information in the Value Chain. The additional element introduced here is the concept of directly engaging managers in all areas affected by the new practices in their execution, and directly approaching the process owners of the relevant corporate practices to get their involvement and input into the proposed practices. The three solutions are part of IT Impact Management.

Practical Problem 2: Legacy and Entitlement Mentality

The company's existing IT applications, infrastructures, and project backlogs are the legacy of the existing strategy-to-bottom-line management practices, which prevent starting with a clean slate. Managers feel entitled to "their" systems and support.

While we may need to assess the alignment of the lights-on application portfolio against business strategy, we have the problem that the current portfolio was produced as a result of previous, probably unconnected, management practices. Similarly, prioritization of the project backlog is useful but, again, the backlog was produced through the existing practices. Prioritization of projects does not assure that we will have the *right* projects in the backlog to prioritize. We need better projects, driven from business strategy.

The influence of legacy extends to organizational relationships between IT and the business units and business management expectations. Particularly with the lights-on budget, everyone behaves as though the current cost base will continue into the future and as if current commitments to continue supporting each manager's applications will also continue, if not increase. In many ways, the IT culture has grown up saying "we do what the user needs."

What this translates into is a generally unexamined commitment to support everything that is currently being supported. This entitlement also applies to the relationship; business managers come to expect to be served by the individual in IT with whom they have built personal relationships. Again, this leads to service requests and support expectations that ignore business strategies. It is a classic case of an entitlement mentality: Managers come to expect what they have always had, irrespective of changes occurring around them. We are confronted with the old way of doing things and the old way of thinking.[2]

Ideally, we need to begin every budget cycle with business strategy, develop the most effective IT strategies and projects to support that strategy, and then go from there in terms of prioritization, budgeting, and measuring performance. We need to reexamine every IT expenditure, whether for new projects or old lights-on support. This works to break through the legacy mindsets and the sense of entitlement.

Though ideal, in practice this result may require several planning cycles to accomplish.

IT Impact Management's Approach to the "Legacy and Entitlement Mentality"

Although not ideal, applying New Information Economics practices immediately, through alignment and prioritization, can lead to considerable progress in changing the management culture. Achieving ideal management practices, from planning and justification through budgeting and performance measurement, is a worthy goal but difficult to achieve in the short term. However making immediate and real (though possibly limited) progress toward this goal is critical.

By using portfolios and portfolio management, all elements of the ongoing IT spend are on the table and subject to discussion. Again, engaging management in aligning IT spend against strategic intentions and assessing service and quality levels can start to address the entitlement culture.

One of our important themes is "affordability." Engaging managers in the holistic, 100 percent view of the IT spend makes it clear that a company's commitment to IT is not open-ended. Rather, it is bounded by the limits of what can be afforded. Consequently, assessing where money is spent, and to what impact, causes considerable increase in awareness that business-as-usual for IT spend has its costs and that choices have to be made.

Practical Problem 3: Management Roles

The company's management culture prevents business and IT management from playing the management roles needed to effectively direct and apply IT resources to achieve maximum bottom-line impact.

For most companies, the solution to driving IT action from business strategy requires a revision to existing management practices and the introduction of new ones. The key change is driving from strategy, but the key consequence is the change in the role that business managers play in directing IT. A difficult part of this change is dealing with the legacy of existing management practices and management culture about the governance of IT. But the real challenge is dealing with the change in the relationships between business and IT, and the consequent change in the roles business and IT managers play. New Information Economics practices work when these roles and relationships change.

Changing roles and relationships, of course, runs up against culture. This can put significant limitations on the change in management behavior needed. As a result, dealing with this practical problem requires considerable pragmatism and, in particular, a learning process. The principles and practices will be successful, but taking management culture into account will be important in determining how rapidly, and how broadly, the changes can occur. Moreover, the very process of applying the principles and practices will accelerate the management culture changes.

The company needs the right management culture to connect strategy to IT and IT's bottom-line impact. As suggested in the previous section, culture and culture disconnects significantly inhibit the ability of the company and the management team to successfully carry out the five management practices.

We introduced the specific roles expected of managers in Chapter 6. They are summarized briefly in Exhibit 7.3.

Note that the list in Exhibit 7.3 includes all elements of the Strategy-to-Bottom-Line Value Chain and the roles in all five NIE practices. As we mentioned above, companies do not typically adopt all practices at once. Note also that company managers no doubt perform most or all of these activities in existing practices. The problem here is to get these things to happen in a connected, coordinated, focused-on-business-and-bottom-line fashion.

The practical problems center on getting the business and IT leadership teams together; getting them to agree about how to do planning, innovation, prioritization, alignment, and performance measurement; and, most importantly, overcoming the people and cultural hurdles to getting things done. In part, the problems are motivating change: The pain of the proposed Right Decisions/Right Results *solution* needs to be less than the pain of the *problems* the management

EXHIBIT 7.3   Management Team Roles

Senior Leadership Team	Technology Leadership Team
• Approve and weight strategic intentions	• Contribute to portfolio information, especially costs
• Review or approve deliverables at several steps	• Assess portfolio for technology
• Make decisions on and approve funding	• Participate in development of the Strategic IT agenda for the use of IT
Business Leadership Team	• Develop IT plan
• Revise and review strategic intentions	• Participate in IT requirements process
• Assess portfolios for alignment, service, quality, intensity of use	• Establish projects and business cases
• Develop IT agenda for the use of IT	• Establish annual project plan and schedules
• Review IT plan	• Advise business leadership
• Develop requirements for projects, based on Strategic IT requirements	• Develop IT plans and establish IT budgets
• Prioritization of requirements, project, annual plan portfolios	• Participate in budget planning
• Recommend decisions on funding	• Initiate action plans
• Establish business unit plans for the use of IT	• Establish IT performance metrics
• Develop budgets	
• Establish business performance metrics	

teams currently experience. Practices and frameworks will not, by themselves, solve them. People must understand their roles and responsibilities, and understand how their participation contributes to the solutions.

We find that management culture presents the single most pervasive hurdle to successfully getting from business strategy to IT action. It is a difficult problem to deal with directly, since a company's culture comes from its history and developed over a long period of time. Culture makes changing management practice most difficult, because culture sets the boundaries on what is accepted by managers with respect to the roles they play, the decisions they make, and the acceptance of roles and decisions made by others.

If existing processes do not effectively engage business management in a continuous and consistent way, the company cannot produce the best use of IT resources. By integrating the strategy-to-results chain and establishing consistent roles and information, management will be more willing to invest themselves in the process. Each NIE practice deals with this problem of integration and connection to the rest of the strategy-to-results, or Strategy-to-Bottom-Line Value Chain.

IT Impact Management's Approach to "Management Roles"

We approach management role change, and the underlying culture challenges, through the five New Information Economics (NIE) practices. These practices make necessary adjustments in the roles that managers are asked to play, and they affect the decisions that managers make or participate in.

The basis for changing roles is directly engaging managers in the processes. Working with a management group, with a common and holistic view of 100 percent of all IT projects and expenditures, changes the roles. This begs the questions of how to get managers to agree to participate and how to get them to believe in the results.[3]

Practical Problem 4: Company Processes

The new or changed management practices that connect business and IT will have to coexist and work with many other existing company management practices (e.g., capital budgets, HR, management performance/compensation, corporate budgets, purchasing, and so forth).

Planning, prioritizing, and operationalizing IT do not occur in a vacuum; they operate within the legacy of existing management practices. This is a significant problem because, in most cases, companies cannot change all management practices at once. The practical problem is doing what is needed to sufficiently connect the business-strategy-driven management practices to the other practices, in order to achieve the benefits of the new practice. (In one case, an insurance company adopted a business-strategy-driven prioritization practice for its IT application development portfolio. However, these new priorities were not fully reflected in the annual operating budget, and the key business managers did not get changes in their personal performance plans. As a result, company management was frustrated that the IT application development did not produce all the business changes intended, in the timeframe expected.)

Companies often have processes for these elements but rarely aggressively coordinate them (see Exhibit 7.4).

- **Corporate Strategic Management Processes.** These are the planning processes (at the beginning of the Value Chain) and strategy-related capital and multi-year budget processes. Without question, if our planning does not influence capital budgeting, or influence final budget decisions, then we have not accomplished anything. For the same reason, if we have not included the outcomes of the businesses planning processes in our activities, we then disconnect from the business. Both connections are essential.

- **Technology Management Processes.** Internal to IT are the Project Management and the Enterprise Architecture processes. Project management is a prime connector for performance metrics as well as for the processes that monitor continuing projects. Questions of reprioritization during the life of projects come into play here. Enterprise Architecture in some companies is a prime mover in planning from the technical perspective. When EA is vigorous, it has to be integrated into the planning and project development activities and involved with the prioritization processes.

EXHIBIT 7.4   Value Chain Connections to Other Processes

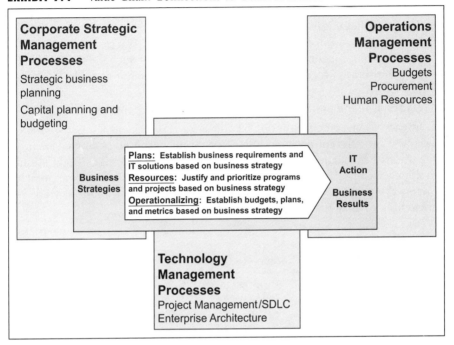

- *Operations Management Processes.* These include the annual budget process, procurement, and human resources. We mentioned budgeting in the corporate strategic processes, from a multiyear and capital perspective. The critical point is that budgeting is what enables actions. Money, after all, is the basic tool for getting things done, and it provides the framework and guidance for what things should be done. It is critical to make the connections between these processes and the budgeting/resource allocation processes.

As Exhibit 7.4 illustrates, the need for connection and integration is not only within the Strategy-to-Bottom-Line Value Chain itself but also between the Strategy-to-Bottom-Line Value Chain and the other elements of the company's management processes. The operational and tactical system requirements (including maintenance and enhancement requests) of individual business units are fed into an IT annual planning process, producing IT programs and initiatives to support those requirements. The programs that result from the collected set of business unit requirements must then somehow be prioritized for business impact, with investment decisions made for high-alignment and affordability programs (IT Strategic Program Review).

In reality, many companies and planning methodologies fumble a critical step: Measuring the actual performance, in both business and IT terms, of the IT organization in putting the plans into action. Very few companies have relevant performance measurement programs that insure that plans are put into action and that the actions have a demonstrable impact on achieving the business' strategic intentions. This undisciplined management of resources results in the continuous erosion of planned strategic resources. As a result, many of IT's activities remain disconnected from the company's strategic intentions, and IT's overall contribution to the business is much smaller than it could be.[4]

IT Impact Management's Approach to "Company Processes"

IT Impact Management solutions emphasize directly engaging the process owners of the relevant process—be it corporate, technology management, or Operations Management—in the evolution of Right Decisions/Right Results developments. In particular, these process owners have to see how our approaches address the problems and concerns *they* have (the optimal solution) while not threatening to change or impact their processes needlessly.

EXHIBIT 7.5   Connecting Processes to Owners

	Process Owner	Their Objectives, Problems, and Concerns	Right Decisions/Right Results Connections and Solutions to their Objectives and Concerns
Corporate Strategic Management Processes	Strategic Business Planning		
	Capital Planning and Multiyear Budgeting		
	Other Processes		
Technology Management Processes	Project Management/ PMO		
	Enterprise Architecture		
	Other Processes		
Operations Management Processes	Budgets		
	Procurement		
	Human Resources		
	Other Processes		

The table in Exhibit 7.5 provides a starting point for connecting the use of NIE practices to the objectives of the owners of corporate, technology, and management processes. This table is, of course, unique to each given company situation. It is a useful exercise to complete the table in order for a company to see exactly how to proceed.

The table provides for other processes as well; each company is likely to have other process owners in addition to those we have suggested. Also, we do not mean to ignore the key CxO offices such as CFO and COO. Typically, they are equally interested and may even be the process owners in some cases.

The five NIE practices,[5] applied in connection with a company's management processes, are the critical steps in creating the integrated Strategy-to-Bottom-Line Value Chain that is required to produce bottom-line impact and control IT spending. Implementing them begins with the process owners.

Practical Problem 5: Management Expectations

Company managers expect simple ROI-based measurement of costs and benefits.

A contributor[7] to our thinking about this book said it well: Senior managers want the issues about IT investments to be simple, and they want the issues expressed in simple financial terms. What are we going to spend, and what will our return be? Unfortunately, much of the complexity around IT planning and management has grown up because existing management practices have made things appear complicated. We have to provide the simplicity and still respond to management expectations for financial returns from IT.

From the very beginning of IT in business, we have experienced a dichotomy between the immediate cost and revenue aspects of IT justification (a hard-line view of ROI) and the "strategic" or "infrastructure" aspects of IT justification. This means that a proposed investment may not have an easily or credibly calculable ROI, even though the investment enables others (managers, business units) to themselves reduce costs or improve revenue.

Often, this latter view is framed in "intangible benefits" terms. The tangible effect may well be to increase IT costs, but the benefits of customer satisfaction, or quality, or time-to-market are expected to reduce costs or improve revenue. When management expectations are solely focused on financial outcomes, the senior management team may take a relatively passive view, reviewing investments and ongoing IT spending solely on a restricted justification basis like ROI.

We do not take sides in this. Making a good financial case for an individual IT investment is always good. But using ROI as the sole basis for deciding on the development portfolio, or as the only arbiter for the ongoing lights-on budget, will not produce the best decisions.

We recommend that management teams always use strategic intentions to express their business goals, and then aggressively link the IT investment portfolio to those goals. This is more effective than relying solely on financial measures for making better decisions. The right decisions means basing decisions on what is important to the business and the management team.

IT Impact Management's Approach to "Management Expectations"

A business case for an individual project may rely largely on ROI calculations. But to fully understand the right decision to improve IT impact on the bottom line, we must consider how the management team expects to improve the bottom line. This is strategic intention, and IT does best when it directly supports those intentions. Focusing on strategic intentions keeps the process simple and understandable.

Practical Problem 6: It Ain't Broke

Business and IT managers get what they need from current processes, and they resist new processes that appear to make it more difficult to obtain what they need.

In most situations, managers have adapted to the processes that currently exist. Managers who can effectively use politics and personal relationships, or even use the "loudest voice" method, are generally comfortable with the existing situation and do not welcome changes in the process. They have worked out ways to get what they need and, therefore, resist new processes that may appear to make this more difficult. This also extends to related process owners such as corporate budgeting, enterprise architecture, systems development managers, and computer support managers. They have all worked out ways to do what they perceive they need to do, using current ways of doing business.

It is no surprise, then, when Right Decisions/Right Results process changes like prioritization and alignment are perceived not as solving their problems but, rather, as adding to them. One of our colleagues has remarked that "managers will always gravitate to the fastest/shortest path to money." This means that when managers need support for applications or new development projects, they will circumvent any complex or potentially unresponsive (to their specific needs) process and go directly to the source, rely on personal relationships, or work through their own hierarchies to find the necessary funds.

Of all the practical problems, this is perhaps the most direct and most threatening. We can talk about culture and disconnected processes and so forth (which are, in fact, real practical problems), but if we cannot control this problem, nothing good will happen.

IT Impact Management's Approach to "It Ain't Broke"

The pain of the solution must be less than the pain of the problem. IT Impact Management works to help management understand that much of the current pain is hidden from the organization, with suboptimal business impact and higher IT costs than would occur using integrated, coordinated processes. A major part of this is establishing the business reasons behind the adoption of the

Strategy-to-Bottom-Line Value Chain and the NIE practices. When senior managers understand the costs (both dollars and organizational inefficiencies) of existing processes, implementing changes becomes easier.

Practical Problem 7: Multiple Perspectives

The company does not speak with one voice.

Even small companies have the problem that different parts of the business have different views of priorities and the best role for IT to play. Larger organizations have multiple business units and functional organizations. Consequently, IT often has to work for multiple and inconsistent business units. A lot of this is a management culture that encourages autonomy and resists coordination. Much is structural as well, where the company itself does not recognize the inconsistencies among business units or treat them as important problems to resolve. For such companies, IT governance and decision-making processes are largely incapable of connecting IT to business strategy. Instead, typically, the loudest voices determine direction and priorities.

For example, a large government agency has several operating divisions and functional divisions, all competing for IT resources from the same IT service organization. Even though division management is involved in IT governance, and prioritization processes require consensus across divisions, the result is most often determined by political clout or maneuvering, rather than connection to strategy. In this case, IT is forced to function as the referee and, in effect, make priority decisions on behalf of the agency.

This is a problem that is often larger than the business/IT processes we are discussing; it involves business and IT governance issues as well. The problem has two related aspects. First, there may be little agreement among senior managers about the basic strategic intentions of the business. Second, partly because of this, decision making and resource allocation operate separately within the silos of the company. IT decisions, however, tend to cross those silos, certainly with common infrastructure and enterprise-wide information requirements, and likely in business processes that benefit from cross-silo participation and information sharing.

This is more than just a practical problem. This problem also underlies the fundamental practical difficulties in attempting to change the basis for making right decisions.

IT Impact Management's Approach to "Multiple Perspectives"

IT Impact Management addresses the single-voice problem by focusing on manager participation in NIE practices. The problem always is getting management to participate and to believe in and follow in the results. These are the problems that IT Impact Management is intended to solve.

It is too easy to expect changing management practices, or adopting new practices, to be simply a matter of telling managers what to do. Giving managers a users manual, or a practice definition, or a good-looking diagram is attractive, but it is not effective. The practical problems are real and substantial and need effective solutions. Unless these problems are solved, the company's investments in IT, and the IT organization's activities, will not be consistent with business strategies; and the company will not get the right bottom-line impact from IT.

THE ROLE OF IT IMPACT MANAGEMENT [8]

IT Impact Management helps companies and managers decide how best to move forward with Right Decisions/Right Results and the NIE practices. The IT Impact Management framework addresses the key practical problems discussed in this chapter. The result is a roadmap for managers to use to craft the specific solution for their company's circumstances.

The goal of the roadmap is to provide guidance for "what's next?" Because companies, cultures, and circumstances are unique, there is no single right answer. There are, however, general guidelines that can be followed.

IT Impact Management provides guidance in three ways. First, it provides alternate methods to establish Right Decisions/Right Results goals for the company and to assess the company as-is and to-be with respect to IT management processes. Second, IT Impact Management looks at the interactions with corporate governance and corporate processes, and provides ideas on how to work with the owners of those processes, Third, IT Impact Management defines a "program" view for managers to adapt to their situations. This specifically deals with the practical problems that have been described here.

◆

The solutions to practical problems and culture require common sense.

We understand we have to work with the corporate budget practice, the existing legacy of applications and infrastructures, the legacy of management practices, and the existing management culture. Our message is that while management practices are important and making changes to them is critical, successfully addressing these practical problems is not just a mechanical process. People are involved, and pragmatism is vital.

	Management Process—Desired Outcomes	**Business—Desired Outcomes**
IT Impact Management	Business and IT management teams execute the processes that improve IT's contribution to business performance.	The total IT spend is effectively controlled. IT's contribution to bottom-line impact is improved.

TACKLE THE PRACTICAL PROBLEMS: MANAGEMENT AGENDA

Management Question	Yes or No?	If No, What Is Our Plan for Correcting This?
Do we have the practical problem of process disconnects?		
Do we have the practical problem of legacy mind-sets and entitlement expectations?		
Does our culture impede business and IT managers from playing the roles they need to?		
Can our IT management processes work well with corporate processes such as budgeting?		
Do our managers expect the wrong things?		
Are our business managers so comfortable with the way things now work that they will resist any significant change?		
Can our business managers speak with one voice about their needs and what IT should do to satisfy them?		

The balance of the book provides answers to the "What is our plan for correcting this?" statements.

ADDITIONAL READING

Additional information can be found in Website Note 8, "Gap Analysis: Closing Disconnects between Business and IT," and at the back of this book in Appendix A, "The Role of Enterprise Architecture in Right Decisions/Right Results."

NOTES

1. In Chapter 11, we suggest a Culture Management approach to help deal with the problems. In Chapter 12, we introduce the Business Value Maturity Model™ as a way to calibrate a company's as-is and establish to-be goals for adopting the Value Chain and NIE practices in the company.
2. Our colleague Mike Luby of USAA Bank calls this a "mind legacy."
3. Chapters 8, 9, and 10 describe these practices and frameworks and, at the same time, address these critical cultural, motivational, people, and political issues.

When we introduce Culture Management in Chapter 11, we explicitly address possible solutions and strategies for getting at the underlying people problems. Right Decisions/Right Results is, fundamentally, an approach for setting the culture rather than simply a mechanical set of practices and tools.

4. We discussed this problem in Chapter 6 when we introduced the details of the Strategy-to-Bottom-Line Value Chain, the deliverables, and the interactions with the corporate business processes. This is just one example of the kinds of disconnects that exist.

5. The detailed solutions to the Company Processes practical problems are covered in Chapters 8, 9, and 10, for each NIE practice.

6. Government and nonprofit managers expect financial returns such as ROI as well, but they are also concerned about IT's impact on mission performance. The practical problems described in this chapter, and their solution, apply just as strongly to government and nonprofit organizations.

7. Conversation with Cecil Smith, Duke Energy.

8. We explore IT Impact Management in more detail in Chapter 13, "Define What's Next."

CHAPTER 8

Make the Right Decisions

This chapter introduces the Prioritization and Alignment NIE practices that enable and support management decision making about new IT investments and existing IT resource allocations. Prioritization looks at new IT development alternatives and ranks them by business impact. Alignment looks at existing IT activities and assesses their effectiveness at supporting the business in the existing environment.

The underlying decision-making philosophy is that company resources devoted to IT are finite. As a consequence, choices have to be made among alternatives: there aren't enough resources to do everything, so choices have to be made as to which things will be funded and which things will not. This is the crucial point. We are not using a "hurdle rate" or strong business case to justify individual projects or ongoing expenses. That is, we are not trying to make a specific go/ no-go decision about a specific project or line item. We proceed as though every potential project or individual

Control Spending and Maximize Impact on the Bottom Line
1   Define the Goals
2   Ask the Right Questions
3   Connect to the Bottom Line
4   Understand Costs and Resources
5   Focus on the Right Things
6   Adopt Effective Process to Produce Action
7   Tackle the Practical Problems
8   Make the Right Decisions
9   Plan for the Right Results
10   Keep Score
11   Deal with Culture
12   Chart the Path to Implementation
13   Define What's Next
14   Answer the "So What?" Question

lights-on line item has been based on an appropriate business case. Rather, the problem is to choose *among* the desirable alternatives that exist in a project portfolio or a lights-on asset pool. "Make the right decision" means choosing the best alternatives, those that will improve IT's bottom-line impact. At the same time, by positing that resources are finite, we enable management to exercise appropriate control over IT spending.

The right decisions are those that improve IT's bottom-line impact and control IT spending. We are concerned about the entire IT spend, which includes new investment in development and enhancement projects, and the ongoing lights-on operational budget. (Note that we include both total capital for projects and expense items when we say IT spend. Fundamentally, we are interested in the overall cash flow that IT requires, rather than the details of accounting decisions. Because many IT expenses are sometimes "hidden" by their accounting treatment (leasing, capitalization, etc.), we prefer to deal with the amount of cash that the company will need to lay out in the budget period, rather than the accounting impact to the bottom line.)

One major purpose of the Prioritization and Alignment decision-making support tools is to give management a complete view of the new investment and lights-on budget alternatives and indicate which alternatives have higher bottom-line impact or control IT spending more effectively. A second major purpose is to fully engage business and IT management *together* in making IT investment decisions. A desired outcome is, as we stated in Chapter 5 in the discussion of Goals and Principles, that "business and IT management have a common, consensus view as to the role of IT to achieve business strategic intentions." Their participation in the decision-making processes, using Prioritization and Alignment, are a large part of achieving that goal.

THE MANAGEMENT CONTEXT FOR "MAKE THE RIGHT DECISIONS"

Affordability and Impact are key to making the right decisions about new investments and ongoing lights-on expense budgets (see Exhibit 8.1). Prioritization

EXHIBIT 8.1   Alignment/Assessment and Prioritization in the Value Chain

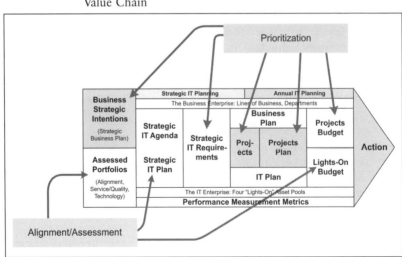

and Alignment occur throughout the Strategy-to-Bottom-Line Value Chain. In Chapter 2, we introduced the basic IT questions about affordability and impact:

Affordability Questions

- What can we afford to spend on IT?
- Can we reduce unnecessary IT costs?
- Can we redeploy expenses to support needed projects?

Impact Questions

- Are we investing IT resources in the right places?
- Do our business strategies drive our IT actions and produce bottom-line impact?
- Are we getting bottom-line impact, and sufficient value, from our current IT assets and resources?
- Are we balancing our strategic and tactical investments?

The answers are based on a comprehensive total portfolio assessment of development and enhancement projects (prioritization) and the lights-on budget (alignment). The key questions are whether the IT development investment options make business sense and whether the lights-on budget is the best way to spend scarce IT dollars. (We continue to note that although most of the IT money in a company is spent in the lights-on area, as in the typical company IT spend shown in Exhibit 8.2, management tends to focus on the new investments in projects. We recommend careful examination of both.)

That this comprehensive portfolio analysis can address senior management questions about IT spending is illustrated by comments from three CEOs who participated in Prioritization and Alignment activities. The first, when shown an aligned lights-on portfolio based on the specific business strategies for his company, remarked, "This is the first time I've understood what IT is contributing to our business success." The second, when working on the prioritized portfolio which had more projects than the company had resources to do them, asked whether work was proceeding on projects that fell below the affordability line. When told the answer was yes, he said, "Stop them. We want to work on the most valuable projects, so put the resources from those lower-value projects to the higher ranked projects." The third, when shown the

EXHIBIT 8.2   Total IT Spend

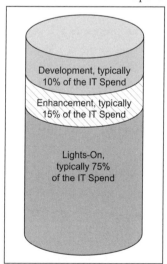

Development, typically 10% of the IT Spend

Enhancement, typically 15% of the IT Spend

Lights-On, typically 75% of the IT Spend

prioritization results, commented on the new credibility of the portfolio's connection to business strategies and goals and then increased the budget available to development.

Side benefits include giving a common view to the management team of all IT projects underway, since the development portfolio displays the complete set of projects, with connections to business strategy and goals. A second benefit is to make resource assignments less of a political process (responding to the most vocal manager) and more of a joint management team process.

ELEMENTS OF RIGHT DECISIONS

Decisions about strategies, plans, and budgets, where resource allocation is the key outcome, occur throughout the management processes in the Strategy-to-Bottom-Line Value Chain.

In all these cases, management needs to decide among alternatives and choose the "best" use of company resources. Strategic decisions determine choices of strategies and the use of IT to fulfill those strategies. Decisions during annual planning determine the projects to be undertaken and the lights-on budget components to be supported and used in operations. Decisions about budgets determine exactly how much should be spent in projects and lights-on. The possible outcomes include:

Development Projects	Insure a high level of strategy support
	Make stronger business cases
	Minimize and/or mitigate business and technical risk
	Balance the overall project portfolio
Enhancement Projects	Invest in applications based on strategic intentions
	Invest in well-performing applications
	Balance the overall project portfolio
Lights-On	Squeeze out poor performing applications
	Reduce support of underutilized applications
	Understand where costs are, and control them

While Prioritization and Alignment highlight these outcomes, the final decisions occur in the context of the management processes portrayed in generic terms in Exhibit 8.3. Budgets define the lights-on expenditures and the overall project pools. Annual project plans define the selection of projects to be done, based on factors like scheduling, skills available, and required sequencing. Strategic plans define the basic directions for development projects and building infrastructures.

But the overall purpose of right decisions is to be sure that the lights-on and project budgets are at the right levels and that the choices within the lights-on and project budgets support the strategic directions of the company. Right decisions should lead the company into the IT Improvement Zone, where IT spending is effectively controlled and IT's bottom-line impact is improved. See Exhibit 8.4.

EXHIBIT 8.3 Decision Points in the Value Chain Management Processes

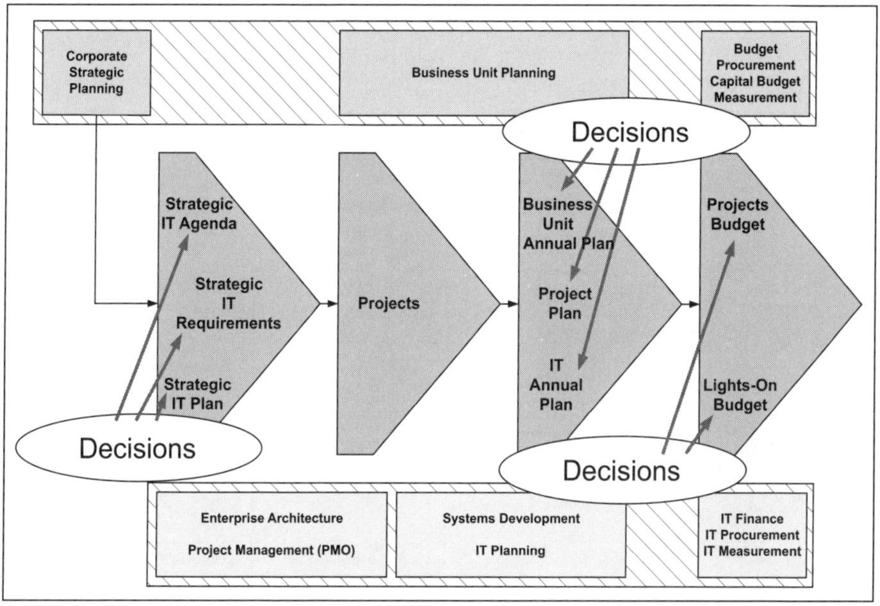

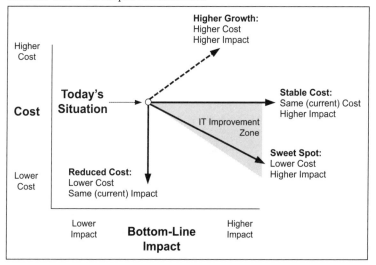

EXHIBIT 8.4 IT Improvement Zone

The Use of Strategic Intentions

Making right decisions is based largely on connection to strategic intentions. Earlier chapters established the importance of strategic intentions; here, we apply them in prioritization and alignment.[1] Exhibit 8.5 gives an example of strategic intentions for a particular company. These would then be applied to Prioritization and Alignment.

EXHIBIT 8.5   Examples of Strategic Intentions

Strategic Intention	Description	Goal	Key Metric	Wt
Wholesale Market Share	Attract, retain, and provide high-quality service to wholesaler.	Strengthen the product line available to dealers. Build the relationship based on wholesaler financial incentives.	Wholesale market share Wholesalers' satisfaction	50
Retail Market Share	Attract, retain, and provide high-quality service to end customers.	Improve ease of doing business. Provide effective products and financial incentives.	Retail market share Customer satisfaction	20
Securitization/ Funding Efficiency	Capability to securitize receivables.	Reduce cost of funds.	Time to market Cost of funds	15
Reduce Losses/ Improve Portfolio Quality	Receivable portfolio quality and collection efficiency.	Reduce collection losses. Improve collection efficiency.	Collection losses Wholesale losses Residual losses	10
Reduce Administrative and Operating Costs	Management and performance of all organizations and functions.	Reduce the total cost of doing business.	Administration percent of revenue	5

The Use of Prioritization and Alignment Assessments

The context for "Make the right decisions" is resource allocation. For Prioritization, the resources are allocated to new IT projects. For Alignment, the resources are the lights-on budget allocated to the applications, infrastructure, services, and management components of the company's existing IT activities. Resources can be funds, staff, or both.

In both cases, the notion of a right decision is directing the allocation of finite resources to the projects (Prioritization) or lights-on budgets (Alignment) that have the greatest potential bottom-line impact. A number of factors enter into the assessments that support such decisions, such as risk, quality, service-level, performance metrics, and status of the technology (e.g., obsolete, unsupported, etc.). The Prioritization and Alignment practices offer many options for decision factors to include in the process, to match the requirements of the management team making resource allocations.

Furthermore, the right decision framework emphasizes broad business management participation in the decision-making process and applying portfolios that cover 100 percent of the IT spend, representing both new development and the ongoing lights-on budgets.

If the alternative projects or lights-on line items are so compelling that the finite resources are determined to be inadequate, the management team can increase the resource pools available. The right decision framework assumes that IT is competing for resources against every other possible use of company resources. When confronted with a candidate pool of projects that, together, represent tremendous potential bottom-line impact, the management team is capable of comparing that against the other demands on resources. This is a very important aspect of the Right Decision/Right Results approach.

Right Decisions: Development and Enhancement

Consider a set of proposed IT investments for a manufacturing company. Through a planning process, a set of strategic IT requirements[2] has been identified. The business organization, with the assistance of the IT organization, has produced a set of proposed projects based on those strategic IT requirements. These projects are put forward as the starting point for an annual project plan. Each project has a defined and acceptable business case.

Using the Prioritization Practice instruments and processes (described below), each project is assessed against business strategic intentions. This company also has chosen to assess the risks to success associated with each project. In this case, a higher Risk number means lower risk and higher potential for success.

Exhibit 8.6 shows the projects sorted in bottom-line Impact sequence. This sequence is the outcome of assessing each project against business strategic intentions. The exhibit also shows the results of the risk assessment. In this case, the company has chosen to combine all risk assessment categories into one single number. The higher the number, the higher the risk. The Dependency column identifies projects that have interdependencies. The Portfolio column indicates the business portfolio classification.

Exhibit 8.7 graphically displays the results, showing Risk (a higher number means lower risk, greater potential for success), Bottom-Line Impact, and Cost (the size of the bubble). Using this, management can discuss which projects to include in the annual project plan. Assuming that resources available will not cover all projects, some projects will need to be put on hold.

Exhibit 8.8 displays the projects in a portfolio view. This gives management insight into the relative investments in the specific portfolio categories such as strategic or business infrastructure. We identified several kinds of portfolio classifications in Chapter 4; here, the company chose the strategic-to-infrastructure classifications.

EXHIBIT 8.6   Development Investment Portfolio

Full Project Name	Impact	Risk	Cost	Dependency	Portfolio
Customer Information System	326	7	892		Strategic
Plant Information System	320	46	2,382		Business Infrastructure
Commodity Code	311	3	654		New Strategy
Marketing—Shipping	301	14	447		Business Infrastructure
Genesis Installation	293	3	213		New Strategy
Manufacturing Management and Planning System	269	40	8,523		Strategic
Product Costing	258	47	333		Business Infrastructure
Replacement Genesis Analysis	237	36	2,099	8	Mandatory
Maintenance Review	233	28	112		Business Infrastructure
Automated Purchasing	229	4	395		Business Infrastructure
Marketing and Sales Region/AR	222	17	433		New Strategy
Laboratory System	222	13	803		Mandatory
Genesis Installation	207	59	1687	8,13	Strategic
Bar Coding in Stores	203	31	3,594		Mandatory
Manufacturing Data Management	198	51	4,016		New Strategy
Procurement	196	10	998		Business Infrastructure
Maintenance Deployment	180	16	1,307		New Strategy
Manufacturing Interfaces	178	59	5,618		Business Infrastructure
Maintenance Planning and Control	163	42	4,334		Strategic
CMMS—Implementation	162	21	158		Mandatory
Quality Management Operator	122	35	297		New Strategy
Total			28,421		Strategic

EXHIBIT 8.7   Project Portfolio for Decision Making

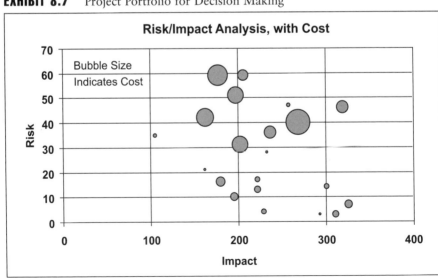

EXHIBIT 8.8   Balancing the Portfolio

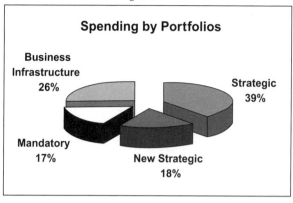

Right decisions is a management process of assessing the projects against business strategic intentions for bottom-line impact, risk, and other factors. The process permits the management team to holistically consider all possibilities and choose those best for the company, based on all the considerations included in the assessments. The Prioritization result itself is not the final decision on the projects. Prioritization is part of the decision-making process that creates the project plan from the candidate list of projects. The Prioritization exercise gives management the tools to make the decisions.

Prioritization deals with projects after they have been developed and business cases have been prepared; it does not help in developing new projects to satisfy business needs. Whether "better" projects are needed, and whether they can be created, is an issue of planning (see Chapter 9). Furthermore, prioritization does not in itself improve project business cases. (See the section on "Implications for Business Cases" below.)

Right Decisions: Lights-On Budgets

Right decisions for the lights-on budget is a management process that examines the investment strategies for each line item in the budget. Two questions are asked. First, is the level of budget support appropriate to the application? For example, if costs are too high for the alignment/quality of the application, then the application might be abandoned, or support levels reduced. Second, should the application be replaced through outsourcing, acquisition, or design/development?

Consider a company that has classified its complete lights-on budget into the four basic asset pools: applications, infrastructure, services, and management. This classification accounts for 100 percent of the IT spend other than projects (development and enhancement). Each asset pool is then described in a set of line items that make up the asset pool. For example, for applications, each line item is a separate application that the company uses.

In the following example, the business leadership team is exploring the investment strategies for applications. (See Appendix B for an explanation of the members of this team.)

The business leadership team has assessed each application for alignment (connection to strategic intentions), service-level and quality, and intensity of use. (Exhibit 8.9 shows the applications together with annual cost and the assessments.) Alignment is the relationship of each application to business strategic intentions. Intensity of Use indicates how widely the application is used in the company and how important it is to the users. Service Level and Quality indicate availability, reliability, functionality, and so forth. Cost is separated into operational costs (e.g., datacenter and infrastructure) and maintenance/support costs (e.g., the personnel assigned to keep each application running). The Alignment practice description later in this chapter explains the management processes and templates used in these assessments.

EXHIBIT 8.9   Portfolio Assessments for Intensity of Use and Service Level/Quality

Application	Alignment	Quality	Intensity of Use	Personnel Cost	Operations Cost
General Ledger	3	3	3	650	1,100
Management Reporting	1	5	5	290	450
Customer Service	4	2	2	1,400	750
Call Center Support	4	4	5	2,300	2,700
Premier Reconciliation	2	5	2	1,750	3,100
DBIS	5	2	2	265	750
Sales Force Toolset	5	2	4	395	800
DB Overbooking	3	5	1	480	520
Traffic Control and Reporting	1	3	1	1,600	2,150
Min/Max Support	3	3	1	250	690
CIS Statements	4	2	3	250	420
Auto Transfer System	2	2	5	1,100	650
Fund and Balance	2	2	2	950	130
TRACON	3	5	4	490	710
Rebate Management	5	3	1	1,600	1,930
CANNON II	3	3	1	100	50
Total				13,870	16,900

In Exhibit 8.10, we portray the Alignment, Quality, and Personnel Cost together in order to examine whether the allocation of personnel is appropriate considering the Alignment and Quality of each application. Managers can see immediately the level of spending for each quality level and for each level of strategic intention support, and begin to frame questions about why money is being spent in some areas (e.g. low quality, low strategic intention support) and not in other areas (high strategic intention support, for example).

Taking the analyses to another level, we can look at combinations of strategic alignment and quality, for example, to help the business leadership team

EXHIBIT 8.10   Portfolio Assessment for Decision Making

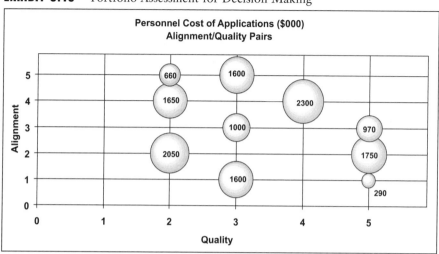

Personnel Cost of Applications ($000)
Alignment/Quality Pairs

identify specific reallocation or abandonment opportunities within the lights-on budget.

Five investment strategies address applications that fall in various alignment/quality pairings (see Exhibit 8.11). By examining the combination of alignment and quality for each application, management can make specific investments decisions, based on bottom-line impact on the business, about where lights-on

EXHIBIT 8.11   Investment Strategies for the Lights-On
Application Portfolio

Investment Category	Investment Strategy
Abandon Alignment is low	Applications should be abandoned.
Crisis Alignment is high (4, 5) Quality is low (1, 2)	Applications are candidates for new investment to improve quality, especially with high alignment (new projects).
Noncritical, Stabilize Alignment is moderate (3)	Alignment is moderate. Spend as little as possible on maintenance and enhancement.
Improve Only as Needed Alignment is high (4, 5) Quality is moderate (3)	Although alignment is high, quality is adequate. Spend money only in emergency or as resources are left over.
Excellent, Monitor Alignment is high (4, 5) Quality is high (4, 5)	Monitor applications for quality issues. Spend money to maintain quality levels, but new investment is likely not necessary.

dollars should be increased, where expenditures can be reduced, and where investment will have the greatest impact on the business. See Exhibit 8.12.

Note that this directly supports our overall objective of controlling IT spend and improving (and maximizing) bottom-line impact. It is through such reallocation or abandonment decisions that we can improve the performance of the overall lights-on budget. We highlight only two possibilities here; others include additional support for applications that are in crisis but are also high in alignment, and therefore deserving of improvement. Personnel currently in stable noncritical categories (candidates perhaps for reallocation) could be pointed at the applications in crisis.

EXHIBIT 8.12   Investment Decisions within Lights-On Application Portfolio

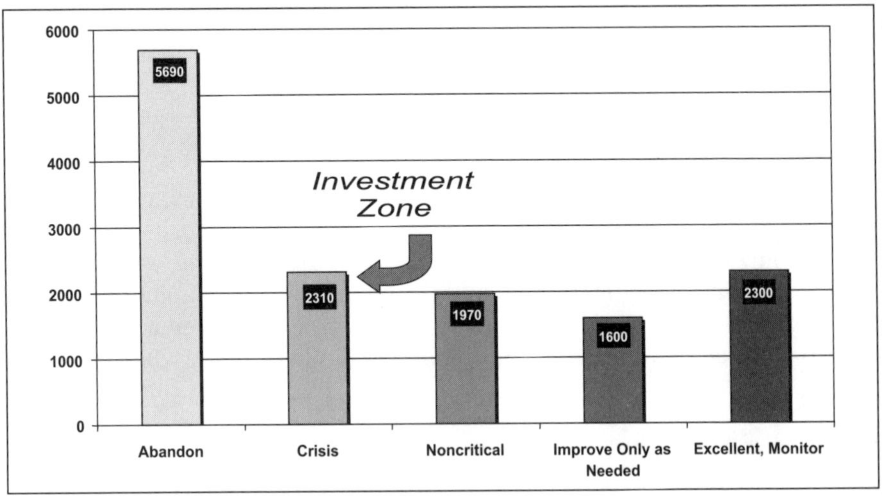

Overall, the business leadership team, in viewing the complete application asset pool, can determine how well the lights-on budget is performing. As an example, Exhibit 8.13 shows the relative alignment of all line items; this indicates the relative amount of lights-on in direct support of business strategic intentions.

As in prioritization, the lights-on alignment and alignment assessment processes do not make the decisions. The business leadership team does this, using the tools and assessments provided.

EXHIBIT 8.13   Alignment of Lights-On Applications Portfolio

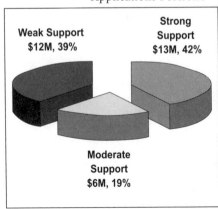

Weak Support
$12M, 39%

Strong Support
$13M, 42%

Moderate Support
$6M, 19%

MAKE THE RIGHT DECISIONS: TWO NIE PRACTICES

This section describes the details of the two decision-making practices: Prioritization and Alignment These descriptions emphasize the steps followed and the participation of the management team. Each is described on a stand-alone basis; that is, it can be implemented by a company without requiring any of the other NIE practices or other elements of the Strategy-to-Bottom-Line Value Chain. Each practice enables the management team to control IT spending (by setting limits on the affordable amount that can be spent on IT) and improve IT's bottom-line impact (by choosing the best projects or most productive line items in the lights-on budget.)

Who Does the Assessments?

Both the Prioritization and the Alignment practices anticipate that business managers will do the assessments. Ideally, this is the best and most effective approach.

However, some companies are not able to do this at first. We deal with this issue in the Maturity Model in Chapter 12, where the maturity of the organization is a key factor in determining how well the NIE processes are being done.

As a practical matter, a company may go thorough stages. Much depends on internal politics and the relationship with the business management group, and how much change is possible in process and management roles. Over several budget and planning cycles, we have seen companies progress as follows:

1. IT or business manager does the assessments individually.
2. IT and business manager do the assessments together.
3. Business Management Group does the assessments as a group.
4. Business Management Group does the assessments individually.

The Prioritization and Alignment practice descriptions below answer the question "who does the assessments" with answer 4 above.

THE PRIORITIZATION PRACTICE

Business-based prioritization is the tool for assessing the bottom-line impact of IT projects and assigning resources to the most valuable. It answers a fundamental management question:

> *How does the company make technology investment decisions, and how can it develop business management consensus on where these investments should be made?*

Companies want to allocate limited resources (dollars, people, time, and management attention) to initiatives that will produce the greatest return to the enterprise. While there are several prioritization methods being used in IT today, the issue goes beyond determining if individual projects contribute to the enterprise's financial or strategic success. Management faces a number of serious questions about how it is assigning IT resources:

- Are IT investments strongly connected to strategic intentions?
- Is the company putting its IT resources into the areas most valuable to the company?
- Is there a partnership between IT and business management for making IT decisions?
- Does company management understand where IT investment resources are going?
- Are IT investments described in business terms?

The next step is to develop a process—and, more importantly, a philosophy—that embraces the following principles:

- Bottom-line impact is based on an initiative's predicted impact on strategic intentions (which can include ROI calculations as one component).
- Business management is responsible for assessing the bottom-line impact of IT initiatives.
- Business managers should understand fully the business impact of *all* of the IT initiatives, not only the ones in their area.
- Investments are assessed individually but prioritized as a complete set across the business unit.
- Investments are described in business terms, addressing the business issue, business requirements and risks, and return on the investment.

The Prioritization practice focuses on assessing the business value, in terms of bottom-line impact, of proposed IT investments. On its surface, Prioritization addresses a straightforward question: Which of the proposed IT investments provides the most return to the company, when assessed by their intended impact on strategic intentions? In practical terms, this is a much more complicated issue, requiring answers to other questions, such as what is assessed, who assesses, against what, how often, and how are resources assigned? These questions occur throughout the Strategy-to-Bottom-Line Value Chain. See Exhibit 8.14.

In the past, companies have equated return with ROI, which limits the bottom-line impact assessment to financial (and, in many cases, questionable) justification. In the Right Decisions/Right Results culture, return includes not only financial justification but also an investment's potential impact on the enterprise's strategic intentions.

EXHIBIT 8.14   Prioritization in the Value Chain

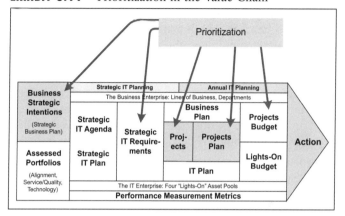

Process Overview

In its simplest form, Prioritization engages the business managers of an enterprise in assessing the bottom-line impact of proposed IT initiatives using the same yardsticks for every project. Risk assessment may also be included in the assessment. The result is a prioritized ranking of projects with which management can rationally allocate resources to the highest value initiatives.

Mechanically, the process involves five steps:[3]

1. First, the process engages senior managers in defining the strategic intentions for the company, assigning a relative weight for the importance of each and coming to a consensus on the definitions and scales with which IT projects will be assessed. Through this consensus-building step, senior managers can be assured of consistent interpretation of strategic intentions, while signaling the organization that IT initiatives will be assessed fairly, consistently, and from an enterprise perspective.

2. All IT projects are described *in business terms* in a short, consistent way, providing a single source description for all proposed IT initiatives. The business sponsor of each project is responsible for this description. In this way, the company has a complete, business-oriented view of its IT initiatives.

    Note that the process requires a short, "one-pager" description of each project. Often, a company finds that the creation of these one-pagers, put together as a complete portfolio, is an important side benefit to doing prioritizations. For example, one CEO remarked that this alone more than justified the effort, as it substantially increased his management team's understanding of IT and what it intended to accomplish for the business.

3. Using a defined cause-and-effect scale for each strategic intent, managers assess the predicted impact of every initiative on each of the strategic intentions.

Managers are looking at cause-and-effect relationships between projects and strategic intentions: If we do this project, what impact will it have on each of our strategic intentions? Each manager must assess all projects. This step results in wide understanding in the business managers of all IT initiatives, how they relate across all parts of the business, and their impact on the strategic intentions.[4] For the simple example shown here, each initiative is assessed for impact on the strategic intention (the Impact column.) In addition, each initiative is rated for business and technical risk, and the resources required are identified. In this case, the company believed the scarcest resource was its professional IT staff, not dollars.

4. In a joint forum, the assessing managers review all assessments. This allows for open discussion of different assessments and subsequent consensus development of the resulting priorities.

5. IT develops a proposed project plan based on priorities, resource constraints, and scheduling dependencies.

Result

The overall result is an across-the-board understanding of IT's complete efforts, their impact on strategic intentions, and the resources required to move forward. Most important, the process foments change in the underlying management culture regarding IT. IT becomes a set of high-value initiatives, focused on the business's strategic intentions, with business management buy-in of the business impact of IT efforts. (These results were discussed in the section on Right Decisions: Development and Enhancement above.) With this portfolio assessment, which shows overall value, cost, and the risks, the management team can make its decisions.

The prioritization of IT initiatives is based on the cause-and-effect connection between the IT initiative and the strategic intention. We ask a specific question: If we invest in this IT initiative, what will be the predicted effect on each of the company's strategic intentions? For example, if the IT initiative is a customer information system, then its expected impact on *cost reduction* might be minor; on *supplier of choice,* perhaps none; but on *Acquisition Capability,* the impact might be a major component of what is required to acquire and integrate a new company.

Prioritization is done through a structured assessment that carries out the logic described above. Exhibit 8.15 shows the specific assessment of a proposed customer information system, against strategic intentions.

By conducting such an assessment for the entire IT initiative portfolio and applying the same tests to every IT initiative, the assessments can be compared, which will yield a rank-ordered portfolio. It is this rank-ordered portfolio that enables the senior management team to make decisions about resource allocation. While this example is a simplified example of the Prioritization practice, note that the assessment of the application project shown in Exhibit 8.15 engages managers from several business departments.

EXHIBIT 8.15 Prioritization Scoring for One Investment Project

Business Value Scorecard for Customer Information System Implementation		Cost Reduction (25)	Supplier of Choice (10)	Targeted Market Growth (10)	Acquisition Capability (10)	Customer Cost (20)	Standards/Best Practices (10)	Capacity Increase (5)	Product Mix Optimization (10)
John Anderson	Controller	0	1	3	3	3	1	0	1
Peter Ecklund	Operations	1	0	0	3	5	1	1	0
Liev Smith	Marketing	1	1	3	5	5	1	1	1
Joan Munson	Product Planning	1	3	3	5	3	1	1	3
Jim Carlson	Finance	0	1	3	3	3	1	0	1
Bill Walton	HR	1	0	0	3	5	1	1	0
Regina Carlson	Engineering	1	1	3	5	5	1	1	1
Chuck Benson	Disribution	1	3	3	5	3	1	1	3
	Total	6	10	18	32	32	8	6	10
	Average	.75	1.2	2.4	4	4	1	.75	1.2
	Score	18	12	24	40	80	10	4	12 · **200**

The prioritization practice can include financial aspects of initiatives such as ROI, risk factors, and the more elaborate forms of option theory that work to quantify the estimates risks and financial returns. All of these are applied in the prioritization rank-ordering process.

Note that, in the above prioritization scorecard, the strategic intentions are:

Strategic Intention	Weight
Cost Reduction	25
Supplier of Choice	10
Targeted Market Growth	10
Acquisition Capability	10
Customer Cost	20
Standard/Best Practices	10
Capacity Increase	5
Product Mix Optimization	10
Total Weight	100

Appendix C, "The Development of Strategic Intentions, with Examples," provides additional discussion of strategic intentions, their format and content, and how they are developed.

Cultural Issues

The changes most needed around this issue are cultural. The Prioritization practice, while describing a process to assess bottom-line impact and assign resources, also helps to evolve the management culture to embrace these principles. While the result of the practice is a ranking of projects, the long-term impact is a change in culture that produces investment options that more effectively support the strategic intentions of the enterprise.

The definition of strategic intentions can include specific metrics for performance measurement, specific targets within tactical and strategic time frames, and weights that reflect the relative importance of each strategic intention.[5]

Using Factors Other than Strategic Intentions

The prioritization process described in the original *Information Economics*[6] project assessment used a standard scorecard with 10 standard factors. These factors fell into three categories, as shown in Exhibit 8.16, which illustrates how two companies applied these basic categories in their prioritization process.

EXHIBIT 8.16   Examples of Company Decisions on Management Factors

Category		Standard Information Economics Management Factors	Company One Example		Company Two Example	
Measurable Business Performance	A	Return on Investment	Internal Rate of Return		Profitability Index	
	B	Competitive Impact	Effect on Market Share		Customer Satisfaction	
Management Agenda (connection to business strategic intentions)	C	Management Information	Connectivity and Decision Support		Product Shelf Life Improvement	
	D	Strategic Alignment	Quality Performance		NA	
	E	Competitive Response	Manufacturing Cycle Reduction		Empowered Employee	
	F	IT Strategic Alignment	Comprehensive Management System		Point of Sale Global	
Risk and Uncertainty	G	Project and Organization Risk	NA		NA	
	H	Definitional Uncertainty	NA		NA	
	I	Technical Uncertainty	NA		Project Milestone Achievements	
	J	IS Infrastructure	NA		Enterprise Network Installation	
			Total Weight	100	*Total Weight*	100

Each company established weights for each factor; for Company 1, Factor A—Return on Investment was 30 percent of the total weight. For Company 2, Factor A—Profitability Index was 25 percent of the total weight.

Companies should consider using financial factors if appropriate in addition to other strategic intentions as a part of the prioritization process. While companies ordinarily use only strategic intentions for prioritization (and alignments), using other factors, such as those shown in Exhibit 8.16, is supported.

Risk Assessment

We define "risk" as threats to the success of a project. We exclude the risk associated with not completing the project, and the business risk associated with the market, customer, or industry acceptance of the results of the project. We deal with these issues as a part of the business strategic intentions for the company.

Some companies choose to use risk assessment as part of the prioritization process. For them, the risk assessment scores, where a higher number is a higher risk, is applied against the bottom-line impact number. Other companies choose to make risk a separate assessment from bottom-line impact and to use tools like portfolio presentations and bubble charts to present risk data to management.

Companies can adapt the original Information Economics risk factors in the current NIE Prioritization Practice. The original *Information Economics* factors were as follows:[7]

- **Project or Organizational Risk:** The degree to which the success of the project depends on new or untested business skills or experience. This risk also considers the degree to which the business organization is capable of carrying out the changes required by the project.

- **Definitional Uncertainty:** The degree to which the business requirements are well defined and well understood, and accurately translated into demand for information and application systems functionality.

- **Technical Uncertainty:** The degree to which the project is dependent on untried technologies, and the degree to which the company possesses the appropriate experience in designing and building applications with the technology.

- **IS Infrastructure Risk:** The degree to which the technical environment possesses the required factors of data administration, communications, project management, and development.

Companies we have worked with have added the following risk assessments:

- **Technical Risk:** The degree to which the use of a particular technology requires new management, analytical, or developmental skills. The risk factor includes whether the requisite skills are available from the vendor or from the marketplace, and whether training or new hires can provide the necessary technical expertise.

- **Investment Risk:** The degree to which other, non-project investments are required to make the project successful.

- **Project Management Risk:** The degree to which project managers are available and capable of dealing with the project's complexities, both technical and organizational.

Some companies choose several risk factors and then weight them according to their specific circumstance. For example, a company in the commodities business chose technical, investment, and project management risk and weighted project management at twice the importance of the other two. This allows a company to establish a risk portfolio for use in the prioritization process.

Implications for Business Case and Project Documentation

The documentation for a development or enhancement project is its business case and "one-pager" for prioritization. The business case format should include a description of exactly what the project expects to accomplish toward each business strategic intention. Ideally, the project business case also references the performance metrics expected to be affected. ROI or related financial measures are an important part of the business case as well and can be included in the decision factors used in prioritization.

Critical Success Factors: Right Decisions/Right Results Principles in Prioritization

Prioritization most directly supports the resource allocation and resource management principles, and indirectly supports the other Right Decisions/Right Results principles. See Exhibit 8.17.

EXHIBIT 8.17   Goals and Practice Principles

Goals	Practice Principles
Actionable, Commonly Understood Strategic Intentions	1. Actionable Strategic Intentions
	2. Actions Tied to Strategy
	3. Common Understanding of Strategic Intentions
The Right Business Results from IT	4. Business-Focused Outcomes
	5. Value-Based Resource Allocation
Management Culture and Consensus View	6. Role-Based Culture Management
Portfolios and Portfolio Management	7. Value/Portfolio-Based Resource Management
The Right Actions and Results	8. Responsive to Change

- *Actionable Strategic Intentions:* Value assessment as described requires clear strategic intentions and assessment scales. Where strategic intentions exist, creating assessment scales forces management to think about operational and strategic impacts that can be used as measures. Where none exist, the process of "discovering" strategic intentions by distilling planning results, budget decisions, business initiatives, and other indicators of a company's strategy force management to develop actionable strategic intention statements that reflect the values of the business.

- *Actions Tied to Strategy:* Project assessment is based directly on the company's strategic intentions. Consequently, management understands the direct contribution (or lack) of each proposed activity and can choose those that best support strategic intentions.

- *Common Understanding of Strategic Intentions:* Business and IT managers reach consensus on the meaning of strategic intentions as a necessary part of assessing bottom-line impact. In addition, creating and using the assessment scales requires a common view of the way that initiatives can impact strategic intentions, reinforcing the understanding of the company's direction. Ultimately, business and IT managers share a common view of the company's direction.

- *Impact-Based Resource Allocation:* Clearly, this principle is the "sweet spot" of prioritization. Using the results of prioritization, IT and business management can make resource decisions explicitly based on bottom-line impact. While other factors are considered as well (skills availability, organization readiness, project interdependencies), the primary focus is connection to strategic intentions.

- *Impact-Based Resource Management:* This brief description has focused on new IT initiatives. However, the process and philosophy is equally applicable to investments in legacy maintenance, infrastructure, and any other categories of IT. By combining these categories into portfolios and pooling resources on the same lines, prioritization can be used to make sure that all resources are being allocated to maximum benefit relative to strategic intentions.

- *Business Outcomes:* This is the second sweet spot for Prioritization. The process and philosophy explicitly requires sponsors to describe initiatives in terms of business issues and business outcomes. During assessment, the only question that is relevant is: What is the cause-and-effect link between doing this initiative and making progress on strategic intentions?

- *Responsive to Change:* Prioritization gives management a quick way to understand the impact of business changes on its priorities. By changing the management factors to reflect new realities in the business, IT and business management can immediately assess where priorities need to change, and direct resources and schedule accordingly.

- *Role-Based Culture Management:* Prioritization requires business, not IT, management to assess the bottom-line impact of IT projects. In addition, it requires all business managers to understand the broad range of company strategic intentions and all proposed IT projects. This change in role (for most companies) changes the way business managers think about IT and its role in the company as a whole, and begins the process of breaking down silo-oriented thinking relative to IT priorities.

Summary: Prioritization Practice

Prioritization is a critical step in moving from business strategy to IT action (see Exhibit 8.18). By providing a common language (strategic intentions and cause-and-effect linkages) for business managers to discuss and assess IT initiatives, Prioritization promotes common understanding and consensus on what the company should do with IT. More importantly, managers can assign resources to the highest value projects, knowing that the assessment is based directly on their views of the business impact of the initiatives.

EXHIBIT 8.18   NIE Practices in the Strategy-to-Bottom-Line Value Chain

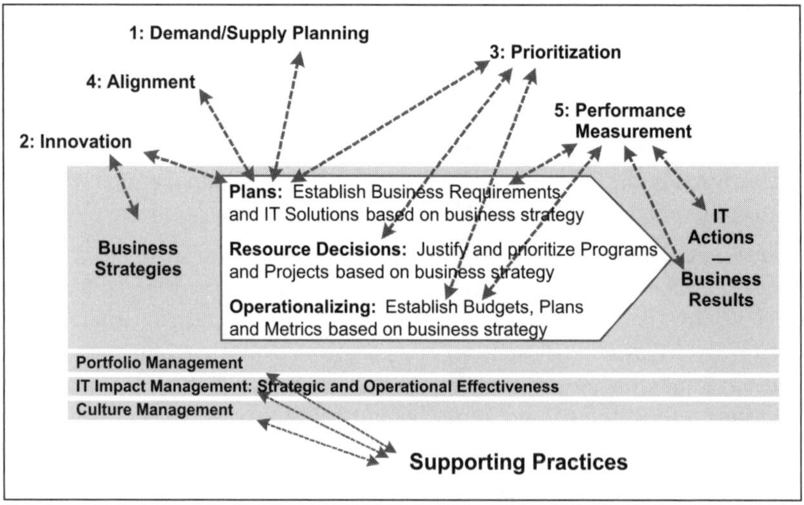

THE ALIGNMENT PRACTICE

Getting business and IT aligned is a prerequisite for delivering IT value and is on the critical path for using IT to improve business performance. Alignment can be measured and, consequently, can be managed and improved. This can occur throughout the Strategy-to-Bottom-Line Value Chain. See Exhibit 8.19.

While the Prioritization practice allows management to assign resources to proposed IT initiatives based on bottom-line impact and connection to strategic intentions, the Alignment practice does the same for existing IT applications and infrastructure. In most companies, IT resources dedicated to existing activities far outweigh resources given for new initiatives. These resources are rarely examined for continuing contribution to the business. The Alignment

EXHIBIT 8.19   Alignment/Assessment

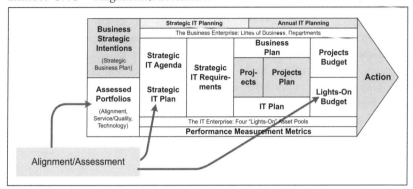

practice looks at these activities and assesses the cause and effect between existing IT activities and the company's strategic intentions and operations.

One of the hardest things to do in any business is stop doing things that are currently in place. Legacy systems and embedded infrastructure, in particular, take on a life of their own, with little formal examination of their continued value. However, every dollar, employee hour, and infrastructure resource that is spent on existing activities is a resource not spent on new initiatives that may have a greater value to the company. The Alignment practice provides a way to look at past resource decisions in the light of present and future needs and to free up resources from lower-value existing activities to be used for higher-value initiatives supporting the existing strategic intentions.

When business managers ask whether the company's IT resources are being invested in the right place, what they really want to understand is whether there is a difference between where IT's energies are being applied and the real business problems. This happens when senior managers are distant from resource decisions, such as when investment decisions are made by middle-level supervisors rather than managers, when maintenance and support overwhelm new development, and when IT leadership resists reallocation to new business areas, when business conditions change.

The Alignment practice is divided into three parts. The first, called "Strategic Alignment," addresses the alignment of IT asset pools (applications, infrastructure, services, and management) to the business strategic intentions. The second, called "Internal IT Alignment," addresses how well each of the four IT asset pools are consistent with each other and, in particular, how well services and infrastructure supports the application asset pool. The third, called "Functional Alignment," addresses the service level, quality, functionality, technology, and intensity of use of each asset pool. (This third part is described in more detail later.)

The Alignment practice asks a fundamental question: Do the existing IT activities promote or inhibit the company's strategic intentions and operational requirements? Each Alignment practice part addresses this question.

Establishing the Portfolios and Costs for Alignment

Properly establishing the portfolios for use in the Alignment practice is a critical step. In Chapter 4, we discussed the basis for development of portfolios in the lights-on budget, and gave some examples of line items within each. Here we reemphasize the importance of selecting the right line items. For applications, the key issue is granularity. Ideally, an application portfolio will contain 30 to 50 line items. This means that, for larger companies, applications will be clustered (e.g., the payroll application contains all of the various reporting elements). For infrastructure, the key is determining the basic infrastructure services (e.g., platforms, networks, e-mail).

For all four portfolios, identifying cost for each line item is the single most critical action. We do not propose a completely detailed cost accounting nor a thorough activity-based costing. We look for costs in the 80 percent accuracy range. This is more than sufficient to drive the data analysis and decision making that needs to occur.

Exhibit 8.20 shows an example of the four portfolios for a company, with annual costs included. This is the level of portfolio development that makes the

EXHIBIT 8.20   Four Lights-On Portfolios with Annual Costs

Service	Annual Cost
Help Desk	4,285,600
On-site Desktop Support	1,029,600
Electronic Report Distribution	550,000
Report Distribution	12,932,000
Job Scheduling	5,526,400
Notes Administration including e-mail	730,800
Hardware/Software evaluation	695,200
Telephone Support	1,012,000
Internet Support	3,400,000
Training (PC and other)	1,806,490
Procurement process	413,600
Records Management	460,560
User hardware maintenance	716,800
Total Services	33,559,050

Infrastructure Element	Annual Cost
Platform—Mainframe	5,051,000
Platform—AS400	5,900,000
Platform—NT	2,297,100
Software Licenses	4,802,221
Data Management (SW)	1,219,200
Security	5,900,000
Disaster Recovery	4,129,250
Network LAN	7,912,120
Network WAN and e-mail and access	3,829,680
MIS Tools (DB2 Table File, Merant)	560,000
Internet/Intranet Security	281,600
Infrastructure Total:	46,344,511

Application	Annual Cost
Consumer Database Marketing	1,087,800
Sales Force Automation	712,000
Sales Budget	88,000
Sales Promotion Inventory	1,020,800
Accounts Receivable	945,260
Banking System	70,400
Budget Application	1,270,400
Capital Projects	545,600
Cash Management	205,695
Cost Sheet Reporting	827,200
EFT	1,295,713
Litigation Support	1,220,320
Retention Manager	125,600
Total Recall Records Management	123,200
Document Control	6,581,524
Green Leaf System	2,868,800
Leaf Forecasting	352,000
Leaf Inventory	1,742,400
Maintenance Management	3,784,000
Applications Total:	24,866,712

Management	Annual Cost
Vendor Relationship Management	800,000
Planning (including upgrades, renewals)	1,188,000
Records Retention/Records Management	380,000
Methodology Development	264,000
Staff and budget mgmt. (administration)	8,212,700
Project Administration	805,200
Planning	1,050,000
Staff Development	3,639,008
Training Program	5,438,063
Management Total:	21,776,970

Services ➜

Applications ➜

Management ➜

Infrastructure ➜

alignment assessments described in the following section so valuable in analysis and decision making.

Strategic Alignment

How well do the applications, infrastructure, and service portfolios support strategic intentions and business operational requirements?

Exhibit 8.21 shows the two dimensions of portfolio alignment and the three portfolios to be aligned. For example, the Applications portfolio is aligned with: (1) the company's strategic intentions, and (2) the company's business processes. Consequently, six different alignment tests are possible, and for each, an alignment assessment template is used. The result is that each portfolio can be examined for alignment gaps. (Alignment information is also a part of the Performance Measurement practice; see Chapter 10.)

EXHIBIT 8.21   Strategic Alignment: Six Tests

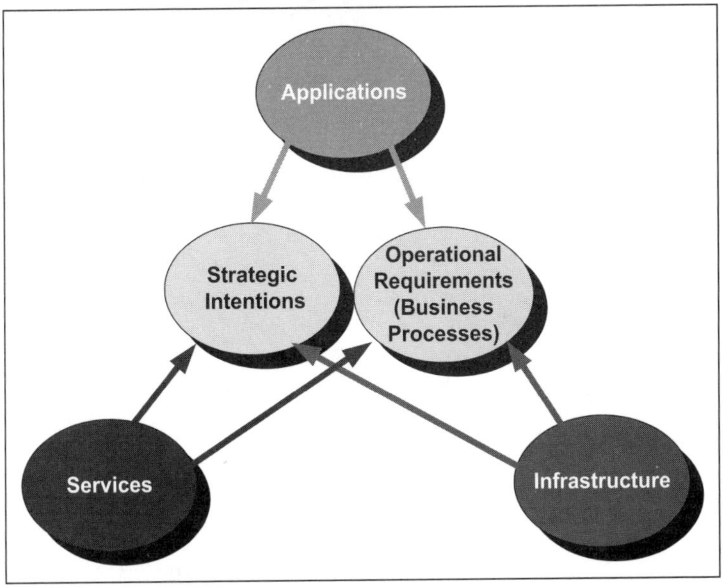

Internal IT Alignment

How well do the IT infrastructure and services portfolios support the highest value components of the IT applications portfolio? That is, if we identify the applications that are (or should be) highly aligned with the business, does the infrastructure adequately support those applications? Are the IT organization's management processes effective in turning business strategy into IT actions?

Exhibit 8.22 pictures the analysis of portfolios against each other. Whereas Portfolio Alignment analyzes the portfolios against the business factors (strategic intentions and business processes), this alignment assesses the consistency of support between the portfolios, such as between applications and infrastructures.

EXHIBIT 8.22   Internal IT Alignment: Six Tests

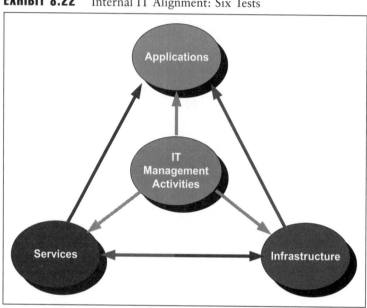

Strategic and Internal Alignment Process Overview

There are two separate alignment assessments performed in the practice. The first, strategic alignment, looks at three elements of IT (applications, services, and infrastructure portfolios) and determines how they support/inhibit two business elements (strategic intentions, and business operational and process requirements).

The second assessment, internal alignment of IT, examines how infrastructure and services support/inhibit applications and each other, as well as how the IT management activities support/inhibit all three.

How Is Alignment Assessed?

The general question for alignment is, "Does an element of the Alignment Model being used support or inhibit the objectives of the other components?" For example:

- **Strategic Alignment:** For every application, does it support or inhibit achieving business goals?

- **Internal IT Alignment:** For each part of the infrastructure element, does it support or inhibit the applications that depend on it?

- **Strategic Alignment:** Does the infrastructure support or inhibit the business goals of the company?

These questions are answered for each of the alignment connections. To obtain the assessment, the service uses a series of matrices that document the alignment relationship. For example, a matrix that assesses the status of alignment between business *goals* and IT *applications* lists, on one axis, the business goals, and along the other, the set of IT applications. The matrix entries document the degree to which the application supports or inhibits the achievement of the business goals. In the example in Exhibit 8.23, we present an assessment of the application portfolio against strategic intentions. Data for the matrix is

EXHIBIT 8.23   Sample Alignment Assessment Scale

3	Critical enabler	Service is a critical enabler in achieving the Strategic Intent. Without this Service, the Strategic Intent cannot be accomplished.
2	Enabler	Service is an enabler in achieving the Strategic Intent. Without this Service, the Strategic Intent can be accomplished, at some additional cost.
1	Indirect enabler	Service is an indirect enabler; it is indirectly related to achieving the Strategic Intent.
0	No effect	Service has no effect on achieving the Strategic Intent.
Blank	NA	Not applicable; Service is not used.
- 1	Minor inhibitor	Service is an indirect inhibitor; it is indirectly related to inhibiting the achievement of the Strategic Intent.
- 2	Inhibitor	Service is an inhibitor to achieving the Strategic Intent. With this Service, the Strategic Intent can be accomplished, but at additional cost.
- 3	Critical inhibitor	Service is a critical inhibitor in achieving the Strategic Intent. With this Service, the Strategic Intent cannot be accomplished.

gathered through interviews, individually completed matrix instruments, and facilitated group processes. (For most of the Alignment connections, a similar table will represent the assessments.)

For each Alignment assessment, a scale is used like the one shown in Exhibit 8.23. Note that this Scale is for an IT services portfolio against business strategic intentions.

Companies may also choose to use a +5 to −5 scale, to be consistent with the scales used in prioritization and in other parts of Alignment assessment.

Who Assesses Alignment?

Alignment is best assessed by the business managers who are responsible for business performance and those who are major users of IT. In a consensus-building and facilitated process, business and IT managers together arrive at an assessment of alignment in each of the alignment connections. This consensus building is a critical element of the process. Fostering and facilitating communication between business and IT managers not only results in assessment but is, in fact, the first step of an ongoing process of organizational development and more effective IT use in the company.

Alignment Assessment Result

Ultimately, Prioritization and Alignment are about allocating resources to high-value activities. Alignment, however, allows a deeper analysis of those activities and allows managers to make resource decisions based on a range of assessments beyond strict bottom-line impact.

For example, in Exhibit 8.24, note several applications which have assessments slightly above neutral or worse for all strategic intentions. Managers can now ask: For that application, should we be spending any resources maintaining this application? Does it need to be a net enabler for strategic intentions, and thus warrant more resources for upgrade or even replacement?

EXHIBIT 8.24   Sample Alignment Data

	Wgt.	20	10	10	10	20	10	5	10		
	Weight	Cost Reduction	Supplier of Choice	Targeted Market Growth	Acquisition Capability	Customer Cost	Standards and Best Practices	Capacity Increase	Product Mix Optimization	Unweighted Total	Weighted Total
Customer Information System	20	1	3	3	0	2	0	-1	2	10	200
Supplier Quality Monitoring	15	-1	2	0	0	2	2	2	2	9	135
Financial Information System	35	0	0	0	1	1	1	1	0	4	140
CORBIT Materials System	15	2	3	2	0	2	3	3	-1	14	210
Product Planning	5	2	1	1	1	0	0	-2	-1	2	10
Manufacturing Expansion Control	10	1	-1	-2	0	-3	2	-1	-3	-7	-70
Unweighted Total		5	8	4	2	4	8	2	-1		
Weighted Total		100	80	40	20	80	80	10	-10		

Additionally, we may look at specific strategic intentions, and examine the application "coverage". In Exhibit 8.24, some strategic intentions have neutral, or worse, overall ratings for application support. Again, managers can ask: Where should we beef up applications to rectify that gap? Are new development projects needed in that area?

Alignment assessments allow managers to look at portfolios (application, infrastructure, services) and decide where the existing applications are supporting the business, where they are weakest, and develop plans for covering gaps in alignment.

Management Issues

Existing applications, infrastructure, services, and management processes were implemented to address strategic intentions of the past, not of the present. Alignment looks at previous resource allocation decisions and examines the continuing bottom-line impact of those decisions in light of present and future strategic intentions and business process needs. As with Prioritization, this practice asks a form of the question: Are IT investments strongly connected to strategic intentions?

Again, culture comes to the fore. The Alignment practice requires that management look at all activities that use IT resources, not just new initiatives, and assess them for bottom-line impact. Management must adopt the philosophy that as the business changes, activities that were valuable in the past may not be so in the future. Over time, the process of Alignment will produce a management mindset that requires all resources to be used for the strategic intentions of the business, not just those targeting new initiatives.

Alignment expresses the degree to which the IT organization can contribute to the company, today and in the future, from the business perspective. By embracing the principles of Right Decisions/Right Results, companies can use the Alignment practice tools to be sure that all of the IT resources in the company, not just new development, are contributing to the business.

Critical Success Factors: Right Decisions/Right Results Principles in Alignment

Alignment most directly supports the resource management and business outcome principles of Right Decisions/Right Results but has an indirect impact on the other as well. See Exhibit 8.25.

- *Actionable Strategic Intentions:* As with Prioritization, Alignment assessment requires a clear statement of strategic intentions, and forces management to develop them as a necessary step in implementing the practice.

- *Actions Tied to Strategy:* Alignment looks directly at the company's strategic intentions and assesses the role that existing IT activities play in meeting

EXHIBIT 8.25   Goals and Practice Principles

Goals	Practice Principles
Actionable, Commonly Understood Strategic Intentions	1. Actionable Strategic Intentions
	2. Actions Tied to Strategy
	3. Common Understanding of Strategic Intentions
The Right Business Results from IT	4. Business-Focused Outcomes
	5. Value-Based Resource Allocation
Management Culture and Consensus View	6. Role-Based Culture Management
Portfolios and Portfolio Management	7. Value/Portfolio-Based Resource Management
The Right Actions and Results	8. Responsive to Change

them. In many companies, for the first time, business and IT management are able to directly assess the impact of existing IT activities and eliminate those that do not contribute to the company's strategies.

- *Common Understanding of Strategic Intentions:* Again echoing the Prioritization practice, business and IT managers must share a common view of the company's direction in order to perform a valid assessment.

- *Impact-Based Resource Allocation:* Alignment is a powerful tool for assessing which existing portfolios and processes produce or inhibit the production of bottom-line impact. By looking at ongoing resource usage for existing portfolios, Alignment allows IT and business management to examine their existing assignment of resources and determine which are and which are not producing bottom-line impact, allowing reassignment where necessary.

- *Impact-Based Resource Management:* Portfolios are explicitly built into the Alignment philosophy and process. Using the results of Alignment, IT and business management can make resource decisions that move resources from existing but low-value activities to higher-valued new and existing initiatives. Additionally, "under-performing" but still necessary portfolios can be identified for added resources and targeted improvement.

- *Business Outcomes:* During assessment, the key question answered is, is this component (application, infrastructure, process) helping or inhibiting the business in a particular area? The issue isn't whether an application, for example, works properly or satisfies its user's needs, but whether or not it is contributing to a desired business outcome. As with Prioritization, business and IT management are forced to focus on how IT supports specific business intentions, processes, and outcomes.

- **Responsive to Change:** As with Prioritization, Alignment explicitly factors in business strategies and directions into assessments. By providing a framework for easily reassessing activities when conditions change, Alignment provides a means for continuous reevaluation.

- **Role-Based Culture Management:** Like Prioritization, Alignment requires business management to participate in assessing the bottom-line impact of ongoing IT activities. By placing this responsibility on business, Alignment begins the process of changing how IT is deployed and forces business managers into the role of helping IT to think about where resources are going and where they can be best utilized, from a company perspective.

Summary: Strategic and Internal Alignment

Business and IT must be aligned if IT is to improve a company's performance. Alignment can be accomplished by examining four aspects of IT and also examining the way that business managers and IT managers plan and execute IT initiatives in each area.

Understanding, measuring, and monitoring IT/business alignment is a prerequisite for delivering and demonstrating IT value. Without alignment, IT and IT management operate in a reactive and uncertain manner, making decisions with limited business input. Proper IT/business alignment satisfies the CIO's need for supporting existing requirements and positioning for tomorrow by promoting management processes, applications, and infrastructure investments that directly support business goals today and for the future.

Functional Alignment

While the Prioritization practice allows management to assign resources to proposed IT initiatives based on bottom-line impact and connection to strategic intentions, the Alignment practice does the same for existing IT applications and infrastructure. In most companies, IT resources dedicated to existing activities far outweigh resources given for new initiatives. These resources are rarely examined for continuing contribution to the business.

Functional Alignment continues this examination by looking at quality, service levels, intensity of use, and technology. The basic assessments are shown in Exhibit 8.26.

The assessment process is identical to the alignment process. In some cases, the technical staff is better suited to do the assessment, particularly for the technology assessments. In all other cases, it is expected that the business leadership group is the provider of assessment information. As discussed earlier, a company may go through stages in this, as described in the above in the section on Assessment Performance. Note 14, "Scoring for Portfolio Assessment," on this book's website contains suggested scoring and further descriptions for each of the Portfolio Assessment components.

EXHIBIT 8.26   Choices for Functional Alignment Assessments

Assessment	Specific Assessment	Assessment Focus
Service Level	Availability	Availability as a problem for workflow or business processes.
	Responsiveness	Responsiveness to the needs of the workflow or business process.
Quality	Functionality	Functionality of the applications, infrastructure, or service, related to the needs of the workflow or business process.
	Accuracy	Accuracy of the data or service performed by the applications, infrastructure, or service, related to the needs of the workflow or business process.
Technology	Architecture	Compliance with enterprise architecture standards.
	Vendor Support and Stability	Degree to which vendor support is a problem in meeting delivery requirements.
	Technical Support	Degree to which support is required of the technical staff (this is an ongoing cost issue).
	Availability of Support in Market or Industry	Degree to which needed support is available.
Intensity of Use	Dependency	Degree to which the application, infrastructure, or service is important to the business process, organization, or individual user.
	Breadth of Use	How widely within the company the application, infrastructure, or service is used.

MAKE THE RIGHT DECISIONS WITH PRIORITIZATION AND ALIGNMENT

The right decisions lead to controlling the IT spend and improving, or maximizing, IT's bottom-line impact. Two NIE Practices provide the tools to support decision making. These decisions occur in the Strategy-to-Bottom-Line Value Chain, as described in Exhibit 8.27.

Note that this is not a mechanical process. Prioritization and alignment practices do not automatically result in resource decisions. Management teams do that, supported by the prioritization and alignment tools. The Prioritization and Alignment NIE practices, though providing critical information for decision making, may not result in the final decisions about projects or lights-on budgets. For projects, considerations such as staff availability, mandatory projects, and scheduling also play a role. For line-item budgets, considerations such as the cost of abandoning applications, organizational dependencies, and corporate budget practices play a role

EXHIBIT 8.27   Management Decision Making Using Alignment Results

	Value Chain Element	Decision Making based on Prioritization	Decision Making based on Alignment/Assessment
1	Business Strategic Intentions	Relative importance of each Business Strategic Intention	
2	Assessed Portfolios		Alignment assessment of lights-on asset pools; identify high- and low-performing resources
4	Strategic IT Plan		Use of alignment assessments to define IT strategic plan
5	Strategic IT Requirements	The priorities of IT requirements (bottom-line impact)	Use of alignment assessments to decide on Strategic IT requirements
6	Projects	(Business case definition of bottom-line impact)	
8	Annual Project Plan	Prioritization of projects (resource allocation)	
9	Annual IT Plan	(Scheduling and technical resource allocation to projects)	Use of alignment assessment to establish tactical objectives
10	Projects Budget	Decision on projects budget (resource allocation)	
11	Lights-On Budget		Use of alignment assessment to decide on lights-on budgets

Notes: 1. Value Chain components without prioritization or alignment are excluded from the table.
2. Items in parenthesis are activities outside of the prioritization decision-making context but that use the results.

The Prioritization and Alignment NIE practices are crucial tools in final decisions, providing the specific bottom-line and IT spend control inputs into those decisions. The final decisions are typically made as part of the "annual project plan," the "projects budget" and "line-item" budgets in the Strategy-to-Bottom-Line Value Chain. See Exhibit 8.28.

The second perspective on resource allocation is to examine decisions as they affect an individual project in its lifecycle, including when it becomes part of the lights-on budget following implementation. Exhibit 8.29 shows how we can define the lifecycle phases from a decision perspective.

From this individual project perspective, the decision to assign resources and the decision to continue its operation, are both driven from the business per-spective—strategic intentions and performance. However, the Prioritization and Alignment NIE practices do not produce better projects or improved perform-ance for lights-on portfolio line items. Both come from planning processes—for example, the Strategic Agenda for the Use of IT, and the Strategic IT Plan (discussed in Chapter 9). These practices do provide a framework for those planning processes—that is, the strategic intentions and the understanding by planners that projects and light-on budgets will be subjected to the prioritiza-tion and alignment processes.

EXHIBIT 8.28   Strategy-to-Bottom-Line Value Chain—Deliverables

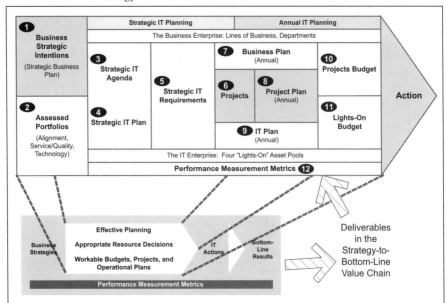

EXHIBIT 8.29   Project Lifecycle Decisions from Prioritization and Alignment

Lifecycle Phase	Prioritization Decisions	Alignment Decisions
Project Formulation/Definition	Make the business case based on bottom-line impact (connection to business strategic intentions).	
Project Selection	Prioritize within overall project portfolio; select the projects with greatest bottom-line impact.	
Project Development	Monitor the project according to risks and bottom-line impact.	
Application Operation (Lights-On Phase)		Continuously assess the status of the project against current strategic intentions, service, quality, functionality, and so forth.

CHAPTER SUMMARY

- *Where is Prioritization applied?*

   The practice is embedded in company processes that produce the IT strategic requirements and the annual project plan. See Exhibit 8.30.

EXHIBIT 8.30   New Information Economics Practices

■ *What outcomes does Prioritization produce?*

Practice Description

□ Assess the business impact of IT initiatives and prioritize them according to strategic intentions.

Desired Management Process Outcomes

□ Business-driven prioritization processes establish the development portfolio.

□ The results of prioritization affect business decision making on IT investments.

Desired Business Outcomes

□ IT investment resources are spent on initiatives that improve impact on achieving the company's strategic intentions.

□ IT investment resources that are being spent on lower-impact investments are reallocated to higher-performing initiatives.

■ *Where is Alignment applied?*

The practice is embedded in company processes that portfolio assessment and annual/capital budgets. The practice is also included in the Performance Measurement practice activities.

■ *What outcomes does Alignment produce?*

Practice Description

□ Assess the business impact of the existing IT infrastructure, applications, and services.

□ Assesses the quality and service levels for existing IT resources, as input to demand/supply planning.

Desired Management Process Outcomes

□ Existing IT infrastructures, applications, and services are validated and aligned against current and future business requirements.

□ Existing IT infrastructures, applications, and services are examined by business management for quality and service levels.

□ All IT investments are reviewed in a routine, consistent basis, assessing connection to strategic intentions.

Desired Business Outcomes

□ Resources are considered interchangeable between new IT investments and existing investments.

□ Only high-impact investments are assigned resources.

MAKE THE RIGHT DECISIONS: MANAGEMENT AGENDA

Management Question	Yes or No?	If No, What Is Our Plan for Correcting This?
Do the business cases we use for project reflect project's support of business strategic intentions?		
Does our current prioritization process prioritize based on connection to business strategic intentions?		
Does our management team understand the complete application development portfolio?		
Do we examine our lights-on budget each budget cycle, and squeeze out the poorly performing elements?		
Do we have an investment strategy in place for the lights-on budget?		
Do we understand where costs are in the lights-on budget?		
Who participates in prioritization?		
Who participates in activities assessing the lights-on budget?		
Is risk formally assessed in project prioritization?		
Does enterprise architecture provide input into prioritization?		

ADDITIONAL READING

The book's website contains additional information:

Website Note 3: IT, Bottom-Line Impact, and Government

Website Note 14: Scoring for Portfolio Assessment

The appendices at the back of the book also contain related information for Chapter 8:

Appendix B: Management Team Roles in Right Decisions/Right Results

Appendix C: The Development of Strategic Intentions, with Examples

Appendix D: Applying Strategic Intentions in Prioritization

NOTES

1. Appendix C, "The Development of Strategic Intentions, with Examples," provides background on how to develop them.
2. Chapter 9 provides for a definition of this and the process that produces it.
3. This prioritization practice description assumes that Prioritization is the only practice being employed by the company. If the company is following other parts of the Strategy-to-Bottom-Line Value Chain—for example, the Demand/Supply planning activities—then strategic intentions would be defined there, and the project plan in Step 5 is included in subsequent Value Chain activities rather than here. Also, this practice description does not include portfolio balancing, an essential element in making a comprehensive project plan and/or a line-item budget.
4. See Appendix D, "Applying Strategic Intentions in Prioritization," for a description of the cause-and-effect scale.
5. See Chapters 3 and 6 for further discussion of strategic intentions, including examples with goal statements and metrics.
6. See Parker and Benson, with Trainor, *Information Economics* (Prentice-Hall 1988), Chapters 13 and 14, pp. 144–176.
7. See *Information Economics,* Chapters 13 and 14, for the definition of these risk factors and the scoring templates associated with them.

CHAPTER 9

Plan for the Right Results

In Chapter 8, we introduced Prioritization and Alignment practices that enable the management team to decide on the most valuable projects and line items in the lights-on budget. This is how managers can achieve what we've termed the "right results": controlled IT spending and improved IT bottom-line impact. By selecting the best projects that have the most potential bottom-line impact and by examining the lights-on budget and eliminating or replacing poorly performing resources, managers can achieve these goals.

When we talked to a CIO about this, though, he remarked that "if all we're doing is prioritizing the same old projects" and "if all we're aligning is the old set of application and infrastructure portfolios" . . . well, that's not enough. "What we need is better projects and better portfolios." In short, we need a new approach to effective planning that creates realistic IT plans (producing new projects and renewed

Control Spending and Maximize Impact on the Bottom Line	
1	Define the Goals
2	Ask the Right Questions
3	Connect to the Bottom Line
4	Understand Costs and Resources
5	Focus on the Right Things
6	Adopt Effective Process to Produce Action
7	Tackle the Practical Problems
8	Make the Right Decisions
9	**Plan for the Right Results**
10	Keep Score
11	Deal with Culture
12	Chart the Path to Implementation
13	Define What's Next
14	Answer the "So What?" Question

portfolios) strongly connected to and driven from real business requirements. See Exhibit 9.1.

Two problems immediately confront us. The first is that connected business/IT planning has two very different aspects: Strategic Demand/Supply Planning and Innovation Planning. The problems to be addressed, the appropriate processes to follow, and the outcomes to be reached are closely related but quite different between the two. The second problem is that business and IT planning are often disconnected in companies. This problem has to be addressed in order to achieve better projects and portfolio line items.

EXHIBIT 9.1   Strategic Demand/Supply Planning and Innovation in the
Value Chain

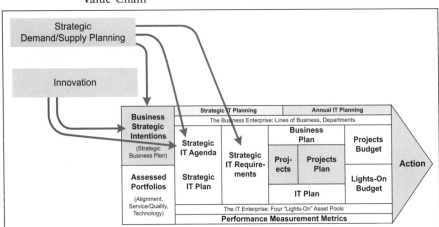

TWO PLANNING PROCESSES

There are two planning relationships between business strategic intentions and
IT. As shown in Exhibit 9.2,[1] the first is where we want IT strategies, plans, and
actions to carry out the business's strategic intentions, to enable them and the
required business changes to achieve the outcomes needed. This relationship is
the basis for Strategic Demand/Supply Planning. Demand represents what the
business requires from IT; supply defines how IT will satisfy that demand. Strategic Demand/Supply Planning assures that supply is consistent with demand.

EXHIBIT 9.2   Demand/Supply and Innovation
Planning Practices

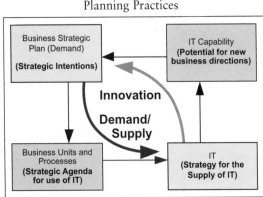

The second relationship is where IT can innovate and contribute new business strategic intentions, as well as new means for achieving the business strategic intentions. This relationship is the basis for Innovation Planning. Impact works to change the demand because of new or different business opportunities created through IT.

This chapter describes two NIE practices: Strategic Demand/Supply Planning and Innovation Planning. Both fit into the Strategy-to-Bottom-Line Value Chain and produce the sort of plans that permit a company to control IT spend while maximizing IT's bottom-line impact.

The Business/IT Planning Disconnect

Although Exhibit 9.2 shows the clear relationship between demand and supply (the demand is defined by strategic intentions and business unit process requirements), and the clear opportunity for innovation (where IT capabilities can impact, or change, the company's strategic intentions), in practice getting business and IT together in a meaningful planning relationship is marred by disconnects.

Many companies find it very difficult to effectively connect business and IT planning. By "effective," we mean producing IT plans (better projects, renewed portfolios) that the business believes in, supports, and carries through to action. Planning disconnects exhibit several symptoms:.

1. IT is not directly engaged in the business planning processes.

2. IT and business strategic planning is essentially shelfware, reflected by the fact that annual plans and budgets are not specifically linked to or driven by the strategic plans.

3. IT and business planning are done separately, with weak or no interaction or linkages. Business planning assumes IT can react and respond to requirements; it does not consider IT-enabled innovations. IT planning focuses on technologies.

4. IT planning itself is highly siloed, with little or no planning across silos and with few company-wide initiatives. These silos are both technical (applications, infrastructures, and IT services are often planned independently) and organizational (multiple business units plan for IT separately).

Doing something about these disconnects can be difficult for a variety of reasons, many of them political or cultural. Unless the senior executive team believes that disconnects are a problem, the team is usually unresponsive to making changes in the planning process. For example, a leading IT consulting organization—a firm where one would expect IT to loom large in planning processes—ignores IT as a factor in its strategic planning process. In another example, a large financial services firm treats IT as a factor to be considered in annual planning, but not in multiyear or strategic planning. In these cases, the executive teams were surprised to learn that IT could be important to their planning; even then, they raised considerable resistance to IT's participation.

Addressing disconnects should be based on the Strategy-to-Bottom-Line Value Chain and the specific processes defined in the Strategic Demand/Supply Planning and Innovation Planning practices. Briefly, we focus on the deliverables in the Value Chain—chiefly, the definition of the business strategic intentions.

The importance of a strategic planning process isn't so much the establishment of a strategic plan itself as it is the definition of the company's strategic intentions. This expression of what is important to management is the starting point for establishing IT projects and plans and, ultimately, its spending and budgets. In order to "control IT spending" and "improve IT's bottom-line impact," we need to know the rules of the game—that is, the basic directions that management is setting for the business.

Connecting IT and Business Planning

The IT organization often does not help build connections to business planning by the manner in which it conducts its own planning. Often, the term "IT strategic plan" conveys a highly technical perspective, focusing on the infrastructure and technical application developments thought to be needed. Any connection to the business that exists in such plans is often a bland chapter listing the company's public, high-level strategy statements, without identifying exactly what IT could contribute to the success of those strategies. Reading such IT strategic plans is an exercise in decoding acronyms and technical terms.

This problem—the business/IT planning disconnect—is complicated by the common idea that business users are responsible for doing something about the business plan, and IT is reduced to planning its own infrastructure requirements and positioning itself to work through the business users. In other words, the IT organization may believe its planning and actions cannot directly impact the company's strategies, because that is the responsibility of the business users. In this view, commonly found in shared-service IT organizations, IT is "run like a business," by which they mean that IT responds to "user needs" as defined by the business users. This approach to IT's role is a great definition of the business/IT planning disconnect.

Is this a problem? For some companies, maybe not. Perhaps the business users are fully capable of translating IT opportunities into their own planning processes and moving these opportunities forward in the development of the company's strategic planning. Perhaps IT isn't a significant factor in the industry, or perhaps IT's role in the company is only supportive.

We believe that in most cases, it *is* a problem. Certainly, the disconnect complicates the development of company strategic visioning about technology and makes implementing company-wide initiatives across silos difficult. Perpetuating business/IT silos and intra-business silos reduces one of IT's major contributions: integrated and common information throughout the company, which enables common processes and capabilities.

Solving the disconnect starts by properly stating some of the objectives to be addressed by an IT plan. Mostly simply, these include:

- A clear statement of the strategic requirements for IT for the company as a whole, and for each business unit.

- A basis for prioritizing those strategic requirements based on support of business strategic intentions.

- Strategic direction for the IT organization for creating and maintaining the necessary infrastructures, and the capabilities for developing, delivering, and supporting the company's applications.

- Clear direction for effectively controlling the IT spend, at the same time as improving, or maximizing, IT's bottom-line impact.

These objectives cannot be met without clear connections between strategic business and IT planning. Business and IT strategic planning has to occur together, in sync.

Connecting Planning to Mission and Right Decisions

As noted in Chapter 5, the first goal we set for management is: "Translate enterprise mission, vision, and strategy into actionable, commonly understood strategic

EXHIBIT 9.3 Mission to Planning (Strategic Intentions) to Right Decisions

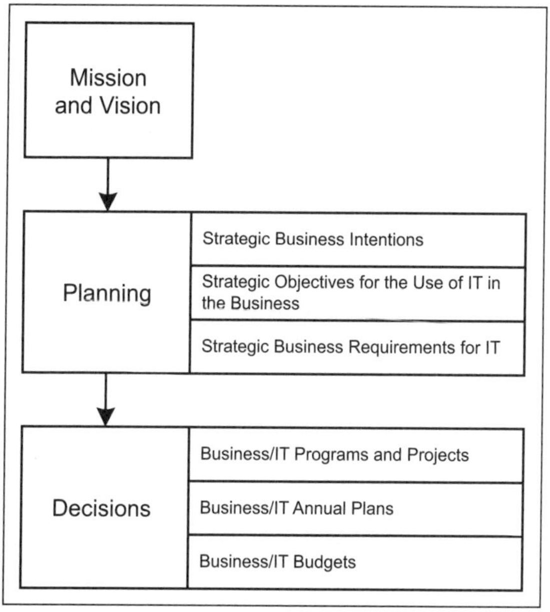

Mission and Vision

Planning	Strategic Business Intentions
	Strategic Objectives for the Use of IT in the Business
	Strategic Business Requirements for IT

Decisions	Business/IT Programs and Projects
	Business/IT Annual Plans
	Business/IT Budgets

intentions." By having good strategic intentions, management can define its strategic objectives for the use of IT, which highlights how IT will directly support and enable each strategic intention. This is further defined into the business capabilities required of IT, stated as strategic business requirements. This then leads to business decisions and choices about programs and projects, plans, and budgets. See Exhibit 9.3.

But it all begins with the definitions of the strategic intentions for the business. As described in Chapter 5, these processes can be formal or informal. Ideally, they are part of the management practices of the company.

THE STRATEGIC DEMAND/SUPPLY PLANNING PRACTICE

Industry is awash in planning processes intended to provide "roadmaps" and "blueprints" for "setting future directions" and "implementing mission statements," and so forth. Typically, these corporate strategic planning processes fail to explicitly account for IT activities and strategies, either on the front end as drivers for new business strategies or on the back end as enablers of strategic intentions. See Exhibit 9.4.

EXHIBIT 9.4 Strategic Demand/Supply Planning in the Value Chain

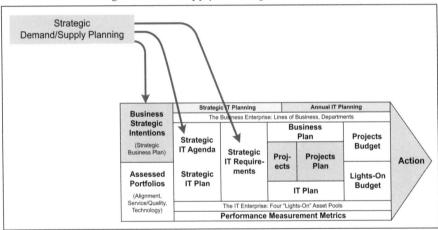

In Right Decisions/Right Results, the point of high-level strategic planning is to translate the company's business strategic intentions into actionable IT strategies and, thereby, create the actions and produce the desired business results. The Strategic Demand/Supply Planning practice starts with high-level business intentions and creates strategies and action plans to drive the IT activities needed to address them.

What Does a Strategic Demand/Supply Plan Look Like?

Properly establishing the IT strategic plan requires a clear definition of the business strategies, as expressed through its strategic intentions, and the relationship between those strategies and what we expect IT to do about them.

Like all such planning descriptions, this should be looked at as a template. Every company is different, and every organizational/political setting is different. Numerous issues such as participants, process, timing, and planning responsibility come into play in approaching the planning process. Nevertheless, the basic concepts are central to addressing the business/IT planning disconnect.

The ideal planning process, shown in Exhibit 9.5, deals with these elements:

Inputs

1. The business's strategic intentions
2. Portfolios and their strategic management
3. Performance management and measurement

Outputs

1. A business strategic agenda for the use of technology
2. An IT (organizational) strategic plan
3. Strategic IT requirements—the programs and projects needed to meet the business strategic agenda

Connections between the Plan and the processes that will implement it

1. Direct connection to the business and IT processes for developing projects
2. Direct connection to the business and IT annual planning
3. Direct connection to the company's and IT annual budgets

EXHIBIT 9.5   Planning Inputs and Outputs in the Value Chain

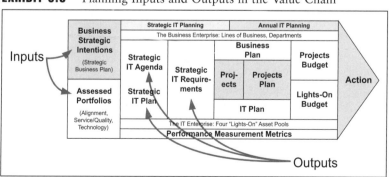

The results are the basic table of contents of a company's strategic plan for information technology. The first, the Strategic Agenda for the Use of IT, defines the strategic intentions of the company and management for applying IT to carry out the company's strategy and goals. This Strategic Agenda, together with the company's business strategic intentions, is the first part of the Strategic IT Plan. It expresses the "demand" for IT—the business strategic intentions together with requirements for technology applications that will address those strategic intentions. This "demand" also defines management's intention to apply IT in the organization, which establishes the business process changes to accommodate and apply IT. The second part of the Strategic IT Plan describes the IT organization's strategies and plans for fulfilling the requirements for IT established in the Strategic Agenda. It expresses the "supply" for IT, including organization, development, and delivery.

Portfolios and their strategic management comprise the critical connecting element among all the pieces. As introduced in Chapter 4, four basic portfolios describe and contain IT organization resources and responsibilities. The application portfolio defines existing and future IT applications. The infrastructure portfolio defines the elements of the supporting technologies. The services portfolio defines the IT organization's interactions with internal company customers and external customers. The management portfolio defines how the internal IT organization manages itself and its portfolios. The planning processes address each portfolio.

What Role Does Enterprise Architecture Play?

For many companies, Enterprise Architecture (EA) is a major part of IT strategic planning. The actual practices followed, however, differ widely from company to company. For some, EA is essentially a standards and to-be definition for IT infrastructure. For these, EA is a major player in constructing and reviewing business projects for compliance with the to-be architecture and in proposing infrastructure development projects. For others, EA also is a major player in defining the to-be for business process and enterprise information. For these, EA also contributes significantly to the business content of projects and, in many cases, the definition of the projects themselves.

For purposes of defining the Strategic Demand/Supply Planning and Innovation Planning practices, we do not explicitly describe a role for Enterprise Architecture. We expect that, in a given company situation, EA will be one of the participants and, in some cases, may be a driver of the management processes described in these practices. Our purpose is to describe the practice, not to specify the specific roles of EA for any participant or, for that matter, any specific part of the IT organization. For example, in the description of portfolio assessment in the previous chapter, much of the technology assessment likely would be done by the EA staff in many companies. This assessment is an important input into the Strategic Demand/Supply Planning practice, but we do not specify precisely who, within IT, would perform it.[2]

Business Strategic Intentions

We defined business strategic intentions as the basic driver for Prioritization and Alignment in Chapter 8, having defined them in Chapter 3. We also described methods for establishing strategic intentions in Chapter 8, as well as in Appendix C, "The Development of Strategic Intentions, with Examples."

In summary, our purpose is not to establish what a company's strategic intentions should be; rather, we use a straightforward framework to document what they are.

The Strategic Agenda for the Use of IT

A critical middle step is required between business strategy (as a source of demand) and IT strategies and actions (as the supply). This middle step is the Strategic Agenda for the Use of IT in the business. This establishes a clear linkage between business strategic intentions and the IT activities the company will undertake to support them.

The Strategic Agenda states what the business expects to do with IT. For example, if a business's strategic intention is to "reduce the cost of logistics between company and customer" (distribution, etc.), then a strategic agenda for the use of IT would state exactly how IT will contribute to that logistics cost reduction. In this case, the Strategic Agenda could be to "apply customer and route data to optimize delivery routes." That's what IT has to deliver—both the data itself and the means for using it in optimizing routes. *How* IT delivers it is based on a separate statement of IT strategy. See Exhibit 9.6.

EXHIBIT 9.6   Elements of Demand/Supply Strategic Plan

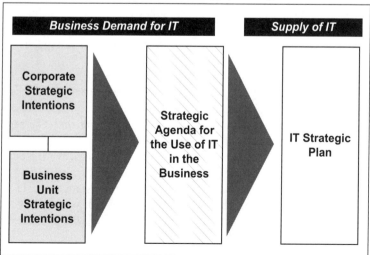

A Strategic Demand/Supply Plan, therefore, has three basic elements at the highest level: (1) the business context via its strategic intentions; (2) the strategic intention for the use of IT to enable the business strategic intentions; and (3) IT's strategic intentions for the means to deliver IT. This is a core idea in the structure of the demand/supply plan. The important NIE innovation is the establishment of the middle ground, the Strategic Agenda for the Use of IT.

Of course, this is no different from saying that there are "requirements" for IT in the business. However, it makes the requirements clear in two ways. First, the use of IT is not, in itself, a business strategy. The business strategy might be to create a close relationship between the customer and the business, or to manage the relationship with the customer (CRM), or to massively adopt supply chain management and reduce supply cost and time. The strategy for the use of IT might be to put database capabilities in the hands of every salesman (e.g., through a sales force automation initiative), or to employ CRM software throughout the company, or to employ an ERP throughout the purchasing and logistics components of the company.

The difference is important. The business strategy establishes the means for improving competitiveness or financial performance. The strategy for the use of IT establishes the means for accomplishing the improved competitiveness—in particular, identifying the specific obligations business management has to use IT for the specific purpose. Saying it another way, Strategic Planning establishes the base strategy and the strategy for using IT to achieve the base strategy.

Strategic Demand/Supply Plan

Our experience at a large financial services institutions was that senior management was willing to define business strategic objectives (e.g., add new products and services, in order to make the bank a dominant part of the customer's financial life) and to define strategies for IT (e.g., to outsource, install internet capabilities, etc.). But the managers failed to take responsibility for the *business* strategies to actually use IT, to make the necessary changes in business processes and business organization that would take advantage of what IT could do.

This structure of *Business Strategy—Business Strategy for the Use of IT—IT Delivery Strategy* directly addresses this problem. It clearly identifies the obligations of business management to make the necessary commitments, process changes, and organizational changes that will accomplish the required result. This structure is a specific example of what we mean by cause and effect. In the first instance, a business strategy's cause and effect is to improve the company's performance. In the second, the strategy for the use of IT's cause-and-effect is to make the business strategy successful. In the third instance, the IT strategy for the delivery of IT is to make the use of IT successful, which in turn makes the business strategy successful, which then achieves the goal of improved business performance. See Exhibit 9.7.

EXHIBIT 9.7　　Strategic IT Demand/Supply Plan

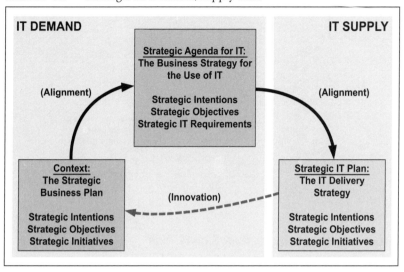

Warren McFarlan has said that "deciding what to do is only 15% of the CIO's job; the rest is managing the transformation."[3] Again, the structure of *Business Strategy—Business Strategy for the Use of IT—IT Delivery Strategy* makes clear where the transformation is. It's twofold. First is the transformation of how IT delivers—a transformation of IT supply. Second is the transformation *in business* in terms of organization, process, relationship to the customer, and so forth to meet the business strategy. Of course, this second transformation is, at the least, jointly accomplished with business management. The CIO can clarify and structure what is necessary, but it is up to business management to see to it that the transformational changes actually occur. The transformation takes place on their turf.

Without the clarity of a Business Strategy for the Use of IT, business management can fall too easily into the trap of expecting the CIO, without partnering or teaming, to single-handedly cause the second transformation to occur. In the absence of extraordinary CIO efforts, this is doomed to failure.

Managers will often claim that a company has no strategic plan and, accordingly, has no strategic intentions from which to develop a strategic IT plan. The Strategic Demand/Supply Planning practice proceeds on the assumption that the business's strategic intentions can be identified and expressed through straightforward processes such as interviews and references to company documents. Our experience has been that strategic intentions always exist, although they may not be documented or even widely understood. The plan structure shown in Exhibit 9.8 permits easy documentation and expression of the company's strategic intentions.

EXHIBIT 9.8   Strategic Plan Table of Contents

Context: **The Strategic Business Plan**	1. Strategic Intentions
	2. Strategic Objectives
	3. Strategic Initiatives
Strategic Agenda for IT: The Business Strategy for the Use of IT	4. Strategic Intentions for the *use* of IT
	5. Strategic Objectives for the *use* of IT
	6. Strategic IT Initiatives (for the *use* of IT in the business)
Strategic IT Plan: The IT Delivery Strategy	7. Strategic Intentions for Applications, Infrastructure, Services, Management
	8. Strategic Objectives
	9. Strategic Initiatives for the *delivery* of IT to the business

Creating the Strategic Demand/Supply Plan

The Strategic Agenda is a framework that clearly expresses enterprise objectives and plans. The clarity lies in two cause-and-effect connections within the framework. The first is the cause and effect between strategic intentions—where the enterprise wants to be—and the strategic initiatives that it is taking to get there. The cause and effect, termed "impact" in Exhibit 9.2, corresponds to "innovation" and assures that the enterprise's actions are consistent with the objectives they address and the intentions they support. In this way, the resources invested in strategic initiatives are assured to be appropriate to achieving the intended results. By expressing enterprise strategies and plans in this simple three-level

EXHIBIT 9.9   Example of a Strategic Business Plan

Strategic Plan Level	Example Description	Example for a Company
Strategic Intention	Example of one of six strategic intentions for the company.	Maximize Marketing Effectiveness—Be the best we can be in our industry.
Strategic Objectives	Example of two out of several strategic objectives for the company. These two relate specifically to the example strategic intention.	Establish and improve customer communications programs. Ensure that customer service is the best in the industry.
Strategic Initiatives	Example of two out of several for each company unit. These two relate specifically to the example strategic intention and the two strategic objectives.	Marketing Department: A new marketing program for dealers and distributors. Distribution Department: A revised call-center organization to maximize time and quality responses to customers.

cause-and-effect framework, the strategies and plans are both made specific and defined in terms of action—the initiatives that connect to the intentions and objectives.

Exhibit 9.9 shows the Strategic Business Plan from Exhibit 4.8. This example shows the cause-and-effect relationship as well as the power of the three-level representation. This strategic business plan leads to the business requirements for the use of IT and then to the strategic plan for delivering the requirements.

It should be emphasized that the purpose of showing this Context: Strategic Business Plan is *not* to suggest that our purpose is to do business strategic planning. Rather, our purpose is to *describe* the *content* of business strategic intentions and so forth, as shown in Exhibit 9.10.

EXHIBIT 9.10   Strategic Intentions to IT Strategic Plan

	Demand		Supply
	Business Strategic Context	**Strategic Plan for the Use of IT**	**Strategic Plan for the Supply of IT**
Strategic Intention	Maximize marketing effectiveness—be the best we can be.	Every marketing and sales person has immediate access to complete customer information.	Establish the infrastructure and staff support to enable an effective, efficient, and complete data warehouse.
Strategic Objectives	Establish and improve customer communication programs. Ensure that customer service is the best in the industry.	Collect and maintain complete information about every customer interaction.	Implement a phased approach to a customer data warehouse.
Strategic Initiatives	Marketing—a new marketing program for dealers and distributors. Distribution—revised call-center organization to maximize time and quality responses to customers.	Establish business processes and organization support for a customer information system, leading to customer relationship management.	Work with Beta Group to identify best approach to a data warehouse. Purchase CRM data package.

We do not expect that companies will have their strategic business plan in this format. Often, companies have very little formal documentation of their strategic plan. Rather, our purpose is to provide a template for stating the business strategic plan. The process of Strategic Demand/Supply Planning will uncover the content and report it using the template.

The second cause-and-effect connection is between the enterprise and IT. The objective is to assure that IT's strategies and plans are consistent with the business strategies and plans. As before, the cause and effect, termed "Alignment" in Chapter 8, assures that IT actions are consistent with the business strategic intentions—where the enterprise wants to be. In this way, the resources invested in initiatives are assured to be appropriate to achieving the intended business results. By expressing business and IT strategies and plans in this three-level cause-and-effect framework, they are defined in terms of action—the specific IT initiatives that connect to the business strategies and plans.

To carry out the example of the Strategic Demand/Supply Plan, Exhibit 9.10 shows how one business strategic intention creates the Strategic Intention for the Use of IT, and the Strategic Plan for the Delivery of IT, all to meet the requirements of the single business strategic intention. It should be noted that Exhibit 9.10 implies a 1 to 1 relationship between business strategic intention and IT delivery strategic intention. This is often not the case; rather, most of the cause-and-effect relationships (shown as 1 to 1 in the Exhibit) are 1 to N.

The Strategic Demand/Supply Planning Process Overview

The key elements of the process are: (1) establish the business drivers—the company's Strategic Intentions; (2) define the role of IT in reaching those business drivers—the company's strategic agenda; and (3) define what IT is to do—the company's IT strategic plan. See Exhibit 9.11.

EXHIBIT 9.11   Step-by-Step Planning Process

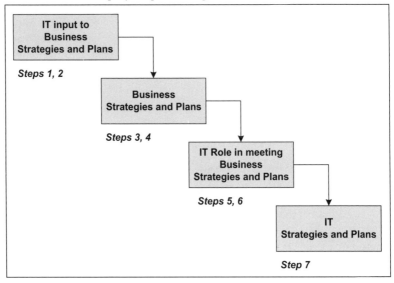

NIE Strategic Demand/Supply Planning operates in a context of existing IT activities and business strategies. Rather than start with the proverbial blank sheet, this planning process begins with existing strategic drivers and an assessment of the current state of IT and how it relates to drivers (discussed in more detail in the Alignment practice description in Chapter 8). Ultimately, the process identifies gaps between existing IT activities and those needed to support the company's current strategic intentions, and fills those gaps with new IT initiatives.

As with other NIE practices, a portfolio view of IT is used as the framework for the planning process: applications, infrastructure, services, and management portfolios become the basis for developing plans to support the strategic intentions.

Management Issues

The two outcomes we look for in Strategic Demand/Supply Planning are:

1. IT resources have a direct and important impact on achieving the company's strategic intentions.
2. IT resources are most effectively allocated to meet the company's strategic needs.

Without a clear statement of strategic intentions and strategic needs, there can be no assessment of impact or intelligent resource allocation to high-impact activities. The key issue is that in many companies, IT management is left to interpret company strategies from the IT perspective, resulting in initiatives that deviate from management's intentions for the business. What is needed is a process that provides the interpretation, gives IT clear statements of management's intentions, and results in consensus among and between business and IT management about the company's directions.

From the process perspective, companies often have not explicitly linked business strategic planning with IT strategic planning, especially in considering the impact that IT can have on the creation of business opportunities. The IT tail should not wag the business dog, but companies do need to understand what IT can contribute to changing the business model or exploiting the existing business capabilities. Companies need a planning bridge that ties together existing business planning processes with IT so that IT ends up with clear strategic intentions to drive the IT planning activities.

The final management issue again comes back to a cultural aspect of planning. Not only do we want a process that ties business and IT planning activities together, but we also want a process that gives business and IT management confidence that each is understanding the needs and role of the other, and is focusing on exactly those things that the business needs to be successful. We are looking not just for new plans, but new understanding.

Process Description

Most IT strategic planning processes start with business objectives and develop IT strategies that are intended to support them. While these are effective as far as they go, this process lacks both the context and the opportunities presented by the existing IT capabilities and activities. With NIE's Strategic Demand/ Supply Planning practice, looking at technology alignment relative to the new strategic intentions identifies business opportunities enabled by the existing technology base, and technology-enabled opportunity scenarios are introduced into the business demand part of the strategic plan. See Exhibit 9.12.

EXHIBIT 9.12   The Fundamental Planning Drivers

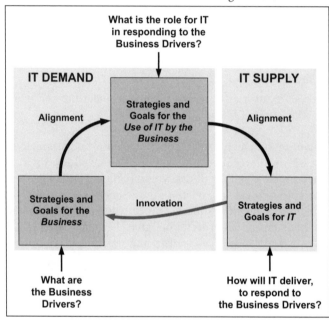

We look to answer three fundamental questions.

1. *What are the business drivers?* We use strategic intentions, objectives, and initiatives to answer this question. It is critical to get down to understanding what the business organizations intend to do to achieve their strategic intentions.

   Note that our purpose is not to do business planning here. We use the three-level structure to identify and communicate the business drivers, not define them. In practical terms, many companies will find that this structure will cause some additional insights into their own plans. But we are not holding ourselves out as performing business planning for them.

   The Innovation Planning practice, however, does provide some opportunity for changing the business strategic intentions and providing additional strategic objectives and initiatives. We provide for this in Step Two of the process (described below).

2. *What is the role for IT in responding to the business drivers?* This is the key innovation of the Strategic Agenda for the Use of IT: the formal expression of exactly what IT can and should do for each of the strategic intentions. This is also a two-edged sword in that the business units find that the statement of intentions for the use of IT also places a burden on them to actually plan for and use IT as specified. We find that this fills a critical gap in strategic planning. Rather than placing all attention on what IT must do, this process places equal attention on what the business organizations must do to employ IT to achieve their objectives.

3. *How will IT deliver, to respond to the business drivers?* This is IT's technology strategy, built to satisfy the role IT needs to play, as defined in the Strategic Agenda.

   The answers, in terms of IT strategic intentions, IT strategic objectives, and IT initiatives, focus the IT organization on achieving the business goals. This also serves to differentiate between IT delivery strategies (e.g., data warehouses, WANs, wireless) from IT *use* strategies (e.g., availability of information to business, access to business information throughout the company, untethered access).

The process occurs at two (or more) levels: at a business unit level and at the enterprise level across all business units. Within both of these levels, the IT portfolios play an important role because they describe the full range of IT applications, resources, and services across the enterprise. This means that, at the first level, business unit managers can see how other business units are successfully using IT resources to achieve strategic goals. This can trigger a new set of ideas about how those same resources can be applied in a similar fashion within their business unit.

The planning process itself is a set of management processes that develop the content of the three-level framework. The objective is to describe doable processes that any executive team can conduct. The management processes are organized into seven steps, moving from business strategies and plans and resulting in IT strategies and plans.

In practical terms, the specific planning process is very dependent on the company circumstances, the relationships between IT planning and business planning staff, and the level of maturity in planning. (See Chapter 12 for a discussion of maturity and process.) The planning process is also dependent on the perception of business and IT management as to the specific goals to be achieved through the planning process. The process steps are shown in Exhibit 9.13.

Note that most other IT strategic planning processes begin with "Define business objectives." Their purpose is to assure that business completely drives the IT planning process. We certainly agree with having business drive IT planning, but we find that business planning needs to have some idea of the possible contributions IT can make to the success of its strategic intentions and, perhaps, in the contribution of new strategic intentions.

EXHIBIT 9.13   Step-by-Step Planning Process

General Process	Step	Primary Purpose
Provide IT Strategic Input into Business Strategies and Plans	Step 1	Identify business mission and key management team objectives.
	Step 2	Visioning and Innovation: Awareness of IT potential for contributing to new and existing business strategy.
Identify Business Strategies and Plans	Step 3	Establish or identify business strategic intentions at a company level.
	Step 4	Establish or identify, for each key business organization, strategic objectives, and initiatives.
Establish IT Role in Meeting Business Strategies and Plans	Step 5	Define the Strategic Agenda for the use of IT; identify strategic intentions for the use of IT in the company.
	Step 6	Define the Strategic Objectives and Initiatives for the use of IT in each key business organization.
Prepare IT Strategies and Plans	Step 7	Define the Strategic IT Plan for the IT organization; define the strategic intentions, objectives, and initiatives for the delivery of IT.

Result

The purpose of the Strategic Demand/Supply Planning practice is to produce an actionable strategic plan for IT, consisting of a statement of business strategic requirements (demand) and IT strategic response (supply). However, given that other parts of the NIE practices also produce potential IT initiatives and resource decisions (Innovation and Alignment), the strategic plan from this phase is a beginning framework for further IT planning at a detailed level.

Consequently, there are two outputs from the Planning practice: the Strategic Agenda and the Strategic Plan.

The Strategic Agenda builds on the company's strategic intentions, and adds clear statements about how the company intends to use IT to achieve the goals of the strategic intentions. The Strategic Agenda is a bridge between the overall corporate strategic plan and the IT strategic plan. It is a high-level directional statement, explicitly tied to strategic intentions, that tells both business and IT management what the company expects IT to do to promote the company's business strategies.

The strategic plan builds on the strategic agenda. Taking a portfolio view, the strategic plan expresses what actions and initiatives IT will undertake, in each of the portfolio areas, to fulfill the objectives of the strategic agenda. Note a major difference between the NIE strategic plan and many traditional IT strategic plans: this plan does not include individual projects. The strategic plan focuses on high level technology-oriented strategies and objectives, and states in broad-brush terms what IT will do, from the technology perspective, to support the strategic agenda. It includes programs and initiatives that IT may undertake in each of the four portfolio areas, but it stops short of articulating specific projects that IT may do as part of those programs.

Beyond the deliverables, the Strategic Demand/Supply Planning practice has a wide impact on the company's planning processes and cultural view of IT and its role in the company. By involving business management in crafting the strategic intentions and strategic agenda for IT, the practice creates two-way understanding between business and IT of the role that IT must play for the company. Clear strategic statements produce clear communication, and communication is the basis for effective IT actions.

Critical Success Factors: Right Decisions/Right Results Principles in Strategic Demand/Supply Planning

- *Actionable Strategic Intentions.* The Planning practice serves to crystallize the business strategies and visions into strategic intentions that IT can act upon. The process explicitly requires business management to "translate" traditional strategy, mission, and vision statements into strategic intentions that communicate to IT, and the business, exactly what management intends to do to improve business performance.

- *Actions Tied to Strategy.* Most top-down planning processes result in planned actions that are driven by the strategic inputs. However, that leaves the existing activities potentially unconnected to new strategies. Strategic Demand/Supply Planning combines both, by driving new programs, initiatives, and strategies from business strategies, but also reexamining all ongoing activities in the context of the company's strategic agenda. In this way, all new *and existing* activities are directly connected to the strategic agenda.

- *Common Understanding of Strategic Intentions.* In many companies, IT managers must interpret business strategies and translate them to IT strategies and actions, often times only approximating the intent of business management. The Planning practice is a way to synthesize business strategic planning results from traditional planning processes into defined strategic intents, eliminating the need for IT to interpret management strategies. The practice requires business and IT management to understand and agree on the strategic and operational meanings of the business strategies, allowing IT to take actions with the explicit understanding of where the business is headed. See Exhibit 9.14.

- *Value-Based Resource Allocation.* Consensus-driven strategic intents are the bedrock for assessing the bottom-line impact of IT activities. Through Prioritization and Alignment practices, strategic intentions that come from the Planning practice drive all resource allocation decisions in each of the IT portfolio areas. Without strategic intentions, there is no basis for making value assessments; without Planning, there are no clear strategic intentions.

EXHIBIT 9.14   Goals and Practice Principles

Goals	Practice Principles
Actionable, Commonly Understood Strategic Intentions	1. Actionable Strategic Intentions
	2. Actions Tied to Strategy
	3. Common Understanding of Strategic Intentions
The Right Business Results from IT	4. Business-Focused Outcomes
	5. Value-Based Resource Allocation
Management Culture and Consensus View	6. Role-Based Culture Management
Portfolios and Portfolio Management	7. Value/Portfolio-Based Resource Management
The Right Actions and Results	8. Responsive to Change

- **Portfolio-Based Resource Management.** The Strategic Demand/Supply Planning practice uses four IT portfolios as the basis for planning analysis. By assessing existing and proposed portfolio elements against the strategic intentions that result from planning, IT and business management can allocate resources to those portfolios based on their existing and potential contribution to the business. There are no anecdotal assessments in this process; all assessments are made by looking at the total portfolio in each area, and acting to maximize the impact of the entire portfolio.

- **Business Outcomes.** Again, strategic intentions that result from the Strategic Demand/Supply Planning practice are the basis for cause-and-effect analysis for IT initiatives. Without this type of strategic intent definition, there is no clear basis for assessing an IT initiatives impact on business initiatives and strategic intentions. Planning again provides the clear context for making these assessments.

- **Responsive to Change.** By splitting the Demand and Supply components of the IT strategy, the strategic agenda and strategic plan are allowed to quickly adjust to changes in the business strategic IT requirements. Changes are easily driven from new strategic requirements into the strategic agenda, driving in turn new programs and initiatives for IT.

- **Role-Based Culture Management.** Strategic Demand/Supply Planning requires that business and IT managers participate in very specific ways to develop the strategic IT requirements, and that IT work closely with business managers to develop the corresponding IT Strategic Agenda. This planning process, by forcing the interaction between these management groups and delineating the roles of each in producing the IT Strategic Plan, begins the overall process of changing the way business and IT interact, and hence the culture of how business will use IT to achieve its strategies.

Summary — Strategic Demand/Supply Planning

The Strategic Demand/Supply Planning practice bridges the gap between business strategic planning and actionable IT strategic plans. By focusing on strategic intentions and the IT strategic agendas needed to accomplish them, the practice builds a consensus view on exactly how IT will be used, and how IT can impact the company's strategies, both tactically and as an influencer of new strategies.

By incorporating a portfolio management perspective into the planning process, the Planning practice ensures that all aspects of IT are considered, and resources are allocated to high-value initiatives, across and within the portfolio

THE INNOVATION PLANNING PRACTICE

Introduction

Historically, IT has been, and still is, primarily a *support* organization. (See Exhibit 9.15.) Its goals and its criteria for success have been related to its ability to respond to the needs of the business through business applications, infrastructure capabilities, and related support services. A key word used to describe IT's role as a support organization has been *automation*—to take an existing business process or function and replace the human processing elements with those of a computer. IT has been judged by its ability to *align* its resources with the needs of the business and to reduce costs, both its own unit costs and those of the business processes that it has automated.

EXHIBIT 9.15   Innovation Planning in the Value Chain

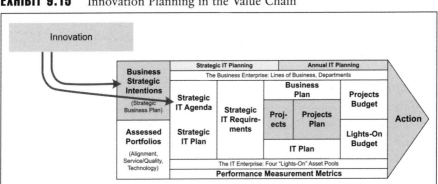

Increasingly, IT is now expected to add value to the enterprise not only by responding to business requests but also by creating business opportunities through the innovative combination of IT capabilities with customer needs and requirements. These business opportunities are not only cost-saving opportunities but also opportunities for new markets and new customer offerings. In other words, IT is expected to deliver value to the business through IT-enabled *innovation.*[4]

A challenge for IT is to find the right balance between these two seemingly contradictory expectations: to maintain alignment with the business as a support organization *and* to be an innovative agent of change. The management expectations and cultures for each are quite different. See Exhibit 9.16.

EXHIBIT 9.16   Alignment/Innovation Planning Practices

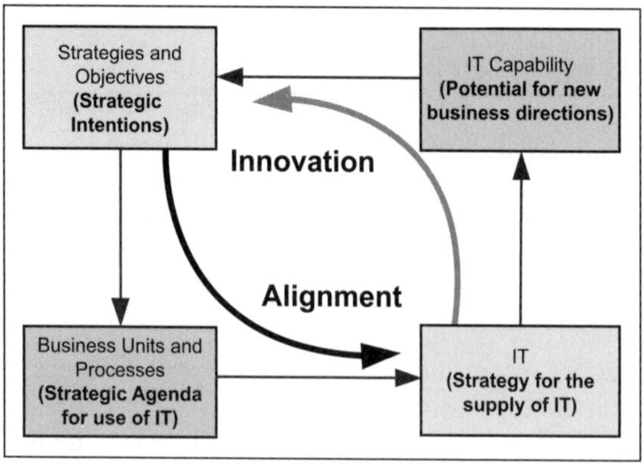

Alignment Culture

An Alignment culture shows up in management's project methodologies, planning methodologies, and attitudes about what IT should be working on. Such methodologies characteristically define the business objective, identify the business initiatives and programs to achieve the objective, and then consider the consequential IT implications (the system and infrastructures necessary to support the achievement of the business objective).

Innovation Culture

IT can enable new objectives, programs, strategies, and plans. IT can create and distinguish products, markets, and potential customers. The management expectation is that IT can actively generate innovations in the company strategies and, ultimately, in its processes to carry out the innovations. The innovation culture creates innovation through IT and rewards IT-driven change.

Innovation has two underlying component parts. The first component is *creativity*, or the generation of new ideas. The second is the *implementation* of the idea. Innovation only happens when both components occur. The dot.com bubble was filled with many creative and new business models. The bubble burst when it became apparent that the implementation of many of these creative ideas could not be financially sustained. The point here is that innovation is not just about being creative and thinking outside of the box. The other necessary piece of the innovation puzzle is having a culture and a set of processes that can cope with new ideas and allow them to develop, be fairly evaluated, and successfully implemented.

What are the key management issues that the practice area addresses?

The key management issue is how IT's role in business innovation can be expanded and improved. This issue really raises two related questions. The first is the cultural question that asks whether IT recognizes its innovation role and encourages that role via a set of management norms. The second question relates to the specific processes that can be used to enhance and bring attention to IT's role in innovation.

Is IT participating as an innovation "partner"? Does IT's management culture actively support IT-enabled innovation?

IT must be able to assess its role within the organization's *innovation chain* and, as needed, enhance and improve its credibility and capability as an innovation partner. During the go-go period of the dot.com rush, many organizations set up separate dot.com divisions that included integrated IT capabilities. The existing IT organization was viewed as being too slow and too cautious to run at Internet speed.

Exhibit 9.17 summarizes some of the characteristics of organizations that successfully encourage and reward innovation.

EXHIBIT 9.17   Cultural Aspects of Innovation

Norms that promote creativity	Norms that promote implementation
Support for risk-taking and change • Rewards and recognition for innovation • Positive attitude and role models for change by management • People are expected to challenge the status quo	Effective group functioning • Teamwork is emphasized • People share common goals • Information is shared openly
Tolerance of mistakes • Mistakes are accepted as a normal part of the job • People are given the freedom to make changes • "It's better to be safe than sorry" is not an accepted practice	Speed of action • Decisions are made quickly • Flexibility and adaptability are emphasized • Sufficient autonomy is given to insure implementation

Can IT's role in business innovation be managed and improved?

Some argue that creativity and innovation cannot be induced or managed through formal processes; that innovation is about improvisation, serendipity, and emergent behaviors caused by the inherently unpredictable juxtaposition and combination of previously unrelated ideas or concepts. We would respond by saying that although specific flashes of creativity cannot be predicted, their probability can be increased through the presence of processes that open up broad conversations between IT and business; and through an environment and culture that creates opportunities for new thinking. The same can be said for an organization's ability to convert new ideas into opportunities and competitive advantages by providing a fertile ground for their germination and development.

How are the management issues addressed by the frameworks and processes that define the practice?

The NIE Innovation Planning practice has four components:

1. *Business and Technology Monitoring* is a review for IT and business management of the business and technology change factors that could affect their business. This process produces a technology and business status report and uses external research, IT architecture and plans, and business information to fully explore the technology and business dynamics affecting business and IT. See Exhibit 9.18.

EXHIBIT 9.18   Innovation Planning Questions and Components

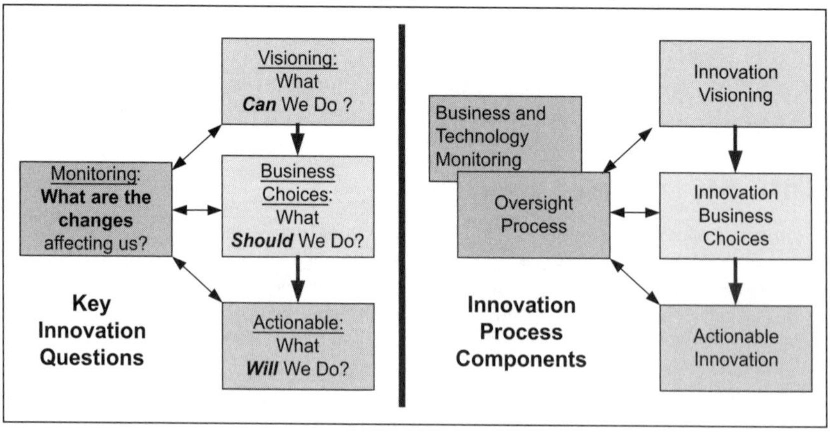

This can be in the form of an ongoing process that engages business and IT management in reviewing current changes and future opportunities. It addresses the question "What are the changes affecting us," both in

technology and business terms. The process can consist of a two- or four-hour session, with the following sample agenda:

- Input from outside experts who are aware of technology and business changes affecting the industry.
- Updates from IT on potentials for addressing key business strategic issues.
- Updates from business management on key business changes occurring in the industry.
- Facilitated discussion on the possible implications for the company.

2. *Innovation Visioning* develops broad alternative visions/directions for the enterprise, responding to technical and business changes, and establishing a consensus set of alternative visions/directions. This process engages the business and technology managers in addressing the question *"What can we do?"* Potential gaps and potential changes in the client's business and IT strategic plans are identified for each scenario. Issues to be addressed include:

- The key business and competitive drivers; which can be causes for business change in industry.
- IT drivers affecting industry; opportunities provided.
- Alternatives for company action in response; possible scenarios describing company action; likely initiatives needed.
- Innovation visioning, which can be in the form of a workshop with both IT and business management participation; a sample agenda.
- Input from outside experts aware of key technology and business issues in the industry; input from business management on the implications for the company.
- Development of alternative scenarios in response to issues and implications.
- Discussion of possible business responses, with IT as a key enabler.

3. *Business Context and Choices* makes choices about the vision/direction for the enterprise that govern how the business can function. This interaction establishes a "problem" statement: "here's what the drivers are, the direction we need to develop, and the ground rules." This process engages the business and technology managers in a full consideration of the possible business scenarios—*What should we do?*—as well as developing those that are most consistent with client business goals and strategies. The process identifies the best scenario and outcome for the client. Issues addressed can include:

- Current goals and strategies, and initiatives; basic principles that drive company actions.

- What company responses are best, in light of current goals and strategies, initiatives, and basic principles?

- What major initiatives are likely in the next two years, given the best company responses?

Business Context and Choices can be in the form of a workshop, engaging business and IT managers in discussion of the implications of business and IT opportunities, and creating potential scenarios for moving forward. A sample agenda would include:

- Presentation of scenarios in response to business and IT change.

- Selection of most appropriate scenarios for the company, in the light of mission, principles, and strategic intentions.

- Discussion of the implications of the scenarios.

4. *Actionable Innovation* develops the scenario and prototype action plan for the innovation (which establishes the outlines of an actionable plan). This event engages the business and technology managers in a planning exercise focused on the defining business and technology scenario based on new technology or business conditions—in other words, *"What will we do?"* The event develops the planning into an actionable plan, including steps to gain commitments, for both business client and technology service provider. Issues that can be considered include:

- What's currently being done in IT and business that relates to the proposed scenario.

- What is specifically required to carry out the scenario; steps needed.

- Effect on existing planning, organization, and budget.

- Leadership roles and responsibilities.

Actionable innovation can be in the form of a workshop, engaging business and IT management in describing the next steps for implementing the innovation. A sample agenda could include:

- Presentation of potential scenarios.

- Practical discussion of the implications.

- A "What's Next?" discussion for business and IT management.

Critical Success Factors: Right Decisions/Right Results Principles in Innovation Planning

- *Actionable Strategic Intentions.* Innovation processes represent the opportunity for IT to influence and shape strategic intentions. Innovation in a narrow context reverses the "traditional" business and IT roles in the planning process, using IT capabilities to create business opportunities to which business can respond with new strategies and initiatives. By focusing business on the things IT makes possible, innovation by its nature forces the business to create strategic intentions that IT can act on.

- *Actions Tied to Strategy.* The "actions" of IT in this case seem to precede the "strategies" from business, as IT has developed capabilities that may be in front of the business's capacity to use them. Regardless, strategic intentions that result from innovation by definition are driven by, and will drive, IT actions in the future. See Exhibit 9.19.

EXHIBIT 9.19   Goals and Practice Principles

Goals	Practice Principles
Actionable, Commonly Understood Strategic Intentions	1. Actionable Strategic Intentions
	2. Actions Tied to Strategy
	3. Common Understanding of Strategic Intentions
The Right Business Results from IT	4. Business-Focused Outcomes
	5. Value-Based Resource Allocation
Management Culture and Consensus View	6. Role-Based Culture Management
Portfolios and Portfolio Management	7. Value/Portfolio-Based Resource Management
The Right Actions and Results	8. Responsive to Change

- *Common Understanding of Strategic Intentions.* Creativity and implementation require a broad view of the enterprise. Common understanding and acceptance of common goals (strategic intentions) is a requirement for success.

- *Value-Based Resource Allocation.* Innovation is an important component of value. The total pool of allocation opportunities is weakened without a process that supports and encourages innovation.

- *Portfolio-Based Resource Management.* Portfolios need to be balanced between innovation-based and enhancement-based resource allocations.

- *Business Outcomes.* Paying closer attention to the cause-and-effect linkages between IT and the business will change IT's perspective from an inwardly-directed "How did we do in supporting the business need?" to an outwardly-directed "What can we do to create new business opportunities?"

- *Responsive to Change.* Innovation is all about being responsive (adaptable) to change—both external (environmental) and internal (organizational).

- *Role-Based Culture Management.* As with the other practices, Planning further defines the roles and responsibilities of IT and business managers in identifying and developing IT-enabled innovations. The combination of role definition and process definition around IT-enabled innovation will establish a new cultural norm.

Summary—Innovation Planning Practice

Processes alone cannot enhance an organization's innovative capabilities. However, when processes, tools, and management actions work together, IT can become an engine of innovation. Without this innovation infrastructure combined with an innovation-receptive culture, great ideas can still happen, but innovation will not.

CHAPTER SUMMARY: PLAN FOR THE RIGHT RESULTS

- *Where is Strategic Demand/Supply Planning applied?*

  The practice is embedded in company processes that produce the Business Strategic Intentions and the Strategic IT Plan.

- *What outcomes does Strategic Demand/Supply Planning produce?*

  The outcomes from Strategic Demand/Supply Planning are detailed in Exhibit 9.20. These outcomes connect to the related business processes (e.g., corporate budget, corporate annual business planning) that will carry out the elements of the Plan.

  Practice Description

  □ Explicitly connects IT strategies and plans to business strategic intentions.

  □ Establishes the business strategic demand for IT, and then IT's strategies and plans for the supply of the necessary IT capabilities.

  Desired Management Process Outcomes

  □ Business and IT planning operate together.

  □ Business planning explicitly considers IT innovations as input and IT consequences as output.

  □ IT planning explicitly considers, and is driven from, business strategic intentions.

  Desired Business Outcomes

  □ The senior management team requires that IT activities directly support business strategies and their strategic intentions, and encourages connected planning. They do enforce it, and work to improve it.

  □ As a result of connected planning, IT investments focus on important business strategies.

  □ Business strategies are dependent on IT contributions to carry them out. The senior management team considers IT implications of their business strategies.

EXHIBIT 9.20   Strategic Demand/Supply Planning and Innovation

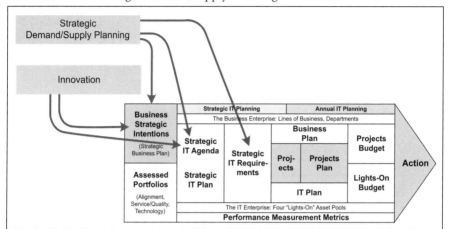

- ☐ IT managers plan based on business strategies.
- ☐ The IT organization is known in the industry as a significant contributor to the company's strategic and operational excellence.

- ■ *Where is the Innovation Planning practice applied?*
  The practice is embedded in company processes that produce the Business Strategic Intentions and the Strategic IT Plan.

- ■ *What outcomes does the Innovation Planning practice produce?*
  Practice Description
  - ☐ Translates IT opportunities into new business strategic intentions, and new ways for IT to support existing strategic intentions

  Desired Management Process Outcomes
  - ☐ Business innovations are considered, and occur, based on new IT opportunities.
  - ☐ New IT opportunities are translated into possible business innovations and strategic intentions, and considered seriously by management.
  - ☐ New IT opportunities are proposed and considered, in order to support existing strategic intentions.

  Desired Business Outcomes
  - ☐ Management expects, as part of its duties, to develop new ideas as a routine part of being in business.
  - ☐ Business plans focus on innovation and are continuously refreshed with new ideas.

PLAN FOR THE RIGHT RESULTS: MANAGEMENT AGENDA

Management Question	Yes or No?	If No, What Is Our Plan for Correcting This?
Business and IT planning operate together.		
Business planning explicitly considers IT innovations as input and IT consequences as output.		
IT planning explicitly considers, and is driven from, business strategic intention.		
The senior management team requires that IT activities directly support business strategies and their strategic intentions, and encourages connected planning. The team enforces this and works to improve it.		
As a result of connected planning, IT investments focus on important business strategies.		
Business strategies are dependent on IT contributions to carry them out. The senior management team considers IT implications of its business strategies.		
IT managers plan based on business strategies.		
The IT organization is known in the industry as a significant contributor to the company's strategic and operational excellence.		
Business innovations are considered, and occur, based on new IT opportunities.		
New IT opportunities are translated into possible business innovations and strategic intentions, and considered seriously by management.		
New IT opportunities are proposed and considered, in order to support existing strategic intentions.		
Management expects, as part of its duties, to develop new ideas as a routine part of being in business.		
Business plans focus on innovation and are continuously refreshed with new ideas.		

ADDITIONAL READING

This book's website contains additional information for Chapter 9:

Note 3: IT, Bottom-Line Impact, and Government

Note 16: What About IT's Performance?

The appendices at the back of the book also contain related information for Chapter 9:

Appendix A: The Role of Enterprise Architecture in Right Decisions/Right Results

Appendix C: The Development of Strategic Intentions, with Examples

NOTES

1. Adapted from the EwIM (Enterprise-wide Information Management) "Impact and Alignment" concepts. See, for example, Marilyn M. Parker and Robert J. Benson, "Enterprise-wide Information Management: State of the Art Strategic Planning," in Robert E. Umbaugh, ed., *Handbook of MIS Management 1990-91 Yearbook* (New York, Auerbach, 1990), pp. S-3–S-15.

2. See Appendix A, "The Role of Enterprise Architecture in Right Decisions/Right Results," for a further discussion of Enterprise Architecture and its role in Right Decisions/Right Results and NIE practices.

3. Warren McFarlan, quoted in Abbie Lundberg, "Survival Strategies," *CIO Magazine,* March 15, 1995.

4. Exhibit 9.16 is adapted from *Information Economics,* p. 59.

CHAPTER 10

Keep Score

The Performance Measurement practice is based on three fundamental ideas:

1. IT managers need to manage their resources and investments to improve their contribution to company strategies and goals, and thereby to the bottom line

2. To accomplish this, IT managers need a measurement capability that brings attention and focus to the activities and behaviors that best support IT's contribution, and

3   This measurement capability must include business-related measures that can be connected to business activities and are relevant to business managers.

Control Spending and Maximize Impact on the Bottom Line	
1	Define the Goals
2	Ask the Right Questions
3	Connect to the Bottom Line
4	Understand Costs and Resources
5	Focus on the Right Things
6	Adopt Effective Process to Produce Action
7	Tackle the Practical Problems
8	Make the Right Decisions
9	Plan for the Right Results
10	**Keep Score**
11	Deal with Culture
12	Chart the Path to Implementation
13	Define What's Next
14	Answer the "So What?" Question

Measurement and management are two sides of the same coin. See Exhibit 10.1. Presumably, all organizations manage IT, albeit with varying levels of quality and effectiveness. By extension, presumably, all organizations also measure IT via some combination of explicit and implicit measures. The question for IT, then, is rarely *whether* to measure but rather *what* and *how* to measure.

Measurements are a manager's as well as an organization's navigational system providing them with information regarding location (where are we?), destination (where are we going?), direction (are we going the right way?), and speed (how fast are we getting there?). To be useful, the attributes or measures used to describe *location* must necessarily also be used to define *destination*. That is, our navigational system is of little use if we describe our location as "the corner of State and Main" but we define our destination as 40N60W.

EXHIBIT 10.1   Performance Measurement in the Value Chain

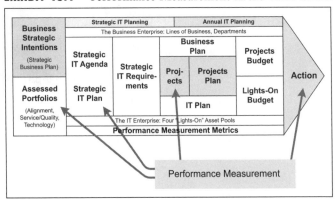

This is the situation in which many IT organizations currently find themselves. The measures or attributes that an IT organization uses to describe its current performance (i.e., IT's location) might be cost efficiency, infrastructure availability, and on-schedule delivery of projects. However, the enterprise uses attributes like business impact, agility, and innovation to describe expected performance (i.e., IT's destination). Without reconciling the terms used to define location and destination, appropriate action cannot be taken. In the terms of the previous example, we cannot effectively navigate from State and Main to 40N60W without adding latitude/longitude measures to our description of location. The key point here is that IT's measurement framework needs to be consistent with IT's role.

As IT's role develops and evolves, its management processes and measurements also need to evolve and develop. The management culture needs to change at the same pace as the organizational role for IT. For many organizations, this is an unrealistic expectation. IT's role is subject to abrupt changes due to rapid changes in technology and the business environment. Management processes and culture change at a more glacial pace. Consequently, management processes and measurements become *out of phase* with IT's role. See Exhibit 10.2.

The challenge for these IT organizations is to accelerate the evolution of their IT management processes, which includes developing appropriate measures for guiding and evaluating IT performance within the context of its changing role. Many CIOs have abundant operational metrics in the areas of systems development and infrastructure operations. These metrics typically focus on internal IT processes, such as up-time, development milestones, and function points per programmer. Our interest within the NIE Performance Measurement practice, however, is in performance measurements that can help bridge the IT/business gap—that is, a Performance Measurement practice that focuses on managing the impact IT has on the business.

EXHIBIT 10.2   Performance Measurement Context

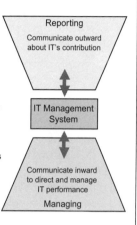

The IT Management (and Measurement) Challenge

IT must master the art of managing to measures that matter to the business:

- Business Process Measures
- Product/Service Innovation
- Value for Money

By addressing these issues, IT can increase its value proposition:

- Elevate the strategic importance of IT
- Improve ability to serve customer segments
- Proactively manage the IT agenda
- Enhance key stakeholder relationships
- Align performance objectives with IT strategy

Reporting
Communicate outward about IT's contribution

IT Management System

Communicate inward to direct and manage IT performance
Managing

MANAGEMENT ISSUES

As stated above, the key management issue around Performance Measurement is having a measurement capability that brings attention and focus to the activities and behaviors that best support and improve IT's contribution to the business. The measurements must be connected to business activities and be relevant to business managers. These issues can be restated in the form of the following management questions:

◆

Is IT doing things right? Are IT's capabilities and services being delivered with appropriate efficiency and effectiveness?

Most IT organizations have existing cost-efficiency metrics. These measures historically reflect the need to manage IT as a cost center. However, these metrics focus on IT's internal operation and do not connect to the needs of the business. Many of these efficiency measures, and even most customer satisfaction surveys, look only at outcomes (lagging measures) rather than at the activities and processes that drive those results (leading measures). Lagging measures are useful for signaling a problem but cannot point to a solution. These organizations need to balance efficiency metrics with process measures and an increased focus on customer-oriented measures like alignment, service level, and quality.

It is necessary to continually match the right measures to the right purpose within the right context.

-- ◆ --

Is IT doing the right things? Are IT resources allocated to the right set of business activities and initiatives?

This question is primarily a question about alignment. An IT organization is exposed to many conflicting demands. Legacy applications require emergency maintenance; new system development timelines shift as requirements evolve; and demands on the infrastructure expand in unexpected ways. IT managers need to have tools that allow them to continually reassign and reallocate resources to the "right" activities and projects. Consequently, IT managers need consistent information about a system's impact on the business to support rational allocation decisions that involve that system.

Importantly, the question of "doing the right things" is a question for both IT and business management. Adequately answering the question is dependent upon fully understanding the strategic and operational goals of the business while also knowing how IT's resources are being deployed.

-- ◆ --

Is IT implementing its strategy? Is IT achieving its own goals for improvement and change?

In addition to business-oriented projects and services, IT will have its own set of strategic initiatives that are also linked to business requirements. For example, IT's strategy for the development of infrastructure—standards, common services, and functional robustness—exists because the business requires, or will require, the resulting capabilities. The Performance Measurement practice needs to have a framework for tracking and reporting progress on the implementation of IT's own strategic agenda. This measurement capability is important because it indicates IT's readiness to fulfill business requirements and IT's readiness to provide (and anticipate) future technical capabilities. This issue is not a *doing things right* issue. Rather, it is about getting the *technical destination* right and succeeding in getting there.

FRAMEWORKS AND PROCESS OVERVIEW

Portfolios

The IT Portfolios form the foundation of the Performance Measurement framework. Two types of portfolios are used. The first are *resource portfolios* that contain and describe IT systems, projects, and services. Examples of resource portfolios are application portfolios and infrastructure portfolios. Attributes of line items within these portfolios include class, cost, service level, quality, and alignment. The second type of portfolio is the *process portfolio* that contains and describes IT management and delivery processes. Examples of process portfolios include Planning/Organization and Delivery/Support. SEI/CMM[1] and COBIT[2] serve as useful models for process portfolio items. Attributes of processes include maturity factors, key performance goals, and key performance indicators.

Strategic Alignment

To address the question of whether IT is doing the right things, the Performance Measurement practice framework uses a strategic alignment[3] assessment process that evaluates the connection between elements of the IT portfolio and the strategic intentions of the company. An important aspect of the strategic alignment assessment is that it actively involves business management in the evaluation and ratings of IT's connections to business goals. See Exhibit 10.3.

EXHIBIT 10.3 Strategic Alignment Gaps

	Wgt.	20	10	10	10	20	10	5	10		
	Weight	Cost Reduction	Supplier of Choice	Targeted Market Growth	Acquisition Capability	Customer Cost	Standards and Best Practices	Capacity Increase	Product Mix Optimization	Unweighted Total	Weighted Total
Customer Information System	20	**Alignment Gaps**				2	0	-1	2	10	200
Supplier Quality Monitoring	15	-1	2	0	0	2	2	2	2	9	135
Financial Information System	35	0	0	0	1	1	1	1	0	4	140
CORBIT Materials System	15	2	3	2	0	2	3	3	-1	14	210
Product Planning	5	2	1	1	**Alignment Gaps**				▶	2	10
Manufacturing Expansion Control	10	1	-1	-2	0	-3	2	-1	-3	-7	-70
Unweighted Total		5	8	4	2	4	8	2	-1		
Weighted Total		100	80	40	20	80	80	10	-10		

Functional Alignment

To address the question of whether IT is doing things right, the Performance Measurement framework uses a multidimensional approach[4] that includes elements of cost performance, service level, and quality and process measurements.

These three dimensions are interconnected, and IT management needs to recognize and be aware of these performance relationships. There is an intuitive understanding of the relationship between cost and quality or service level. Less intuitive is the fact that the specific relationship between cost and quality is determined by the quality of the processes involved (i.e., the marginal cost of an improvement in project delivery is determined by the quality of our project management processes). See Exhibit 10.4.

EXHIBIT 10.4   Performance Dimensions

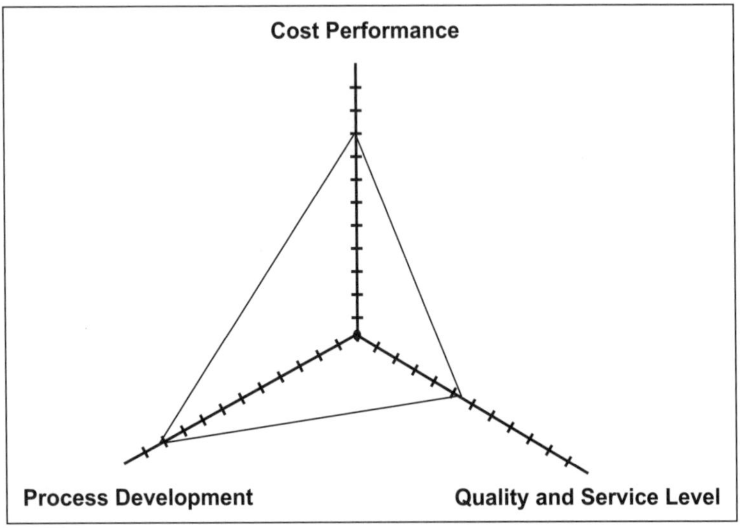

Cost Performance

Cost performance and cost metrics will always be part of the IT Performance Measurement suite of measures. Organizations are continually looking to save IT-related costs wherever possible, but the methods for doing so are not always obvious and cost analysis is not always straightforward. For example, although the value of e-mail systems is indisputable, the cost of operating them can be the subject of much controversy. Ascertaining costs is a crucial aspect of any cost-saving exercise: A granular and accurate breakdown of system expenses is mandatory for identifying potential savings. Organizations pursuing a managed approach to investment in e-mail systems require an in-depth understanding of mail system costs to formulate a strategy for reducing overall mail system expenses.

Within the context of IT as a cost center and with the *primary* goal of IT being to manage and control costs, then cost measures are appropriate indicators of success. When the context changes and IT is expected to *add value*, then new measures are needed to support the new criteria for success. Indeed, within the new added-value context, managing with cost performance as the guiding star could land the organization on rocky shores. Additional performance measurement dimensions are needed.

Quality and Service Levels

As the performance context for IT shifts toward added-value services, the measurement framework must give more emphasis to customer-focused metrics such as service level and quality. See Exhibit 10.5.

EXHIBIT 10.5 Elements of Service Level and Quality

	Elements of Service Level	Elements of Quality
Application Development Portfolio	• Availability of the development resource • Responsiveness of the development resource	• Reliability of the development process • Reliability of the development result
Applications Portfolio	• Availability of the application • Responsiveness of the application	• Functionality of the application • Accuracy of the application and its data
Infrastructure Portfolio	• Availability of the infrastructure element • Responsiveness of the infrastructure element	• Functionality of the infrastructure element • Reliability of the infrastructure element
Services Portfolio	• Availability of the service resource • Responsiveness of the service resource	• Reliability of the service process • Reliability of the service result

Process Measurement

Although cost and service level data are useful, they are lagging indicators that communicate results but are not useful as levers to manage or implement change. Process measurement (and management) is a way to affect the IT organization's performance drivers. Measuring and managing processes is about measuring and managing the causes behind cost and service-level results.

The NIE Performance Measurement practice recommends a combination of operational and management processes for assessment. Example processes are shown in Exhibit 10.6. *These processes will not be equally important, as their impact will depend on the specific needs of the IT organization within its specific business context.* The framework for assessing and managing processes, including assessment categories, is illustrated in Exhibit 10.7.

EXHIBIT 10.6   Example of Available IT Process Models

Software Development (SEI)	IT Management (COBIT)
Requirements Management	Define a Strategic IT Plan
Software Project Planning	Define the Information Architecture
Software Project Tracking and Oversight	Define the IT Organization and Relationships
Software Quality Assurance	Manage the IT Investment
Software Configuration Management	Manage Human Resources
Organization Process Definition	
Integrated Software Management	**System Engineering (SEI)**
Software Product Engineering	Derive and Allocate Requirements
	Integrate System
	Verify and Validate System
	Ensure Quality
	Monitor and Control Technical Effort

EXHIBIT 10.7   Process Measurement Example

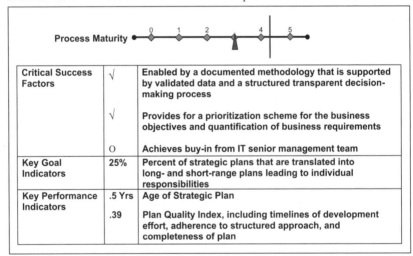

Managing IT Strategy Implementation

It is critical that IT be able to implement its own strategic objectives. The fundamental framework for this is to track each strategic objective as a project, which means naming an owner for that objective, identifying related initiatives, assigning resources, and establishing milestones (see Exhibit 10.8). An additional component of the Strategy Implementation framework is the identification of linkages to IT portfolios from which specific measures can be obtained to assess the impact of the strategic objective as it is implemented. The purpose of any

EXHIBIT 10.8   Tracking IT Strategy Implementation

Strategic Objective:	Planning and Budgeting Process Enhancement
Owners	John Barnes, IT/CFO Brad Snyder, IT Budget Director
Related Initiatives	Project Management Office (PMO) implementation Portfolio Management tool implementation Common IT Metrics initiative
Resources	IT Budget staff Budget staff in each business unit Consultants
Milestones and Indicators	Step 1 Template development Step 2 FY2003 Baseline Step 3 FY2004 Budget
Linkages to Process and Resource Portfolios	Management Portfolio—Connect budgets to business objectives Project Portfolio—Address project resource allocation Lights-On Portfolio—Address alignment issues and the retirement of low-value systems

strategic objective is to improve the performance of IT services and capabilities as reflected in the portfolios.

RESULT

IT, like most organizations, needs to pay attention to short-term, tactical performance as well as to long-term, strategic performance. Correspondingly, there are measures needed for the identification and diagnosis of operational issues, and measures necessary to maintain focus on strategic goals and assess progress toward their achievement.

The measures described within the Performance Measurement practice provide a broad spectrum of metrics that can be used for diagnostic as well as strategic purposes. The metrics included in this scorecard are identified through a process that links strategic objectives to specific resource and process drivers and to specific metrics associated with those drivers. Most, if not all, of an IT Performance Scorecard's measures will come from the Performance Measurement framework as presented in this book.

Exhibit 10.9 shows the overall results of portfolio assessment in Performance Measurement. Each application in the Application Portfolio can be assessed, first for alignment, then service level/quality, then for current and future resources. Taken together, this begins to comprise a complete picture of the Application Portfolio. Management can assess the components of the Portfolio and make reasonable decisions about retirement, future investment, or operational concerns about services and quality. For example, in the exhibit, Financial Information is the lowest from the Alignment perspective. Does that mean that the

EXHIBIT 10.9   Integrating Performance Measures with IT Portfolios

	Alignment	Service Level	Quality	Current Budget	Future Budget
Applications					
Customer Care Systems	2.9	1.9	2.2	$7M	-
Manufacturing	1.1	1.2	1.2	$30M	-
Sales Force Automation	2.4	2.1	2.5	$2M	++
Manufacturing	2.5	1.1	2.1	$46M	+
Product Planning	1.5	1.2	1.6	$3M	+
E-Business	2.2	1.6	1.8	$9M	-
Financial Information	.8	2.2	2.3	$3M	-
Data Warehouse	1.1	2.1	1.1	$1M	+

Alignment
Connection to Strategy

Efficiency
Budget Conformance

Service Level
Availability
Responsiveness

Quality
Functionality
Accuracy

financial system needs a refresh? Does it signal a need to consider alternatives? Similarly, the Manufacturing application ranks lowest in service and quality. The same questions apply, particularly since that application area is consuming the largest amount of resources. Again, this means that management can make informed decisions.

CRITICAL SUCCESS FACTORS: RIGHT DECISIONS/RIGHT RESULTS PRINCIPLES IN PERFORMANCE MEASUREMENT

Performance Measurement most directly supports the actions tied to strategy and resource management principles of Right Decisions/Right Results, but has an indirect impact on the others as well.

- *Actionable Strategic Intentions.* Performance Measurement starts with the company's strategic intentions and maps key IT activities (and related measures) to them. Through Performance Measurement, IT's actions can be focused on the connection to strategic intentions. This focus will improve how IT contributes to the achievement of the strategic intentions.

- *Actions Tied to Strategy.* Performance Measurement closes the loop from strategy to action. When IT measures the right things and ties its actions to strategy through measurement, it can be sure that it is doing exactly the right things for the business, with its measures and activities driven by business strategies. See Exhibit 10.10.

EXHIBIT 10.10   Goals and Practice Principles

Goals	Practice Principles
Actionable, Commonly Understood Strategic Intentions	1. Actionable Strategic Intentions
	2. Actions Tied to Strategy
	3. Common Understanding of Strategic Intentions
The Right Business Results from IT	4. Business-Focused Outcomes
	5. Value-Based Resource Allocation
Management Culture and Consensus View	6. Role-Based Culture Management
Portfolios and Portfolio Management	7. Value/Portfolio-Based Resource Management
The Right Actions and Results	8. Responsive to Change

- *Common Understanding of Strategic Intentions.* Leadership team consensus on the goals for performance is the basis for a performance management process. Additionally, measuring the right things, and communicating and reviewing performance with business management, leads to a better understanding of: (1) what IT is about, (2) the business strategic intentions that IT is supporting, and (3) IT's ability to get there.

- *Impact-Based Resource Allocation.* Performance Measurement works to support the achievement of planning, prioritization, and alignment, all aimed at achieving resource allocation consistent with strategic intentions. Performance Measurement provides the information that supports decisions regarding the reallocation of resources.

- *Portfolio-Based Resource Management.* Performance Measurement applies to all the portfolios and tracks the performance of all portfolios against strategic intentions. Performance Measurement is at the center of portfolio management; it is a necessary tool to using portfolios throughout IT and business management.

- *Business Outcomes.* Performance Measurement data indicate the success of the enterprise in establishing the cause and effect between business and IT.

- *Responsive to Change.* Performance Measurement's contribution is based on enhancing IT's ability to detect and respond to changes in business priorities and strategic intentions. Performance Measurement substantially improves IT's responsiveness and flexibility.

- *Role-Based Culture Management.* A key component of the Performance Measurement practice is the active involvement of business managers in shaping and providing the context for the specific measures for performance. Too often, IT performance measures are developed from IT's inward-looking perspective. The Performance Measurement practice balances this existing inward perspective with an outward perspective that reinforces the important role that business managers should play in establishing relevant performance measure for IT.

SUMMARY: PERFORMANCE MEASUREMENT PRACTICE

Improving IT's contribution to the business is a complex task that requires a set of robust management tools. The power of the Performance Measurement framework comes not from its individual pieces but from their integration. Managing IT's contribution to the business is a process of understanding cause-and-effect relationships and continually balancing and (re-)allocating resources. The effectiveness of the framework comes from looking at cost, service level, quality, alignment, and process measurements as a set of interrelated elements that, taken together, form a holistic model for managing and improving IT performance. The Performance Measurement practice provides IT and business management with the tools necessary to improve IT's performance with respect to achieving strategic and operational effectiveness.

- ***Where is Performance Measurement applied?***

  The practice is embedded in company processes that produce portfolio assessments, metrics, and annual plans.

- ***What outcomes does Performance Measurement produce?***

  Practice Description

  ☐ Measures IT performance in ways related to the business and its strategic intentions.

  Desired Management Process Outcomes

  ☐ IT's performance measurement methods connect IT to business requirements and strategic intentions.

  ☐ All IT assets and resources are described in portfolios, covering both new investments and current resources and assets.

  ☐ IT is able to clearly communicate its performance goals and achievements with the business.

  ☐ IT's performance measurement and portfolio frameworks provide data for continuous improvement of IT service delivery and management processes.

  Desired Business Outcomes

  ☐ IT is aligned with the company's strategic intentions.

  ☐ Applications are abandoned or renewed because of poor alignment or service/quality levels.

  ☐ The overall IT portfolio is regarded as high-quality.

  ☐ Overall, the entire IT investment is considered as valuable to the company.

KEEP SCORE: MANAGEMENT AGENDA

Management Question	Yes or No?	If No, What Is Our Plan for Correcting This?
Portfolio information is actively used at all levels of IT management. Portfolio information includes measures of annual cost, service level, quality, intensity of use, and categories of use.		
Resource allocation decisions and project priorities are regularly reviewed between budget cycles.		
IT performance measures are linked to business impact using cause-and-effect linkages and alignment assessments.		
Responsibility for the ongoing management of IT performance measurement is clearly defined.		
The tracking of IT performance occurs regularly through documented measurement processes for which training and support are available.		
Management has made a commitment to one or more IT process maturity models (e.g., COBIT, SEI/CMM).		
IT management is able to answer the question "Are we doing (working on) the right things?"		
IT management is able to answer the question "Are we doing things right?"		
Business-oriented measures of service level and quality are in place.		

NOTES

1. For the Software Engineering Institute's Capability Maturity Model, see Software Engineering Institute, Carnegie Mellon University, *The Capability Maturity Model: Guidelines for Improving the Software Process* (Reading, MA: Addison-Wesley, 1995).
2. Information Systems Audit and Control Foundation (ISACF), *Control Objectives for Information and Related Technology (COBIT)—Management Guidelines,* 3rd edition (Rolling Meadow, IL, 2000).
3. See Chapter 8 for detailed discussions of Strategic Alignment.
4. See Chapter 8 for detailed discussions of Functional Alignment.

Deal with Culture

Management culture can be defined as the "underlying values, beliefs, and principles that serve as a foundation for the organization's management system, as well as the set of management practices and behaviors that both exemplify and reinforce those principles."[1] Using this definition as a starting point, Chapter 11 covers management culture in four parts. First, we describe the impact of culture and explain it as a set of factors that need to be identified, understood, and dealt with in the course of applying the five NIE practices. Second, we explore the need for management culture change in the Strategy-to-Bottom-Line Value Chain, and how this affects the ability of a company to change its processes and adopt NIE practices. Third, we introduce 15 categories of culture issues that separate business and IT managers. Fourth, we define the culture management support practice to deal with the culture issues.

Control Spending and Maximize Impact on the Bottom Line	
1	Define the Goals
2	Ask the Right Questions
3	Connect to the Bottom Line
4	Understand Costs and Resources
5	Focus on the Right Things
6	Adopt Effective Process to Produce Action
7	Tackle the Practical Problems
8	Make the Right Decisions
9	Plan for the Right Results
10	Keep Score
11	**Deal with Culture**
12	Chart the Path to Implementation
13	Define What's Next
14	Answer the "So What?" Question

Our intention is to offer a set of diagnostics that enable a management team to understand the specific cultural hurdles they face and what they may do to overcome them.

We examine a very small slice of the overall culture issues facing a company, focusing narrowly on how we can do something about influencing the attitudes managers have about IT and their role in managing it. We need to change the way managers work with IT, their role with respect to IT, and the mental models that managers have about IT.

PART 1: THE IMPACT OF MANAGEMENT CULTURE

Four basic themes about the impact of management culture have been discussed in this book. These themes focus on the barriers that culture can erect to the Strategy-to-Bottom-Line Value Chain, and they will lead us to the best approaches for reducing these barriers.

1. *Weak management support for processes causes disconnects in the Strategy-to-Bottom-Line Value Chain.* Such disconnects are based in culture, where the culture discounts the importance of connecting IT to business strategy or the importance of business and IT management working together to meet business strategic goals. Without management support and commitment, processes don't work, and the outcomes of processes such as planning and prioritization simply don't make it to the next steps, such as budgeting and annual planning.

2. *Culture restricts management roles.* The Strategy-to-Bottom-Line Value Chain depends on business and IT managers playing specific roles throughout the steps of planning, innovation, prioritization, alignment, and performance measurement. This is partly a disconnect, where the culture discounts the importance of playing the planning and decision-making roles about IT, and partly management misunderstanding, where the culture gives predefined limits and boundaries to the levels and categories of roles management plays. This is especially true in siloed organizations, where NIE practices have managers playing roles across silos.

3. *Culture limits IT's role.* Business and IT management can have inappropriate or conflicting views about IT's role in helping set and fulfill business's strategic directions, and in management processes. Culture predefines IT's role in the business, and limits what and how IT can contribute.

4. *Culture resists change.* Management groups are reluctant to change how they do business, particularly if the initiative to change is not theirs. To the extent the Strategy-to-Bottom-Line Value Chain requires process and role changes, this resistance kicks in.

The most critical resistance is to changes in how decisions are made. Reluctance to accept the results of decisions made in new NIE-based planning and prioritization processes, which is a great change in "how things are done," is a great inhibitor to connecting strategy to results. This is especially apparent in siloed organizations, where managers are reluctant to change how decisions affect individual (especially their own) silos.[2]

These four culture themes can determine whether an individual manager believes that business/IT processes are important enough to spend time on, and devote energy to, whether those process outcomes should be paid attention to, and whether there is enough importance/incentive to change or affect the assignment of resources based on those process outcomes. The four themes, which obviously overlap, can be traced throughout the management culture discussions in Chapters 1–4. The bottom line, however, is that management culture looms large, and we have to be able to deal with it.

New Management Processes Alone Are Not Sufficient

In order to embed NIE practices in a company's processes, we need to affect how business and IT view each other within the context of their respective roles and responsibilities. We need to influence the beliefs that each management group has about managing the impact of IT, the processes needed to produce that impact, and the belief in the needed outcomes.

The particular importance of dealing with culture is more than whether a process works. In particular, culture determines whether the sort of changes represented by NIE "take" in the company and become a permanent change in management behavior. Often, a new process works in its first cycle, when management is trained and there is a support team to help in using the new tools and methods. Whether the process change persists, however, is not dependent on the training, or even on the management support for the process, but rather on whether the values, roles, and objectives have become a part of the mental models held by management about business and IT.

In short, change in management process does not persist without culture change.

Effect of Culture on Management Roles: Involvement and Commitment

The potential effect of culture is highlighted in the extent of the roles managers need to fulfill in the Strategy-to-Bottom-Line Value Chain. Exhibit 11.1 provides a summary of the roles that the NIE practices need in order to produce the significant deliverables, ranging from the business strategy to the annual plan.[3]

In NIE, three management groups[4] play key roles: the senior leadership team typically is comprised of the CEO and direct reports; the business leadership team typically is made up of direct reports to the senior management team; and the technology management team typically is the CIO and direct reports. These management roles define the *involvement* and the *commitment* expected from each management group. By involvement, we mean the expenditure of time and energy to participate. By commitment, we mean not only involvement but also an agreement that the process is important and, more importantly, that the results of the process are important. Culture, of course, is a significant determiner of each manager's involvement and commitment, particularly for the business management team.

The critical role that culture plays is dramatically demonstrated when we do install an NIE practice, but subsequently the results do not affect other processes of the Strategy-to-Bottom-Line Value Chain. For example, we recently worked with a financial services organization to assist with the prioritization of projects, as a part of the annual project planning cycle. Prioritization is mechanically easy to do, but the business managers were very uneasy about their participation, rejected the notion that they should understand something about projects not in

EXHIBIT 11.1   Management Roles in the Strategy-to-Bottom-Line Value Chain

		Deliverable Name	Senior Leadership Team	Business Leadership Team	Technology Leadership Team
Strategic Planning Cycle	1	Business Strategic Intentions	Approve and weight strategic intentions	Revise and review strategic intentions	
	2	Assessed Portfolios	Review	Assess portfolios/ alignment, service, quality	Contribute to portfolio development Assess portfolio/ technology
	3	Strategic IT Agenda for Use of IT	Approve	Develop IT agenda	Participate in IT agenda process
	4	Strategic IT Plan	Review	Review IT plan	Develop IT plan
	5	IT Strategic Requirements	Review	Develop requirements Prioritization Recommend decisions	Participate in IT require-ments process
	6	Projects	Review and approve large projects	Create project requirements and business cases	Form detailed projects and technical requirements
Annual/Tactical Planning Cycle	7	Annual Project Plan	Make decisions or approve funding	Prioritization Recommend funding	Establish annual project plan and schedules
	8	Annual Business Plan	Approve	Review IT plans Establish business unit plans	Advise
	9	Annual IT Plan	Approve	Review	Develop IT plans Establish budgets
	10	Annual and Capital Projects Budgets	Approve	Develop budgets	Participate in budget planning
	11	Annual Lights-On Budget	Review	Review	Develop budget Initiate plans
	12	Performance Measurement Metrics	Approve	Establish business performance metrics	Establish IT performance metrics

their direct sphere of responsibility, and were especially uncomfortable about shar-ing knowledge about their own area's projects with other management groups.

We encountered another typical scenario in a consumer products company, where midlevel managers throughout the company were simply unable to ren-der judgments about IT projects without previously vetting their judgments with their most senior managers. In this case, the company was such a heavily siloed company, run with almost military precision, that midlevel managers were accustomed to following the clear directions of their leaders and were unac-customed to expressing their own business judgments.

Process change alone is not enough to close the gaps in the Strategy-to-Bottom-Line Value Chain; the culture, represented by the willingness of individ-ual managers to be involved and be committed to the results, is equally critical.

Management Culture Limits IT

Management culture can pigeonhole IT into a predetermined role that limits the goals IT can accomplish and how IT can accomplish them.

For example, in a consumer products company, the prevailing culture viewed IT as a cost center. The culture limited IT management's access to senior business managers by not including IT in the company strategic planning process and senior corporate retreats. Management simply never thought IT was strategic enough for IT to participate. In a financial services company, on the other hand, the prevailing culture saw IT as a central element of the company's operational and competitive strategies, and IT was included as a full business partner. Management culture in the first company strictly bounded the management processes in which IT participated and clearly separated IT into a secondary, and even unconnected, role in the company. IT people weren't "company people" in the culture. Management culture in the second company did not attach "not really our business" labels to people; someone who worked in the IT area was as much a company manager or professional as anyone else. Everyone was a financial services person first, and only secondarily specifically connected to IT.

These are simple examples of management culture at work. Neither are good or bad cultures per se (although the first example is less than ideal, from an IT person's perspective). The culture conflict arises when it inhibits the planning, innovation, prioritization, alignment, and performance measurement processes required for the company to fully exploit IT's capabilities.

Culture's importance is in the roles and responsibilities each manager carries out, establishing expectations for outcomes and defining what is important to the management teams. Culture, perhaps even more than strategy, can set the basis for priorities and determine the level of attention given to prescribed roles and responsibilities. When values, beliefs, principles, management practices, and behaviors that make up culture limit IT, this prevents the company moving from strategy to IT action to bottom-line results.

PART 2: THE NEED FOR CULTURE CHANGE

Our experience shows that, however successful and appealing the five management practices may be, their success cannot be sustained or repeated year after year unless the culture in both business and IT is compatible. In all cases, these culture issues get in the way of the fundamental goal of NIE: enabling the company to move from Business Strategy to IT Action to Results.

Most managers do understand that "our management culture has to change" in order to make the kind of progress that is possible with New Information Economics. We encounter very little argument about the need for, or the value of, the five practices we suggest; rather, we hear about the practical problems in actually applying the practices due to existing attitudes among both senior and midlevel managers directly affected by IT.

The biggest single impediment to any IT-enabled innovation is resistance to change, when the underlying culture supports the old way and resists and resents the new way of doing things. Here, the problem is even more severe, because we are dealing with basic management processes of planning, prioritization, and so forth, directly changing the role managers play in those processes and changing the expectations managers have about the outcomes to be produced.

The five practices do affect the relationships between business and IT, and change the existing roles and relationships between business and IT managers. While the NIE solutions introduce effective management processes, they require both IT and business managers to do new things, to play new roles. IT and business managers have to change their views of their roles and responsibilities with respect to IT and business.

But what if the company's management culture, for some reason, is unsuited for a manager playing the kind of role the NIE practice demands? Or what if the business management culture is different in some substantial way from the IT management culture and, accordingly, the requirement for them to work together causes culture conflict. The answer, of course, is that the culture has to change.

These problems arise from many sources, and their consequence is that the kinds of processes represented by the NIE five practices will not succeed. Moreover, this issue is not limited to individual NIE practices; the problem is that the idea of "Strategy to IT Action to Bottom-Line Results" demands new roles and responsibilities. The problems are based on the inability of business managers to carry out the roles or responsibilities, work together or with other business and IT managers, or work with IT managers across their internal IT silos.

Culture strongly affects whether innovations in management process can succeed. We talk in this book in terms of culture disconnects or conflicts, but this may sound too mechanical or binary. What management teams believe about IT's role, about organizational relationships, and about processes that connect IT and business, very much sets limits on what can be accomplished. Similarly, what management does in its practices for managing business and IT itself helps to establish or modify the culture.

PART 3: CLASSIFICATION OF BUSINESS/IT CULTURE

We make the case that management culture must accept the process changes and management role changes required by New Information Economics, and this may mean culture change. But what do we mean by "culture change?" As we deal with the ideas and practicalities of change, we will benefit from an "as-is" description and a "to-be" target. To help with this, we describe a classification of different aspects of business/IT management culture. In Part 4, we describe ways to obtain the "to-be".

Culture shapes and colors management attitude and behavior, but it rarely is dealt with directly by management action. Our objective is to identify attitudes and behaviors that are indicators of the management culture at work. For clarification, we offer a classification of these cultures in order to clarify their sources and, ultimately, find the right kind of actions to deal with them.

These indicators of management culture about IT fall into three categories.

- *IT's Business Role:* Culture that defines IT's business role and impact.

- *Business and IT Relationships:* Culture that defines the organizational relationships between business and IT.

- *Business and IT Process:* Culture that defines the way that IT and business managers work together.

The boundaries between these categories are gray. Management attitude and behavior about IT's role and impact also influences the organization's structure and, consequently, the kinds of management processes that operate between business and IT. Nevertheless, it is helpful to understand and diagnose the culture characteristics in these three categories.

Category 1: IT's Business Role—Culture Defines IT's Business Role and Impact

This category is about management beliefs, values, and principles pertaining to the role and impact of IT. It deals with the underlying assumptions about how IT contributes to the business. The management attitudes and behaviors get into the differences between IT's strategic and operational benefits, management insistence on using ROI or other metrics to measure impact, and so forth. As stated before, these characteristics are not black and white, and they overlap. The question is whether we can recognize them in a particular company circumstance, and then do something in response.

IT's Business Importance

This characteristic is the degree to which business management believes IT is an important part of the business. A consequence is whether IT issues are managed and planned as part of the business management and planning processes. Sometimes people glibly talk about the integration of IT and business. The question is, on the business side, does management "think IT" when it thinks of the

EXHIBIT 11.2 Culture and IT's Role

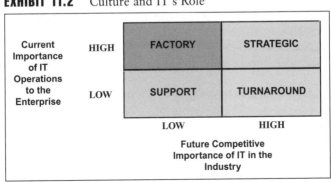

business? Are IT considerations part of the planning process, included in the considerations when business strategies are hashed out?

IT's Cost versus IT's Impact

This characteristic is the degree to which business management believes that IT produces impact, rather than considering IT to be just a cost of doing business. Does IT, in actual terms, add value? The answer can be ingrained in the management culture; it becomes the default assumption when any new IT investment is presented.

IT's Justification

This characteristic is whether IT is justified solely on ROI or other hard measurement, or whether justification also takes into account other business impact measures. In the first case, the culture may expect methods such as ROI and require an ROI-based business case as a part of IT planning and individual systems development. The second case addresses strategic and other business performance effects.

IT's Contribution to Business Innovation

The characteristic is management expectations for IT's contribution to changing the business. Management expectations could range from operational support to strategic business innovation.

We mentioned in Chapter 4 that Warren McFarlan and others have developed a simple matrix that captures much of this cultural concept. Briefly, this matrix characterizes the strategic importance and the operational importance of IT in the business.[5] See Exhibit 11.2.

The matrix focuses on the actual role of IT as it applies to operational issues (Would the company stop work if the systems stopped?) and the competitive issues (Are customers choosing the company because of its IT activities? Does IT give the company value or cost competitive advantages?).

The matrix also characterizes the cultural implications. If a company is truly in the *support* quadrant, meaning that IT has neither operational nor competitive importance, then it is likely that the management culture also does not treat IT as an integral part of the business. On the other hand, if the business is in fact strategic, with both high operational and competitive dependencies on IT, then a management culture rooted in the *support* quadrant would pose a real culture conflict.

Such a culture conflict would limit IT's business role. If the culture is "Support" or "Factory," then IT's role in the business is based solely on aligning itself with the current business strategies and operational requirements. "Strategic" and "Turnaround," on the other hand, would add *innovation* to the culture, where IT's effect comes from enabling new business strategies.

Summary of Category 1: IT's Business Role

Culture issues about the role of IT cover all NIE practices. If IT is not seen to be important, then business managers are predisposed not to pay attention to planning, not to participate fully in prioritization and alignment, not to view performance measures as important, and not to see IT as a source of innovation and future business strength.

IT's role will change over time as the business context changes and the management culture surrounding IT lags. IT's expected role is subject to the external forces of new technologies and business competition. Again referring to McFarlan's matrix, this means that the expected role of IT can quickly move from Factory to Strategic. However, the internal management culture and the processes that successfully supported the Factory role are now less appropriate and, indeed, can become active inhibitors to IT's moving to its new Strategic role. This ongoing dynamic is characterized by the expected changing of IT's role in advance of the culture and management processes. This means that the Strategy-to-Bottom-Line Value Chain can operate with greater effectiveness and efficiency when cultural and management process gaps and inhibitors can be regularly identified and addressed (corrected or compensated for).

Category 2: Business and IT Relationship — Culture Defines the Organizational Relationships between Business and IT

This class of culture elements is about the beliefs, values, and principles about how business and IT work together, and deals with such matters as governance and accountability. These elements are certainly connected to the role and impact of IT; the way managers view IT impacts the organizational relationships between business and IT.

These elements deal with the separation of business and IT, whether expressed in terms of silos, individual line of business autonomy, separate IT organizations, poor governance processes, or poorly working business/IT teams.

Silo Orientation

The common theme in the silo culture is a parochial, localized focus on those things that will make the silo successful. Decision making is often decentralized and relatively autonomous, with an emphasis on locally optimized solutions that may or may not support an enterprise goal or strategy. Silo priorities are viewed by silo management as *the* priorities. In this context, IT is viewed as an operation to support the silo, and IT resources that are spent in other areas of the company are of little concern except as resources that could be redirected to the silo. IT planning is usually done on a silo-by-silo basis, with IT management responsible for balancing resources across silos, often in a politically sensitive process. Silo orientation is very similar to line-of-business autonomy.

Line-of-Business Autonomy

This is a powerful cultural characteristic, which describes whether individual business units have corporate permission to go their own way in matters like IT. It is related to the silo orientation, but here, the goals are just part of the problem. Even if the corporate goals across all business units are the same, individual business units may still be able to pursue their own strategies and initiatives, and their own IT implementations. The implications for IT lie in both infrastructure and applications. The degree to which infrastructure needs to be common and company-wide is ultimately a business decision, but things are certainly more difficult, the more diverse the infrastructure is. In this culture, company-wide initiatives are made much more complicated.

IT/Business Separation

This characteristic is that the IT organization and the business organization are separated, perhaps physically and organizationally, certainly culturally. Outsourcing can be a major contributor to this culture characteristic, as can shared-services organizations.

IT/Business Integration

This cultural issue is simple. Are the IT managers a normal part of the business leadership teams that produce results? Or is IT management an add-on, someone who brings special skills when necessary but ordinarily is not assumed to be part of the management team? This issue goes beyond management. Do IT professionals participate in normal business management councils and activities? Or is the IT organization separate and apart, conducting its management processes without the benefit of teaming? The issue goes the other way as well. Does IT include business managers and professionals in its normal activities and events?

IT Governance

This culture characteristic is whether management believes that the processes for guiding and controlling IT are working or broken. If management believes governance is working, then it is easier to adopt NIE practices that change the existing governance environment. For example, doing prioritization immediately raises questions about authority, decision making, who should be involved, and so forth. If management believes these processes are broken, then there is greater difficulty and resistance to change in adopting such NIE practices.

Summary of Category 2: Business and IT Relationships

In all of these aspects of the business/IT organizational culture, the underlying point is the cohesiveness of the business itself, together with the cohesiveness of business and IT organizations. Any degree of separation—whether expressed in terms of silos, individual lines of business autonomy, IT itself being separate, poorly working governance, or poorly working teams—has significant implications for the success of company-wide IT activities.

Category 3: Business and IT Process—Culture Defines the Way IT and Business Managers Work Together

This category is about management systems and management practices and behaviors. It deals with the specific processes and practices connecting IT and business. This includes planning processes, planning results, business and IT teams, and so forth.

The cultural characteristics in this area are related to the first set of culture elements about the importance of IT in the business as well as the second set, about the degrees of separation of IT and business in the company. Here, the focus is on the ways IT and business managers work together. Although there are connections to the first two, these characteristics exist in any company setting.

The significance of this culture category lies in the capability of the company to successfully undertake initiatives, particularly strategic initiatives, intended to bring about change in the business itself. Whether this is in terms of internal process change or competitive/customer change, the problems are more severe if IT and business managers cannot work together.

IT/Business Planning Integration

These characteristics lie in management expectations for connection of IT and business planning. The issue is what management expects about the following: (1) IT may or not be involved in business planning; (2) annual plans and budgets may or may not be specifically linked to or driven by strategic plans; (3) IT and business planning may or may not be done separately, with weak or no interactions and linkages; business planning assumes IT can react and respond to requirements, and does not consider IT-enabled innovations; IT planning focuses on technologies; and (4) IT planning may or may not be highly siloed, with little or no planning across silos and with few company-wide initiatives.

In a culture that does not expect IT connection to planning, none of the hoped-for objectives for connecting business and IT, or maximizing the impact IT brings to the business, can be achieved. The consequences are easy to spot. Organizations substitute tactical planning for strategic thinking and strategic direction. IT organizations march to a technology drummer, seemingly unaware of business direction and opportunity. Senior managers express frustration with the large operational investments in IT, but without the clear strategic and competitive results that they had hoped for.

IT Solution Orientation

In the minds of business managers, an IT solution can easily substitute for a business goal. For example, the IT implementation of an enterprise resource planning (ERP) system can be management's definition of the business goal. However, the underlying business goal, such as standard operating processes throughout the company and consolidated supply-chain management, is independent of the technology. ERP is the means, but it is not the same as the business problem or the business goal.

Strategic Understanding

The problem in many companies is there is little grip on exactly what the company's strategies are. To be sure, most companies do have formal mission statements, often with a high-level strategy statement. Strategic planning often is ineffective, producing strategy statements that do not easily translate into actions that people can take. An organization needs plans that let people know what they should be doing tomorrow.

Role of Plans

The characteristic is whether managers think plans, and the planning activities that produce them, are important and should guide their behavior. When thought to be unimportant, plans fail to be specific and, consequently, cannot be used as guideposts leading to the specific programs or initiatives needed to achieve the strategies. Too often, the enterprise strategic plan is not actionable; business units and IT cannot determine from the strategic plan what they should be doing.

Undefined IT Role

This culture issue is the unstated expectation for the IT organization. No one typically needs to define the role of marketing, or the role of finance, in carrying out the enterprise activities. However, often the leadership team may not fully understand what role IT *could* play. Here is where there's opportunity for innovation and new leadership expectations.

Accountability

This issue has to do with senior management's expectations for the accountability for creating business results with IT. In one typical case, business managers were passive participants in business changes brought about by IT. The view was that IT was responsible for producing not only the technology components of an initiative but also the process change or other innovations. A different culture would have business managers take the leadership role, with IT providing the technology but leaving accountability for the business result in the hands of business management. The significance is both leadership and accountability. From the leadership perspective, in the one kind of culture, IT bears the brunt of finding business opportunities and responding to them with effective new initiatives. In the other, business leadership is expected to take this role. From the accountability perspective, a similar dichotomy exists. A key difference lies in business sponsorship of IT projects. In the one case, business management sponsors new projects and is accountable for the business results. In the other case, IT sponsors new projects, is responsible for demonstrating the business case, and is accountable for the results.

Summary of Category 3: Business and IT Process

As we noted in Category 1, culture about the role and impact of IT can prevent companies from making progress with IT. In Category 2, culture about the business/IT organizational relationships, especially those that separate business and IT, can prevent companies from achieving strategic and operational excellence that crosses organizational lines. Here in Category 3, culture impedes business and IT managers getting together and inhibits their working together in integrated and connected processes.

PART 4: APPLYING CULTURE MANAGEMENT CONCEPTS

Our goal is to enable a company to move from its business strategies to IT action to the right business results, and to surmount the obstacles presented by its management culture. The culture management support practice will help change the underlying management culture to reduce barriers to changing management processes and using the NIE practices.

We address culture management in three ways: (1) by identifying the as-is and to-be culture; (2) by assessing the maturity level of the company's management

EXHIBIT 11.3   Identifying As-Is and To-Be Culture

Section		Description	Focus
IT's Role and Value in the Business	1	IT's Business Performance	Whether IT is important enough to include in business planning and business thinking
	2	IT's Cost versus IT's Value	Whether management has confidence that IT's value, in the aggregate, is more than IT's costs
	3	IT's Justification	Management's use of metrics (e.g., ROI) versus achievement of strategic intentions
	4	IT as Business Innovation	Management expectations for alignment or new business innovations
Organizational Relationships between IT and the Business	5	Silo Orientation	Whether there is an enterprise-wide view of IT as an organization and a role being played
	6	Line of Business Autonomy	Degree to which lines of business are autonomous
	7	IT/Business Separation	Degree to which IT and business are separate, in culture, practices, and people
	8	IT Governance	Degree to which IT is driven by the business through governance
	9	IT/Business Integration	Whether business and IT operate as a team
Management Processes	10	IT/Business Planning Integration	Whether the IT Planning process, and the resulting plan, is IT-driven versus business-driven
	11	IT Solution Orientation	Degree to which technology-focused goals are surrogates for Business Goals
	12	Strategic Understanding	Degree to which actionable strategic intentions; planning drives from strategic intentions
	13	Role of Plans	Whether planning is ineffective, shelfware
	14	Undefined IT Role	Whether IT is proactive versus reactive with respect to delivering business results
	15	Accountability	Is IT or business management accountable for applying IT to produce business results?

processes; and (3) by changing managers' experiences. This section provides a set of tools and diagnostics that enables managers to understand the specific cultural hurdles they face and what they can do about them.

Tool 1: Identify the As-Is and To-Be Management Culture

Culture is based on management beliefs, values, principles, and practices, and can be expressed in terms of the focus statements in Exhibit 11.3. Management culture can be identified by examining what managers believe and what they can do with respect to business and IT and the processes that connect them. The 15 classifications of IT/business culture are the starting point for the identification. Exhibit 11.3 shows the focus for each class of management culture, and gives the framework for possible as-is and to-be statements.

EXHIBIT 11.4   Sample Questions for Identifying Culture

Management Culture Template 1			
Management Beliefs and Actions	**As-Is Statement:** *Is this statement true?*	**Are Current Plans and Actions Consistent with this Statement?**	**To-Be Statement:** *Should this statement be true in the future?*
IT activities—new initiatives and current operations—are integral to the achievement of our business strategy.	❏ Yes ❏ No ❏ Don't Know	❏ Yes ❏ No ❏ Don't Know	❏ Yes ❏ No ❏ Don't Know
IT is an important component of our strategic business initiatives.	❏ Yes ❏ No ❏ Don't Know	❏ Yes ❏ No ❏ Don't Know	❏ Yes ❏ No ❏ Don't Know
IT is an important component of, and consideration in, our business plans and business planning processes.	❏ Yes ❏ No ❏ Don't Know	❏ Yes ❏ No ❏ Don't Know	❏ Yes ❏ No ❏ Don't Know
IT planning is integral to, and done concurrently with, our business plans.	❏ Yes ❏ No ❏ Don't Know	❏ Yes ❏ No ❏ Don't Know	❏ Yes ❏ No ❏ Don't Know
Our business initiatives stand alone; any necessary technology support is filled in as needed.	❏ Yes ❏ No ❏ Don't Know	❏ Yes ❏ No ❏ Don't Know	❏ Yes ❏ No ❏ Don't Know
Our business unit annual and strategic plans specifically include IT initiatives.	❏ Yes ❏ No ❏ Don't Know	❏ Yes ❏ No ❏ Don't Know	❏ Yes ❏ No ❏ Don't Know

Exhibit 11.4 lists a sample focus for identifying the culture within the first of the 15 culture classifications shown in Exhibit 11.3. The sample statements in Exhibit 11.4 express some aspects of the business-to-IT connection. We do not suggest that any of these culture situations is right or wrong. However, some culture situations are better for successfully adopting NIE practices. Consequently, we identify the as-is situation within a company for each culture classification,

and then the to-be. The gap between the as-is and to-be establishes a target for change.

The assessment is based on a set of questions for each of the 15 culture classifications. While Exhibit 11.4 is a sample, the complete questionnaire process is tailored to the individual company's situation in three important ways. First, the relative significance of the 15 culture classifications is determined. This prioritizes them, to assure the most important ones to the company's situation are addressed. Second, the questions themselves are selected to meet the exact company circumstances. For example, we will employ a different set of questions for companies that are organized functionally rather than around lines of business. Finally, the set of managers answering the questions depends on the company circumstances.

Exhibit 11.4 is a sample questionnaire template for the first culture classification, IT's importance to the business. Two specific objectives are addressed: first, the as-is to to-be gives a sense of the gaps to be filled. Second, the "consistent with statements" gives direction for the real culture impact on management processes, and the prospects for embedding NIE practices within them.

Tool 2: Assess the Maturity Level of the Company's Management Processes

Chapter 12 will introduce the Business Value Maturity Model as a tool for assessing the company's process maturity in areas covered by NIE practices. Although the focus is on process, there is a close connection between where a company is with respect to its processes and its culture about the importance and acceptance of those processes.

In Chapter 12, we point out that maturity assessment establishes the current as-is ability of companies to perform strategy-to-results processes, and enables a decision on what the company needs to do to improve its ability to perform those processes. The Chapter 12 goals are overcoming management culture barriers and improving the company's ability to act.

Culture sets the boundaries of what is possible for a company to do through its management processes. The maturity of those processes is dependent on the culture accepting and acting upon the outcomes of the processes. The ability to connect the processes (i.e., whether the Strategy-to-Bottom-Line Value Chain can actually function within an organization) is dependent on management culture.

Tool 3: Change Managers' Experiences

Culture change is experiential in nature. While Tools 1 and 2 above are about assessing culture and process maturity, this section is about changing the culture and impacting process maturity. Our approach is based on the principle that culture is not changed by dictate or decision or rational arguments. *Culture changes when managers' experiences lead them to new ways to think about the business.* Culture changes when managers are required, whether by crisis or by new circumstances, to perform different tasks and different roles.

Accordingly, our approach focuses on managers performing new roles and tasks, through participating in and owning NIE processes. Exhibit 11.1 lists many of the roles to be played by various leadership teams in the steps of the Value Chain. We assert that the experience of playing the roles changes that culture.

Peter Senge provides one way to think about culture, its influence, and what needs to change. He uses the term "mental model" to describe how a manager views the world: "Mental models are deeply held internal images of how the world works, images that limit us to familiar ways of thinking and acting. Very often, we are not consciously aware of our mental models or the effects they have on our behavior."[6] In this view, moving managers to new ways of thinking and acting requires changing the mental models managers have.

This is what our experience approach is about: changing the mental models, the culture, that managers have about business and IT.

Changing Culture through Experience

Traditional thinking about management culture emphasizes the role of senior management in setting and changing it, through, for example, using world-class performance targets, leadership changes, major reorganization, or changing reward structures. While these techniques may be useful, they are not sufficient. Management culture about IT is created, and exists, as an accumulation of the observations and experience of individual managers. If their experience is not changed, the culture will endure.

Our approach moves business managers from passive, reactive observers of IT to active participants in managing and directing IT. Management culture is a collection of experiences, and the Culture Management principles affirmatively change the experiences of managers. For example, when the business leadership team participates in an enterprise-level prioritization process, the team gets an enterprise view of business strategy, a view of what each of the company's silos is doing and relative importance of that to the company. The culture changes as individual managers participate and engage in processes that affect what they know and what they experience about IT and business.

Again, our approach to changing culture through management experience has three basic elements:

1. *Identify the mental models managers have about business and IT.* This analysis is based on the as-is assessment, and leads to understanding the culture hurdles we face in making the Strategy-to-Results process changes and adapting NIE practices.

2. *Establish to-be culture goals* and through the Maturity Model (see Chapter 12) establish process targets; these goals and targets explicitly define the new roles and experiences expected of managers.

3. *Engage the appropriate managers* and give them the experience of working with NIE practices; this gives them hands-on experience with the values and

processes represented by the NIE goals and critical success factors. The identities of appropriate managers are defined partly by their roles (see Exhibit 11.1) and partly by the degree of support for this process from senior management (discussed further below).

The third point above is key. Our experience tells us that managers change their attitudes and opinions *only* as a result of successful experience and learning based on experience. Rarely do managers change because they're told to. Even more rarely do managers change their attitudes based on logic and persuasion. Management culture grows out of experience, and changes in management culture are based on experience.

Summary of Part 4: Concepts of Culture Management

In an ideal world, the idea of addressing culture in three steps is very appealing. First, identify the as-is for culture. Then establish the to-be management process target and assess the current management process status, thereby highlighting the requirements for culture change. Then provide a method for achieving culture change.

In reality, the process is much more circular and much less serial. Assessing culture and process maturity, and changing managers' experiences, are all part of the same set of problems and issues. We know that culture is critical and that it limits (or enables) what needs to be done. By shedding some light on it through assessment, establishing targets for process maturity change, and changing management's experiences, we get closer to our overall goal of increasing IT's impact.

We have emphasized throughout this book that culture inhibits these new roles, as well as inhibiting the adoption of the new practices and processes. In practical terms, how can we get managers to expend time and energy and to commit to the results of the process when the culture doesn't support their doing so? The answer is that certain standard management roles are important to beginning the process of culture change. The first role is senior management support. This is where the importance of assessing the current culture and assessing the process maturity level becomes so critical. These tools make it possible to communicate the problem, and the nature of the solution, to senior management. Indeed, this is vital. Whereas making a rational argument for change will not work (only experience will work), support does need to exist for gaining the experience. Getting this support is important, and making the case for the support and for adopting one or more NIE practices, is based on the understanding and assessment that comes through assessment of culture and process maturity. A second role is leadership, exercised by the management team most directly concerned about the company's success in Strategy-to-Bottom-Line-Results. This leadership provides the energy to carry out the assessments and process changes.

DEAL WITH CULTURE: MANAGEMENT AGENDA

Management Question	Yes or No?	If No, What Is Our Plan for Correcting This?
Our management culture supports business and IT planning processes being fully connected and integrated.		
Our management culture supports IT-enabled innovations that impact business planning and result in new business strategies and better ways to implement existing strategies.		
Business and IT managers can work together so that IT investments are prioritized in relation to business strategy.		
The entire IT spend, including development, operations, maintenance, and services, aligns with business strategy.		
Performance measurement is a part of our culture, so IT business and technical performance is tracked.		
Business and IT management teams can work together to consistently execute the management processes that improve IT's contribution to the business's bottom-line performance.		
Business managers can participate in the planning and management processes that focus on the entire IT investment, both lights-on and projects.		
IT and business managers participate effectively in these management processes.		

ADDITIONAL READING

The book's website contains additional information:

Website Note 3: IT, Bottom-Line Impact, and Government

Website Note 10: Stage Theory and Management Culture

Website Note 11: Right and Wrong in Management Culture

Website Note 12: Value and Values

The appendices also contain related information for Chapter 11:

Appendix B: Management Team Roles in Right Decisions/Right Results

NOTES

1. Taylor Cox, Jr., *Cultural Diversity in Organizations: Theory, Research & Practice* (San Francisco: Berrett-Koehler, 1993), p. 161.

2. A company CFO once told us that a business manager complained that "the prioritization process wasn't working." The CFO pressed the issue, and the business manager reported that the projects "which we know are important" weren't scoring high on the business impact assessments. The CFO understood: prioritization was working, it just wasn't giving the answers that the business manager wanted.

3. This exhibit is a complete specification of possible leadership team roles. The exhibit implies that a company must simultaneously and immediately adopt all nine deliverables and all nine roles for each leadership team. This implication could be a barrier to doing anything. Rather, adopting NIE practices is an incremental process, and a company can approach the development of these management roles incrementally as well.

4. See Appendix B for a complete discussion of the management teams and their roles and responsibilities for processes and outcomes in the Strategy-to-IT-Action-to-Results Value Chain.

5. F. Warren McFarlan, "Portfolio Approach to Information Systems," *Harvard Business Review,* September–October 1981, pp. 142–150.

6. Peter M. Senge, *The Fifth Discipline: The Art and Practice of the Learning Organization* (Doubleday Currency, 1990), p. 8.

Chart the Path to Implementation

Chapter 12 introduces the *Business Value Maturity Model*™ as a tool to improve how the company directs and applies IT for maximum value. The chapter briefly describes this maturity model, shows how it can be used, and introduces maturity model specifics as applied to each area of New Information Economics practices. Here, we make four points:

1. *Business strategy to IT action to results is a chain of events and processes. This chain is constrained by the weakest process and the disconnects between processes.* Management should examine the chain to find the weakest links and disconnects, and fix them.

2. *To examine the chain, management should assess the maturity of the company's strategy-to-bottom-line processes, focusing on those that do planning, innovation, prioritization, alignment, and performance measurement as well as portfolio and culture management.*

Control Spending and Maximize Impact on the Bottom Line	
1	Define the Goals
2	Ask the Right Questions
3	Connect to the Bottom Line
4	Understand Costs and Resources
5	Focus on the Right Things
6	Adopt Effective Process to Produce Action
7	Tackle the Practical Problems
8	Make the Right Decisions
9	Plan for the Right Results
10	Keep Score
11	Deal with Culture
12	**Chart the Path to Implementation**
13	Define What's Next
14	Answer the "So What?" Question

The maturity assessment establishes the current as-is ability of companies to perform Strategy-to-Bottom-Line Value Chain processes and enables a decision on what the company needs to do to improve its ability to perform those processes.

The Maturity Model will identify the weaker, less capable processes, which the company can then improve. The model can also be used to set targets for improvement. Such an assessment begins by considering the business outcomes such processes should produce, including:

- The company gains maximum strategic and operational impact from its IT investments.

- The company excels in innovating through IT in its products, processes, and performance.

- The company consistently chooses the highest impact IT investments.

- The company achieves increased returns from its IT activities.

- Performance measures lead to improved IT and business performance.

- The entire IT investment contributes to business performance.

Once management determines that the company needs improvement in these areas, the Business Value Maturity Model™ helps identify specific opportunities to use NIE practices. The model can also be used to set targets for making the appropriate improvements.

3. *Management should determine and eliminate the management culture barriers to changing its Strategy-to-Bottom-Line processes and adopting NIE practices.* NIE practices give management teams new experiences in dealing with business and IT decisions. The Business Value Maturity Model™ helps to identify the as-is—and by extension the to-be—targets of the culture related to management's new roles and responsibilities. This is part of changing the processes, which makes them more effective and raises their maturity levels.

4. *Management should connect the company processes that lead from strategy to the bottom line.* While improving the maturity of each management process is vital, it is equally important to assess the maturity of the collection of processes, taken together, that move the company from strategy to results. Each individual process can be a silo, unconnected to related processes. This is the "disconnect" problem described in previous chapters. To be successful, the company's management processes need to connect, both to each other within the Strategy-to-Bottom-Line realm and to the affected company processes such as budgeting, business strategic planning, and operational/annual planning. The Business Value Maturity Model™ is used to make this assessment, leading to an understanding of the disconnects and what actions are needed.

Improving the company's strategy-to-IT-actions-to-results processes, and improving their connections, is critical to achieving the business results listed previously and thereby obtaining greater impact from IT. Our goal is to assess *all* of the related management processes, show how to improve and better connect them, and thereby vastly increase the impact IT has on a company's bottom-line performance.

INTRODUCTION TO THE BUSINESS VALUE MATURITY MODEL™

In previous chapters, we discussed NIE practices and their application through the company's management processes. NIE practices such as planning, prioritization, and alignment are embedded in the company's own management processes, with the result that the desired business outcomes are produced. *NIE goals*[1] set the framework for adopting and using NIE practices. *Culture* creates the environment in which the practices, and management processes, successfully produce the desired results. *Expected business outcomes* states a simple business outcome for the use of the practice.

Considerable limitations on the capability of a company to successfully employ NIE practices originate from the company's culture and the company's own capabilities for performing the practice. It is the purpose of this chapter to introduce a powerful tool, the Business Value Maturity Model™, to help a company overcome the two limitations. In short, previously we described the desired *business outcomes* that we want to produce through the NIE practices; now we introduce "maturity" as an indicator of whether the company can, in fact, produce the outcomes based on a combination of culture barriers and company capability to act on the results.

Maturity models have evolved over the last 20 years in areas as disparate as software engineering, project management, non-IT business processes, and data management. They share two basic characteristics. First, they are based on the original work of the Software Engineering Institute, supported by the federal government, in developing the Capability Maturity Model (SEI/CMM) for processes around the development of software. Second, they are used to assess the "maturity" of related management processes as a means to improve those processes in order to achieve organizational goals. This is based on the assumption that more effective and more mature management processes will produce better results: better software, better projects, better financial decisions, and so forth.

The Business Value Maturity Model™ follows the structure first introduced by the work of the Software Engineering Institute. Beginning in the 1980s, Watts Humphreys[2] and others formalized ideas of growth and organizational change in SEI's Capability Maturity Model,[3] which focused on the processes and management practices an organization should apply to software development. SEI's maturity model defines five levels and is used to describe both the goals a company should establish for its processes and the current as-is state of the processes it uses.

The Business Value Maturity Model™ is built around similar basic expressions of maturity as shown in generic terms Exhibit 12.1. The description of each level includes the characteristics of the management processes and their maturity with respect to achieving the desired outcome. The complete Business Value Maturity Model™ includes specific descriptions for each NIE goal, culture, and practice.

EXHIBIT 12.1   Business Value Maturity Model™

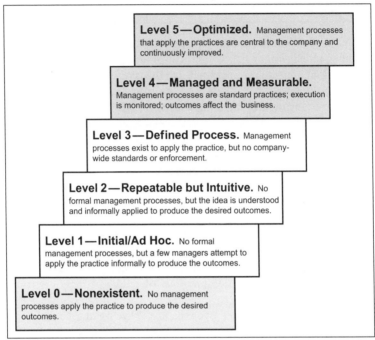

The Business Value Maturity Model™ enables, through assessment and subsequent improvement, more effective and better-connected management processes. "More effective processes" that produce those results can be described as follows:

- IT and business planning are fully connected and integrated.
- IT-enabled innovations impact business planning and offer new strategies.
- IT investments are prioritized against business strategy.
- The entire IT spend is aligned with business strategy.
- IT business and technical performance is tracked.
- Business and IT management teams execute the processes that improve IT's contribution to business performance.
- Planning and management processes focus on the entire IT investment.
- IT and business managers participate effectively in all NIE-enabled processes.

What Does the Business Value Maturity Model™ Cover?

We are concerned with the maturity of the company's management processes that carry out planning, prioritization, and so forth. The Maturity Model, accordingly, is based on the five NIE practices and three supporting practices. At the same time, we are equally concerned with the overall connections of the management process, both among themselves and with other company processes. Consequently, the Business Value Maturity Model™ also assesses the maturity of the *connection* of management processes that deal with IT planning to business results, for the purpose of assessing the *connections* among the processes.

MATURITY MODEL GOALS

The goal for using the Business Value Maturity Model™ is to overcome management culture barriers and improve the company's ability to act.

A basic point made in Chapter 11 was that management culture is the main determinant of success in adopting NIE practices such as prioritization, alignment, and so forth. These practices enable management teams to make the best decisions and take the best actions. This requires the active, and accepting, participation of both business and IT management teams. As we pointed out earlier, these management teams need to play certain roles, and the management culture may not support those roles. More to the point, the management culture may not respect the *results* of the processes or the desired outcomes they are intended to produce.

For example, we successfully introduced the innovation and prioritization practices into their strategic business and IT planning processes of a large financial services institution. By "successfully introduced," we mean the practices were understood, the management teams participated fully in the exercises we conducted, and the CEO felt that the exercises were valuable to the management team. However, *none* of the results appeared in any of the senior managers' annual plans for the coming year; none of the IT-enabled innovations produced any lasting changes to the company's strategic plan. Why not? The pervasive management culture did not support the manner in which the practice results were produced, did not support the idea of IT-enabled innovation in the business, and was not capable of producing actions based on "interesting" meetings. However, some progress was made. For the first time, the senior leadership team understood the problem. The individual managers who participated observed the potential for changing how planning was done. A sense of disappointment was shown when the meetings didn't produce lasting results, along with a sense of missed opportunities. In the long run, progress in changing the culture had begun.

The second main determinant of success in adopting new practices such as alignment and prioritization is the company's capability of executing the business process in which they are embedded, and acting on the results produced. As we discussed in Chapter 1, this is partly an issue of process connections; for example, will the results of a strategic planning process connect to the annual planning and budgeting process?

But we are also dealing with the larger issues: How does one fundamentally change how a company manages its IT? For example, Exhibit 12.2 shows the deliverables in the Strategy-to-Bottom-Line Value Chain; in order to produce them, how does one fundamentally affect the behavior of the company itself?

EXHIBIT 12.2   Management Process Deliverables in the
Strategy-to-Bottom-Line Value Chain

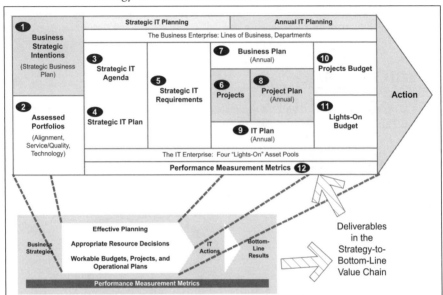

The answers lie in setting goals, adopting new practices, and influencing the culture of the company, in a way that shows both the long-term goal—where we want to be—and the roadmap for getting there.

REQUIREMENT FOR MANAGEMENT ACTION

Management action is necessary to produce the desired outcomes.

The combination of process execution and taking action based on process results was captured in the deliverables and roles charts introduced in Chapter 6 and repeated here.

Without regard to whether NIE practices are used, each of the nine deliverables is part of how the company manages itself and its IT. Success in getting from strategy to action (through the budget, annual, and operational plans of every component in the business) depends on the holistic collection of management actions. Management has to act, and the maturity of the processes themselves, along with the connections between them, determines the likelihood of getting the right actions.[4]

Every deliverable important to getting from strategy to action is tied to an NIE practice. See Exhibit 12.3. In other words, the management processes that perform strategic planning, or prioritization, or creating the annual plan, require the kind of activity and discipline that the NIE practice brings.

EXHIBIT 12.3 NIE Practice: Detailed Deliverables

Strategy-to-Bottom-Line Value Chain			
		Deliverable Name / Deliverable Description	NIE Practice

		Deliverable Name	Deliverable Description	NIE Practice
Strategic Planning	1	Business Strategic Intentions	Mission plus weighted Strategic Intentions	Demand/Supply Planning Innovation
	2	Assessed Portfolios	As-is alignment, service, quality, technology, use	Alignment Performance Measurement
	3	Strategic IT Agenda for the Use of IT	Strategic Intentions to Strategic Initiatives	Demand/Supply Planning
	4	Strategic IT Plan	Strategic Intentions to Strategic Initiatives	Demand/Supply Planning Innovation
	5	IT Strategic Requirements	Initiatives—3 to 5 years horizon—portfolio format	Demand/Supply Planning Prioritization
Annual/Tactical Planning	6	Projects	Real, doable projects	Not an NIE deliverable
	7	Annual Project Plan	One year annual horizon— with portfolio format	Prioritization
	8	Annual Business Plan	Documentation according to company practices	Not an NIE deliverable
	9	Annual IT Plan	Documentation according to company practices	Not an NIE deliverable
	10	Annual and Capital Project Budgets	Documentation according to company practices	Alignment, Prioritization
	11	Annual Lights-On Budget	Documentation according to company practices	Alignment
	12	Performance Measurement Metrics	Documentation according to company practices	Performance Measurement

Furthermore, each of the NIE practices requires considerable involvement and commitment by business and IT management teams. The heart of each practice is how the management team makes decisions about the relative importance of business strategies, about the priorities for IT initiatives supporting those strategies, about the alignment of current IT investments, and so forth. The involvement lies in making the decisions. The commitment lies in following through to the next step and creating the desired business outcomes.[5]

While this is being described in management process terms, the implications are more fundamental. The situation can be described by the statement: "Without action, strategy is meaningless." Here, without action, all of the ideas, benefits, and potential outcomes to be delivered by NIE practices are equally meaningless. In process terms, this means getting to the annual plans and budgets, and getting management to commit to actions that will implement the decisions made, the priorities established, and the strategies identified.

Management roles are critical as well (see Exhibit 12.4). In Chapter 11, we introduced the management roles required, as a descriptor of the problems of culture that we need to understand and overcome. In order to get to action, management has to play the needed roles, and this may require dealing with culture as well.

EXHIBIT 12.4   Management Roles

		Deliverable Name	Senior Leadership Team	Business Leadership Team	Technology Leadership Team	Planning Process Owner
Strategic Planning Cycle	1	Business Strategic Intentions	Approve and weight strategic intentions	Revise and review strategic intentions		Create initial draft strategic intentions (strawman)
	2	Assessed Portfolios	Review	Assess portfolios/ alignment, service, quality	Contribute to portfolio development Assess portfolio/ technology	Manage portfolio development Manage the assessment process
	3	Strategic IT Agenda for Use of IT	Approve	Develop IT agenda	Participate in IT agenda process	Create the initial drafts (strawman)
	4	Strategic IT Plan	Review	Review IT plan	Develop IT plan	Create the initial drafts (strawman)
	5	IT Strategic Requirements	Review	Develop Requirements Prioritization Recommend decisions	Participate in IT requirements process	Drive the process
Annual/Tactical Planning Cycle	6	Projects	Review and Approve large projects	Create project requirements and business cases	Form detailed projects and technical requirements	Assure that project formation works right
	7	Annual Project Plan	Make decisions or approve funding	Prioritization Recommend funding	Establish annual project plan and schedules	Drive the process
	8	Annual Business Plan	Approve	Review IT plans Establish business unit plans	Advise	Assure this happens
	9	Annual IT Plan	Approve	Review	Develop IT plans Establish budgets	Assure this happens
	10	Annual and Capital Project Budgets	Approve	Develop budgets	Participate in budget planning	Create initial draft (strawman)
	11	Annual Lights-On Budget	Review	Review	Develop budget Initiate plans	Create initial draft (strawman)
	12	Performance Measurement Metrics	Approve	Establish business performance metrics	Establish IT performance metrics	Assure this happens Create initial drafts (strawman)

EMBEDDING NIE PRACTICES INTO MANAGEMENT PROCESSES

It comes down to changing management processes.

To be effective, NIE practices need to be embedded in the company's management processes. While these management processes are company-specific, the NIE practices are standard toolsets that can be applied to any company's situation. The key is how the company's management processes apply the NIE practices and the concepts and principles that underlie them. The company cannot consistently achieve its goals of applying IT more effectively and increasing shareholder value through IT without integrating strategy-to-bottom-line practices into its existing management processes.

Effective processes make things happen. The better defined and followed the processes are, the better the performance of managers and organizations becomes. Watts Humphreys said it best: Mature processes lead to disciplined work, and disciplined work is what produces better and more predictable results.[6] Good practices enable their underlying processes to consistently achieve their goals, while also establishing and reinforcing a congruent culture about those goals. It is important to assess the maturity of management processes with respect to the specific practices they use in order to determine the likelihood that those processes will actually proceed from business strategy to IT action to results—the basic goal of New Information Economics.

Improving Management Process Connections

Increasing maturity by improving management process connections is equally important.

As we noted above, we are equally concerned with the connection of processes, both within the NIE framework and between the IT-related processes and the rest of the company's business processes. If a company uses NIE's Prioritization practice, higher impact projects will come to the top of the project queue. But this is significant *only if* the result is connected to budgeting processes, management performance evaluation processes, tactical planning processes, and so forth (see Exhibit 12.5). Using only the NIE Prioritization practice will achieve little unless the prioritization outcome drives budgeting and resource decisions.

As stated previously, the overall problem is to translate a company's business strategies and goals into the right IT actions that produce the right business results. *But just the adoption of one or more new practices isn't enough.* Ever since *Information Economics* appeared in 1988, there's been a continual evolution and advancement of "point solutions" to improving IT's business impact. (For example, the idea of investment portfolio management has emerged, with many consultants and authors promoting its virtues. This follows management's interest in prioritization and strategic alignment.)

As a result, the Business Value Maturity Model™ looks at the individual practice areas, as well as the overall, holistic set of processes that takes a company from its Strategy to IT Action to Results.

Maturity Model Goals—Summary

The goals are overcoming management culture barriers and improving the company's ability to act.

Culture affects and limits management processes by defining roles and expectations, especially what roles managers play in and around IT and how they play

EXHIBIT 12.5   Connecting NIE Practices to Other Company Processes

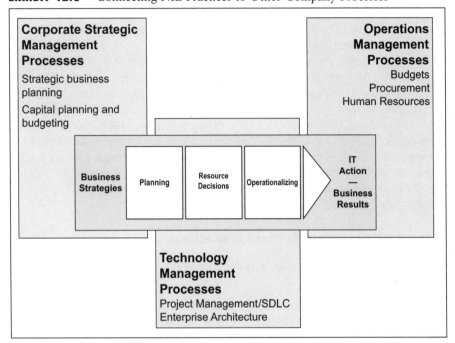

them. We want to assess the maturity of the management processes used to establish, encourage, and strengthen the desired culture. The critically important point is that the simple adoption of new practices such as prioritization is not enough to significantly change company performance. The worldwide CIO for a multi-business Fortune 500 company expressed the issue this way: *"The CIOs in each of our business units understand the principles. How do I get them to apply them?"* This is the problem of organizational change and cultural change. Getting managers to adopt new ways of doing and thinking about things is never easy.

The Business Value Maturity Model™, through assessing as-is management processes, helps identify the cultural problems and disconnects that limit the company's ability to act. It enables the establishment of targets for process improvement and helps the company determine where improvement initiatives are needed.

USING THE BUSINESS VALUE MATURITY MODEL™

A company uses the Business Value Maturity Model™ for two primary purposes:

1. To assess where the company is with its current practices relative to a standard model and relative to where the practices need to be to meet the company's strategic requirements. In this way, the model helps the company to identify process gaps that can impact IT's contribution to shareholder value.

EXHIBIT 12.6 Business Value Maturity Assessment

Business Value Maturity Model™ High-Level Assessment Form									
Practice Title	**Practice Description** (The description is established in Chapter 4.)	Instructions • Check the one that most closely describes the current state of affairs. • Circle the one that most closely states *what you believe is necessary* to achieve *Strategy to IT Actions to Results.*							Rank 1 to 9
		Nonexistent	Initial/Ad Hoc	Repeatable/ Intuitive	Defined Process	Managed and Measurable	Optimized Processes	Importance
Demand/ Supply Planning	Explicitly connecting IT strategies and plans to business strategic intentions. Establishing the business strategic demand for IT, and then IT's strategies and plans for the supply of the necessary IT capabilities.	0 ☑	1 ☑	2 ☑	3 ☑	4 ☑	5 ☑	
Innovation	Translating IT opportunities into new business strategic intentions and finding new ways for IT to support existing strategic intentions.	0 ☑	1 ☑	2 ☑	3 ☑	4 ☑	5 ☑	
Prioritization	Assessing the business impact of new IT initiatives and prioritizing them according to strategic intentions.	0 ☑	1 ☑	2 ☑	3 ☑	4 ☑	5 ☑	
Alignment	Assessing the business impact and support of business strategic intentions of the existing IT infrastructure, applications, and services. Assessing the quality and service levels for existing IT resources, as input to demand/supply planning.	0 ☑	1 ☑	2 ☑	3 ☑	4 ☑	5 ☑	
Performance Measurement	Measuring IT performance in ways related to the business and its strategic intentions.	0 ☑	1 ☑	2 ☑	3 ☑	4 ☑	5 ☑	
Strategy-to- Bottom-Line Value Chain	Connecting the processes doing planning, innovation, prioritization, alignment, and performance measurement with themselves and with the other appropriate company processes.	0 ☑	1 ☑	2 ☑	3 ☑	4 ☑	5 ☑	
IT Impact Management	Establishing and achieving IT's business value proposition. Managing IT based on business value outcomes.	0 ☑	1 ☑	2 ☑	3 ☑	4 ☑	5 ☑	
Portfolio Management	Establishing baseline, business value, and performance information for the entire IT investment.	0 ☑	1 ☑	2 ☑	3 ☑	4 ☑	5 ☑	
Culture Management	Establishing baseline, business value, and performance information for the entire IT investment.	0 ☑	1 ☑	2 ☑	3 ☑	4 ☑	5 ☑	

2. To establish the targets for process improvement. Because the model describes the characteristics and requirements for each maturity level, a company can use the model as a set of trail markers that indicate where the opportunities are for improving a specific practice. In this way, the company can set targets to improve its processes.

Using the Business Value Maturity Model™ for Assessment

The Business Value Assessment (see Exhibit 12.6) is a high-level simple instrument that illustrates how a manager can self-assess the current maturity situation for the company. The instrument also provides for defining the "to be" situation that the manager believes is necessary for the company to achieve its goals.

This high-level instrument does not show the detailed descriptions of each maturity level—for example, what describes "defined process" for a given process. A full maturity assessment uses more detailed instruments that include the description of each maturity level. However, a generic set of maturity level descriptions is shown below:

- *Level 0: Nonexistent.* No management processes apply the NIE practice to produce the business outcome and thereby improve IT's bottom-line impact and control the IT spend.

- *Level 1: Initial/Ad Hoc.* No formal management processes exist, but a few managers attempt to apply the NIE practice to produce the business outcome and thereby improve IT's bottom-line impact and control the IT spend.

- *Level 2: Repeatable but Intuitive.* No formal management processes exist, but the idea of the NIE practice is understood and informally applied to produce the business outcome and thereby improve IT's bottom-line impact and control the IT spend.

- *Level 3: Defined Process.* Management processes exist to apply the NIE practice, but there are no company-wide standards or enforcement to produce the business outcome and thereby improve IT's bottom-line impact and control the IT spend.

- *Level 4: Managed and Measurable.* Management processes are standard practices throughout the company, execution is monitored, and outcomes are recognized to affect business in terms of producing the business outcome and thereby improve IT's bottom-line impact and control the IT spend.

- *Level 5: Optimized.* Management processes that apply the NIE practice are central to the company and continuously improved.

The person completing the surveys marks each goal, culture, or practice by answering two basic questions:

1. Which maturity level best describes the situation in the company today? What is the maturity of the company's management process with respect to seeking the goal, influencing the culture, or applying the practice?

2. Which maturity level best describes what the maturity *should* be, in order for the company to realize its strategic intentions with the aid of IT?

Using the Business Value Maturity Model™ for Process Improvement

Assessments using the Business Value Maturity Model™ are useful for determining where a company is in regard to a specific practice and describing where a company wants to be in its use of that practice. As with the SEI/CMM, not all companies need to achieve, or can achieve, Level 5 in all practice areas. It is important that management prioritize the implementation and improvement of NIE practices based upon their expected impact on IT's contribution to shareholder value. Once these priorities have been established, implementation and improvement plans can be developed to address the Key Process and Cultural Elements associated with the achievement of a given Maturity Level within a specific practice.

For example, as expressed in the generic maturity model (see Exhibit 12.1), to move from Level 1 to Level 2 requires developing the relationship between business and IT so that repeatable collaboration is possible and both parties deem the results of this collaboration useful. Moving from Level 2 to Level 3 requires actionable and commonly understood strategic intentions as a necessary part of the defined process. Documentation and training around the defined process is also required. In this way, the Business Value Maturity Model™ becomes a roadmap for practice improvement.

SUMMARY: THE BUSINESS VALUE MATURITY MODEL™

We have introduced five business-driven NIE practices, portfolio management, and the management culture hurdles that come with them. Taken together, they raise key questions: How does one fundamentally change the way a company manages IT? How do you fundamentally affect the behavior of your company? The answers lie in setting appropriate goals, adopting new practices, and influencing the culture of the company in a way that identifies both the long-term goal and the roadmap for getting there.

Two main ideas summarize the use of the Business Value Maturity Model™. First, *deciding exactly which NIE practices to introduce depends on where the company is with respect to its needs and its ability to employ the practice effectively.* The correct starting point cannot be selected using a simple shotgun approach; the appropriate choices depend on the state of current management processes, expectations, and understanding and acceptance of the problems to be solved. Second, *new management practices aren't effective without considering all of the interactions between them and how the company behaves in related areas.* For example, prioritizing projects does not achieve anything unless the results of prioritization affect budgets, affect actual work priorities, and change business management's expectations about what IT is to accomplish. The prioritization process must also impact business managers' understanding of what *they* must do to make the process and management behavior changes, in order to fully implement the IT projects being prioritized.

The Business Value Maturity Model™ addresses both points. It serves as a method to help determine the next steps in adopting the principles and practices of NIE and helps in understanding the relationship between NIE practices and other related management activities.

The Business Value Maturity Model™ represents a rational framework that a company can use to assess and improve its practices to better connect IT activities to business strategies and, thereby, increase IT's contribution to shareholder value.

CHAPTER 12 APPENDIX A: DETAILS OF THE BUSINESS VALUE MATURITY MODEL™

We adapt the generic maturity model to each of the NIE practices. The idea is to apply the resulting Business Value Maturity Model™ to the company's processes that address the same issues as the NIE practice. For example, the Prioritization model is applied to any company process that prioritizes IT investments. Of course, in the absence of any such process, the company's maturity would be 0.

The Business Value Maturity Model™ description is in four parts: (1) a practice description (from Chapters 8–10); (2) critical success factors (CSF) for the application of the practice; (3) keys to maturity for the practice; and (4) the six-level description of the specific levels of maturity. This appendix gives details for Parts 1, 2, and 3, including the complete Business Value Maturity Model™ for all five NIE practices and the three NIE support practices. This appendix also includes the process outcome and business outcomes for each practice, at each maturity level.

We use the Business Value Maturity Model™ in two contexts. The first deals with each NIE practice area individually and is described in the following section. The second deals with the complete set of processes from Strategy-to-IT-Action-to-Bottom-Line Results and assesses the maturity of the company's processes taken as a group, focusing on connection and completeness.

1. Business Value Maturity Model™—Process Area Descriptions

Chapters 8–10 describe each of the practices, and Exhibit 12.7 repeats the high-level description. The practice description establishes what the NIE practice is intended to accomplish in the company's management processes. This description is the same for each maturity level.

2. Business Value Maturity Model™—Critical Success Factors

The CSFs express the important factors leading to increased process maturity using the NIE practices. A close inspection will show that many of these CSFs are, in fact, culture-based. See Exhibit 12.8. This shows the close connection between process maturity and the company's management culture.

This also demonstrates why we use the maturity model approach to deal with culture change as well as process effectiveness. The same initiatives that

EXHIBIT 12.7 Business Value Maturity Model—Process Descriptions

New Information Economics Practices

Strategic Demand/Supply Planning	Innovation	Prioritization	Alignment	Performance Measurement
Explicitly connects IT strategies and plans to business strategic intentions. Establishes the business strategic demand for IT, and then IT's strategies and plans for the supply of the necessary IT capabilities.	Translates IT opportunities into new business strategic intentions and finds new ways for IT to support existing strategic intentions.	Assesses the business impact of proposed IT initiatives and prioritizes them according to their judged impact on the strategic intentions.	Assesses the business impact of the existing IT infrastructure, applications, and services. Assesses the quality and service levels for existing IT resources, as input to demand/supply planning.	Measures and communicates IT performance in ways related to the business and its strategic intentions.

Strategy-to-Bottom-Line Value Chain—Management Process Connection

Connects the processes doing planning, innovation, prioritization, alignment, and performance management with themselves and with the other appropriate company processes.

New Information Economics Support Practices

IT Impact Management	Portfolio Management	Culture Management
Focuses business and IT management on IT's value proposition—IT's current and potential contributions to the business—in order to produce the greatest value for the businesses IT serves. Develops senior IT and business management's capability to enable and execute the key management processes required to achieve IT's value proposition.	Obtains, manages, and reports consistent and complete information about all IT assets and resources, covering applications, infrastructure, IT services, and IT management. Establishes baseline, business value, and performance information for the entire IT investment.	Understands and shapes management beliefs, values, and principles pertaining to the role and value of IT, including how IT can contribute to the shareholder value.

EXHIBIT 12.8 Business Value Maturity Model—Critical Success Factors

Strategic Demand/Supply Planning	New Information Economics Practices			
	Innovation	Prioritization	Alignment	Performance Measurement
Company strategy is defined in understandable terms. Business and IT managers have common understanding and commitment to company strategies. Business and IT organizations understand how IT activities support company strategies. IT planning is intended to derive IT actions from company strategies.	Management monitors IT's performance and contribution to business success, and understands business impact. Management understands cause and effect of existing efforts and can extrapolate into new business opportunities. Business and IT have a common view on how IT can contribute to the business. Business and IT managers have clear roles and participate actively in shaping new business opportunities with IT.	Company strategy is defined in understandable terms. New IT investments are described in business terms, especially their proposed impact on strategic intentions. Business management is responsible for assessing the likely impact of IT initiatives on strategic intentions. New IT investments are organized into resource and process portfolios for purposes of value assessment.	Company strategy is defined in understandable terms. Business management is responsible for assessing the existing service and quality levels and support for strategic intentions of existing IT investments. Resources for support of existing investments are allocated and budgeted based on explicit contributions to strategic intentions. Existing IT investments are organized into resource and process portfolios.	The value of current IT activities is assessed by evaluating their impact on strategic intentions. Resources are allocated and budgeted based on explicit cause-and-effect connection to strategic intentions. Resource and process portfolios exist for purposes of value assessment, performance management, quality and service level assessment, and resource commitment.

Strategy-to-Bottom-Line Value Chain Management Process Connections

Managers and business functions responsible for each company process understand the goals for connecting the processes.

Capability of senior management team to understand and enable the connection of the appropriate management processes.

New Information Economics Support Practices		
IT Impact Management	Portfolio Management	Culture Management
Capability of senior management team to understand, enable, and execute the key management processes on which IT's contribution to the business depend. Capability of IT management to define the IT value proposition—its current and potential contributions to the business—and communicate it within the IT organization and to the business organizations IT serves. Success in communicating IT's value proposition throughout the company, and the role each organization and manager plays in carrying it out.	IT management processes to obtain and apply portfolio information. IT management understands how to apply portfolios and portfolio information in planning, innovation, prioritization, alignment, and performance measurement. Business management understands how to apply portfolios and portfolio information in making investment decisions.	Managers in all areas of the business have a common understanding of and commitment to enterprise strategic intentions. Manager's roles are clearly defined to assure proper participation and avoid any disconnects created by an organization's existing culture. Managers are expected to be responsive to change combining "strategy to action" thinking with the ability to react to unexpected events and business change.

248

EXHIBIT 12.9 Business Value Maturity Model—Keys to Maturity

New Information Economics Practices

Strategic Demand/Supply Planning	Innovation	Prioritization	Alignment	Performance Measurement
The degree to which business and IT planning operate together.	The degree to which business and IT planning operate together.	The degree to which business and IT planning operate together.	The degree to which business and IT planning operate together.	The degree to which IT performance measures are linked to business impact.
How, and the degree to which, business planning explicitly considered IT innovations and inputs, and IT consequences as outputs.	How, and the degree to which, business planning explicitly considered IT innovations and inputs, and IT consequences as outputs.	The capability of business managers to assume an enterprise view of, and understand the business impact of, IT initiatives.	Ability of business management to understand existing IT investments and judge their impact on strategic intentions.	The degree to which IT performance measures are tracked and integrated into IT planning and other decision-making processes.
How, and the degree to which, IT planning explicitly considers business strategies.	The degree to which business and IT can accept and react to new visions, potentials, and opportunities created by IT.	Ability of managers across the enterprise to take an enterprise-wide view of initiatives and strategic intentions.	Willingness of business management to examine all investments periodically, and assign and re-assign resources based on current assessments rather than historic patterns.	
	Cultural willingness of the company to investigate new business ideas, especially those not originating with business management.			

Strategy-to-Bottom-Line Value Chain—Management Process Connections

The degree to which senior management supports the goals of connection.

The degree to which the management process owners understand the goals for connection.

The maturity of the individual company processes—consistent with the NIE practices and support practice areas.

New Information Economics—Support Practices

IT Impact Management	Portfolio Management	Culture Management
Degree to which senior business management understands the IT value proposition: its current and potential contributions to the business.	The degree to which IT assets and resources are described in portfolios.	The degree to which business and IT managers have a common understanding of and commitment to enterprise strategic intentions.
Degree to which senior business and IT management understands, and enables, the processes necessary to carry out IT's value proposition.	The degree to which management processes effectively acquire, maintain, and apply portfolio information.	The degree to which managers' roles are clearly defined to assure proper participation and avoid disconnects created by an organization's existing culture.
Degree to which the IT organization, its management and staff, understand the IT value proposition and the role each plays in carrying it out.	The degree to which portfolios and portfolio information are used in management decision-making processes.	
Degree to which the business organization understands IT value proposition and the role the business organization plays in carrying it out.		

are needed to make the processes effective are also needed to affect the culture. More important, the experience that the senior business and IT management teams have in applying the NIE practices and achieving increased levels of maturity, are exactly the experiences necessary to change the underlying management culture.

Examination will also show that the CSFs have considerable commonality. This is probably not surprising since all of the NIE practices are targeted on similar objectives.

3. Business Value Maturity Model™—Keys to Maturity

Each NIE practice produces deliverables that move the company from strategy to action. The keys to maturity, shown in Exhibit 12.9, combine CSFs with the essential outcomes for each practice. These keys to maturity form the foundation for the maturity model, and the expression of increased levels of maturity are based on these keys. Just like the CSFs, many of these keys to maturity are management culture-based.

CHAPTER 12 APPENDIX B: THE DEVELOPMENT OF MATURITY MODELS

The ideas of maturity models have developed over the last three decades to describe how a company and its management team can develop and grow in the use of information technology. Their origins lie in the ideas of "stages" or "phases" that a company goes through as it adapts its cultures and management practices to manage and apply technology. These ideas represent the organizational growth and learning that occurs as new methods and technologies affect how managers operate.

Richard Nolan had perhaps the earliest and most widely understood message, expressed in his Four Stages of EDP.[7] The four stages (Initiation, Contagion, Control, and Integration) were used to describe how management issues changed as the organization gained more experience with information technology. Nolan's stage theory expresses the organizational development and growth that occurs as the organization matures in the use of information technology.

Nolan observed that the transformation from one stage to the next requires explicit changes in organizational process and policy.

Beginning in the 1980s, Watts Humphrey and others formalized ideas of growth and organizational change in the Capability Maturity Model, focused on the processes and management practices that a company applies to software development. This maturity model expressed five stages of maturity and was used to define the goals a company may have for its processes and the current as-is state of its current processes. The Capability Maturity Model has been developed extensively by the Software Engineering Institute and is widely used in companies to assess and develop their capabilities in software development.

As stated, the maturity model that SEI has developed identifies the characteristics of each stage. For example, at maturity level X, a management process has the characteristics of Y. Those characteristics of Y then also serve, in advanced stages, as the definition of the goals the company would set for its management processes. Consequently, the maturity model is both an assessment tool and a roadmap for process improvement.

Others have adapted the ideas of the maturity model. For example, SEI itself has developed a People Maturity Model,[8] which deals with the management of people in software development. Others have developed a Project Management Maturity Model,[9] an E-Business Maturity Model,[10] and so forth. The Information Systems and Audit and Control Foundation (ASACF), in conjunction with PricewaterhouseCoopers (PwC) and Gartner, developed a set of maturity models that cover 34 IT management processes. This set of maturity models is collectively called Control Objectives for Information and Related Technology (COBIT).[11]

The COBIT models follow the SEI precedent of using a five-level maturity scale with descriptions of the characteristics of each IT management process at each of its maturity levels. The COBIT model also includes CSFs, key goal indicators (KGIs), and key performance indicators (KPIs). The relationship between these three elements can be expressed as:

> CSFs are what you need to do based on the choices made in the maturity model, while monitoring through KPIs whether you will reach the goals set by the KGIs.[12]

COBIT applies the idea of maturity models to 34 IT management processes. Its description of the generic maturity model states very well the basic characteristics of each level. See Exhibit 12.10.

EXHIBIT 12.10   COBIT Generic Maturity Model

		COBIT's Statement of Generic Maturity Model
1	Initial/Ad Hoc	There is evidence that the organization has recognized that the issues exist and need to be addressed. There are, however, no standardized processes but instead there are ad hoc approaches that tend to be applied on an individual or case-by-case basis. The overall approach to management is disorganized.
2	Repeatable but Intuitive	Processes have developed to the stage where similar procedures are followed by different people undertaking the same task. There is no formal training or communication of standard procedures, and responsibility is left to the individual. There is a high degree of reliance on the knowledge of individuals and, therefore, errors are likely.
3	Defined Process	Procedures have been standardized, documented, and communicated through training. It is, however, left to the individual to follow these processes, and it is unlikely that deviations will be detected. The procedures themselves are not sophisticated but are the formalization of existing practices.
4	Managed and Measurable	It is possible to monitor and measure compliance with procedures and to take action where processes appear to be working effectively. Processes are under constant improvement and provide good practice. Automation and tools are used in a limited or fragmented way.
5	Optimized	Processes have been refined to a level of best practice, based on the results of continuous improvement and maturity modeling with other organizations. IT is used in an integrated way to automate the workflow, providing tools to improve quality and effectiveness, making the enterprise quick to adapt.

COBIT is emerging as an important framework and standard that can support benchmarking between organizations while also allowing for company-specific elements that connect to company-specific performance issues and requirements.

ADDITIONAL READING

Appendix F contains detailed Business Value Maturity Model™ descriptions for each NIE practice.

NOTES

1. For example, the goal of "Produce action and use budgets, projects, and performance measurement to achieve business results" sets the foundation for employing the NIE Performance Measurement practice. See Chapter 1 for the definition of the NIE goals.
2. Watts S. Humphrey, *Managing the Software Process* (Reading, MA: Addison-Wesley, 1989) and *A Discipline for Software Engineering* (Reading, MA: Addison-Wesley, 1996).
3. Software Engineering Institute, Carnegie Mellon University, *The Capability Maturity Model: Guidelines for Improving the Software Process* (Reading, MA: Addison-Wesley, 1995).
4. Note that we do not disagree with constructs like the Balanced Scorecard that highlight the importance of measurement and management incentives that flow from business strategy. Indeed, we highlight performance measurement as an important NIE component. Our focus here is on the means for getting action to occur—that is, the maturity of individual processes and the maturity of the holistic connection of those processes.
5. See Chapter 1 for a statement of process and business outcomes expected from NIE practices.
6. Watts S. Humphrey, *Managing the Software Process.* Humphrey applied management process maturity concepts to software development and systems engineering, on the premise that more mature processes produce better software.
7. Richard Nolan, "Managing the Computer Resource: A Stage Hypothesis," *Communications of the ACM,* vol. 16, no. 7, July 1973.
8. SEI, People Capability Maturity Model® (P-CMM®) Version 2.0, July 2001, *www.sei.cmu.edu/publications/documents/01.reports/01mm001.html.*
9. Harold Kerzner, *Strategic Planning for Project Management Using a Project Management Maturity Model* (Hoboken, NJ: John Wiley & Sons, 2001).
10. PricewaterhouseCoopers, with the assistance of Carnegie Mellon University, has developed the E-Business Maturity Model (emm@™).
11. Information Systems Audit and Control Association, *COBIT,* 3rd edition. Available at: *www.isaca.org/cobit.htm.*
12. Ibid.

CHAPTER 13

Define What's Next

This chapter introduces IT Impact Management as a framework for helping companies and managers decide how to move forward with Right Decisions/ Right Results and the NIE practices. The goal is to give managers guidance for "what's next." Because companies, cultures, and circumstances are unique, there is no single right answer. There are, however, general guidelines that can be followed.

This chapter provides guidance in three ways. First, we present three alternate methods to establish goals for adopting Right Decisions/Right Results. Each method assesses the as-is and to-be with respect to IT management processes, which then become the basis for defining the goals. Second, we present a method to set goals from the perspective of corporate governance and processes. Third, we describe how a company can establish a program for the adoption of Right Decisions/Right Results, which we call "IT Impact Management."

Control Spending and Maximize Impact on the Bottom Line	
1	Define the Goals
2	Ask the Right Questions
3	Connect to the Bottom Line
4	Understand Costs and Resources
5	Focus on the Right Things
6	Adopt Effective Process to Produce Action
7	Tackle the Practical Problems
8	Make the Right Decisions
9	Plan for the Right Results
10	Keep Score
11	Deal with Culture
12	Chart the Path to Implementation
13	**Define What's Next**
14	Answer the "So What?" Question

Exactly what are the Right Decisions/Right Results goals? They fall into three categories:

1. Where should we start? Which NIE practice should be done first?

2. Who should be involved? IT management? Business management?

3. What should the outcomes be? (See, for example, Exhibit 13.17).

This chapter shows how to answer these questions.

THREE METHODS TO ESTABLISH RIGHT DECISIONS/ RIGHT RESULTS GOALS

We offer three related methods to establish goals. In all three methods, the approach is to determine the as-is, decide what the company's goal should be to achieve a to-be state, and then decide where to start and how to establish the set of actions needed to reach the to-be goal.

The first method starts with the current performance stage of IT in the company, based on the stage model introduced in Chapter 2. This establishes an as-is starting point for applying Right Decisions/Right Results. Companies then can begin with one or two practices such as prioritization or alignment, based on their as-is starting point.

The second method applies the Business Value Maturity Model™ from Chapter 12. This establishes an as-is and to-be for each basic NIE practice, and permits management to set goals to address maturity-level gaps. Management decides which of the to-be gaps will become a "should be" and sets the roadmap accordingly.

The third method works from the practical problems described in Chapter 7 and establishes an as-is and to-be goal. As with the maturity model approach, management then decides what the priority should be and plans accordingly.

Method 1: Setting Goals Based on the Stage of IT Performance

The status of stakeholders, current management processes, and business/IT governance comprise an important as-is in terms of applying the concepts and practices of Right Decisions/Right Results.

The stakeholders fall into four groups:

1. IT management (referred to as the Technology Leadership Team elsewhere in the book).

2. Senior management (called the senior management team elsewhere in the book), including business unit managers with bottom-line accountability for the units they manage.

3. Business unit and functional managers (referred to as the Business Leadership Team elsewhere).

4. Managers of related management processes in the company (e.g., corporate budget, program management offices, and financial officers such as CFOs).

Each group's perspective on current IT performance has a substantial effect on what its members will regard as solutions to the problems they care about. (It certainly is possible to go forward with individual NIE practices without careful consideration of these groups' points of view. The risk, however, is the initiative won't stick and will simply be a one-time exercise; worse, the experience can serve to harden management attitudes concerning IT management processes.)

EXHIBIT 13.1   Five IT Performance Stages

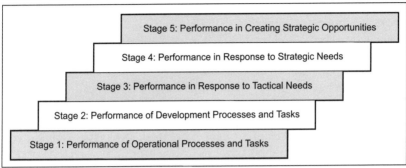

A company begins by determining the stakeholders' attitudes about the current stage of IT performance. In Chapter 2, we introduced a simple stage analysis of IT performance. See Exhibit 13.1.

A company is at Stage 1 when IT can competently perform IT operations. A company is at Stage 2 when IT is conducting systems development competently. A company is at Stage 3 when governance and planning processes react well to new tactical needs. A company is at Stage 4 when governance and planning processes react well to new strategic requirements. Finally, a company is at Stage 5 when IT significantly contributes to business planning with new, innovative directions that lead to new strategic intentions or new ways to address current strategic intentions.

EXHIBIT 13.2   Management Views on IT Performance

Company Stage		Management View on IT Performance				
Stage	**Stage Description**	Senior Management	Business Unit Management with P/L Accountability	Functional Managers	IT Management	Corporate Process Management
Stage 1	IT competently performs operations.					
Stage 2	IT competently conducts systems development.					
Stage 3	IT's governance and planning processes react well to new tactical needs.					
Stage 4	IT's governance and planning processes react well to strategic requirements.					
Stage 5	IT contributes innovative directions leading to new strategic intentions.					

Understanding where management believes IT is, in these stages, leads to appropriate goals and strategies for adapting Right Decisions/Right Results. A simple test is shown in Exhibit 13.2. The answers are simple yes's and no's. The company's stage is the highest at which a "yes" is the answer. Where there are differences between senior management and profit/loss managers, senior managers' views should prevail. The answers can be obtained directly from management, or can be estimated by the CIO or CFO. If the answer is "don't know," this shows an opportunity for addressing planning and management disconnects between the management groups and IT management.

The results are useful from several perspectives. The first is using the results to set the stage for determining where to begin using Right Decisions/Right Results. This is shown in Exhibit 13.3. A second perspective is the differences between management groups. See Exhibit 13.2 for the data collection on perspectives. Senior management's views are important, but from the perspective of success in adopting new processes, the views of process managers and business functional managers are at least as important. A third perspective is differences between IT management and the other business managers. This is particularly important in identifying disconnects between the management groups.

Based on the stage answers, management can consider the appropriate starting place for Right Decisions/Right Results initiatives. The table that follows identifies the focus of efforts according to the as-is stage; it does not preclude the

EXHIBIT 13.3   Establishing a Focus for Action

Company Stage	Possible Focus for Management Efforts
Stage 1: IT does operations well but does not do systems development well.	*Prioritization:* Controls the system backlog and improves overall project formation process, documentation, and business case development. *Demand/Supply Planning:* Leads to IT improvement strategies and actions about systems development and project management.
Stage 2: IT does both operations and systems development well but does not respond well to new tactical needs.	*Alignment:* Leads to a better understanding of the match of the current portfolios to business requirements. Assures current resources applied to right problems. *Prioritization:* Better matches projects to business requirements.
Stage 3: IT does operations, development, and tactical responses well but does not respond well to new strategic requirements.	*Strategy-to-Bottom-Line Value Chain:* Establishes process connections from strategic plan to IT plans and actions. *Innovation:* IT contributes to business plans. *Demand/Supply Planning:* Defines IT responses to strategic requirements. *Prioritization:* Matches projects to strategic requirements. *Alignment:* Assures current resources applied to the right problems.
Stage 4: IT does operations, development, tactical, and strategic responses well but does not contribute innovative directions to business planning.	*Strategy-to-Bottom-Line Value Chain:* Establishes process connections from strategic plan to IT plans and actions. *Innovation:* IT contributes to business plans. *Demand/Supply Planning:* Defines IT responses to strategic requirements.
Stage 5: IT does innovation well.	*Strategy-to-Bottom-Line Value Chain:* Establishes improved process connections from strategic plan to IT plans and actions.

use of other NIE practices. The practices identified can be adopted as a first step. The roadmap then consists of moving forward in the stages of IT performance.

Method 2: Setting Goals Based on Business Value Maturity Model™

The Business Value Maturity Model™ is another way to define the goals, based on an as-is, to-be assessment of management processes. As we showed in Chapter 12, a maturity model enables a management team to decide on what the company needs to do to improve its ability to perform the individual NIE practices described in the Strategy-to-Bottom-Line Value Chain, as well as to connect them effectively.

EXHIBIT 13.4 Business Value Maturity Model™ Applied to NIE Practices—Scorecard

The Right Decisions/Right Results Maturity Model Scorecard			
NIE Practice	**Business Bottom-Line Impact**	**Maturity As-Is**	**Maturity To-Be**
Strategic Demand/ Supply Planning	The company gains maximum strategic and operational impact from its IT investments.		
Innovation	The company excels in innovating through IT in its products, processes, and performance.		
Prioritization	The company chooses the most valuable IT investments.		
Alignment	The company achieves maximum returns from its IT activities.		
Performance Measurement	Performance measures lead to improved IT and business performance.		
Strategy-to-Bottom-Line Value Chain	IT processes, NIE Practices, and corporate processes are connected and consistent.		
IT Impact Management	IT's contribution to business performance is maximized.		
Portfolio Management	The entire IT investment contributes to business performance.		
Culture Management	IT's contribution to business performance is maximized.		

By conducting a maturity assessment and completing the Scorecard (see Exhibit 13.4) using a framework such as that shown in the list below, the as-is can be defined for a company. A to-be determination of where the company wants to be identifies exactly where focus should be placed, to establish a goal for process improvement. By doing so, company management can substantially improve how it controls the IT spend, and produces improved IT bottom-line impact.

The basic indicators for maturity levels, described in Chapter 12, are:

Level 0—Nonexistent,

Level 1—Initial/Ad Hoc

Level 2—Repeatable but Intuitive

Level 3—Defined Process

Level 4—Managed and Measurable

Level 5—Optimized

Chapter 12 contains detailed definitions of each level as applied to each NIE practice.

EXHIBIT 13.5   Assessment Form—Part I

Business Value Maturity Model™ High-Level Assessment Form								
Practice Title	**Practice Description** (The description is established in Chapters 8 through 10.)	**Instructions** • Check the one that most closely describes the *current state of affairs. This is the As-Is.* • Circle the one that most closely states *what you believe is necessary* to achieve *Strategy-to-Bottom-Line Value Chain goals.* This is the To-Be.						Rank 1 to 9
		Nonexistent	Initial/Ad Hoc	Repeatable/ Intuitive	Defined Process	Managed and Measurable	Optimized Processes	Importance
Demand/ Supply Planning	Explicitly connecting IT strategies and plans to business strategic intentions. Establishing the business strategic demand for IT, and then IT's strategies and plans for the supply of the necessary IT capabilities.	0 ☑	1 ☑	2 ☑	3 ☑	4 ☑	5 ☑	
Innovation	Translating IT opportunities into new business strategic intentions and finding new ways for IT to support existing strategic intentions.	0 ☑	1 ☑	2 ☑	3 ☑	4 ☑	5 ☑	
Prioritization	Assessing the business impact of new IT initiatives and prioritizing them according to strategic intentions.	0 ☑	1 ☑	2 ☑	3 ☑	4 ☑	5 ☑	
Alignment	Assessing the business impact and support of business strategic intentions of the existing IT infrastructure, applications, and services. Assessing the quality and service levels for existing IT resources, as input to demand/supply planning.	0 ☑	1 ☑	2 ☑	3 ☑	4 ☑	5 ☑	
Performance Measurement	Measuring IT performance in ways related to the business and its strategic intentions.	0 ☑	1 ☑	2 ☑	3 ☑	4 ☑	5 ☑	
Strategy-to-Bottom-Line Value Chain	Connecting the processes doing planning, innovation, prioritization, alignment, and performance measurement with themselves and with the other appropriate company processes.	0 ☑	1 ☑	2 ☑	3 ☑	4 ☑	5 ☑	

Exhibit 13.5 shows the scoring that can be used to define the as-is and to-be. The scoring provides for both the as-is and the to-be on the same sheet. A second scoring sheet that covers the NIE support areas is shown in Exhibit 13. 6. This provides for rank-ordering the importance of the practice, and consequently the steps to be followed in establishing a roadmap.

EXHIBIT 13.6　　Assessment Form—Part II

Business Value Maturity Model™								
High-Level Assessment Form								
Practice Title	**Practice Description** (The description is established in Chapters 8 through 10.)	**Instructions** • Check the one that most closely describes the *current state of affairs. This is the As-Is.* • Circle the one that most closely states *what you believe is necessary* to achieve *Strategy-to-Bottom-Line Value Chain goals. This is the To-Be.*						Rank 1 to 9
		Nonexistent	Initial/Ad Hoc	Repeatable/ Intuitive	Defined Process	Managed and Measurable	Optimized Processes	Importance
IT Impact Management	Establishing and achieving IT's business value proposition. Managing IT based on business value outcomes.	0 ☑	1 ☑	2 ☑	3 ☑	4 ☑	5 ☑	
Portfolio Management	Establishing baseline, business value, and performance information for the entire IT investment.	0 ☑	1 ☑	2 ☑	3 ☑	4 ☑	5 ☑	
Culture Management	Establishing baseline, business value, and performance information for the entire IT investment.	0 ☑	1 ☑	2 ☑	3 ☑	4 ☑	5 ☑	

Note that Chapter 12's Appendix A offers considerably more information about the maturity model for each practice, which can assist in determining the best as-is and to-be answers.

Method 3: Setting Goals Based on Practical Problems

Chapter 7 introduced seven basic problems affecting management perspectives about IT. By determining whether the problems discussed in Chapter 7 apply to a company, management can set goals adopting Right Decisions/Right Results. Exhibit 13.7 provides a short instrument for this purpose; each Practical Problem statement can be answered with a simple "yes" or "no."

Based on "yes" answers to the questions in Exhibit 13.7, goals for addressing the problems can be adopted. Exhibit 13.8 identifies specific goals that can be accomplished, in terms of specific directions for overcoming culture and process difficulties. These solutions were suggested in Chapter 7 as part of IT Impact Management, discussed below.

EXHIBIT 13.7 Establishing the As-Is for Practical Problems

Practical Problem	Current Company Situation	As-Is—Practical Problem Description
Process Disconnects		Existing management processes are unable to consistently carry through from business planning to IT action to bottom-line results.
Legacy and Entitlement		The company's existing IT applications, infrastructures, and project backlogs are the legacy of the current inadequate strategy-to-results management practices and prevent starting with a clean slate. Managers feel entitled to "their" systems and support.
Management Roles		The company's management culture prevents business and IT management from playing the roles needed to effectively direct and apply IT resources to achieve maximum bottom-line impact.
Company Processes		The new or changed management practices that connect business and IT will have to coexist and work with many other existing company management practices (e.g., capital budgets, HR, management performance/compensation, corporate budgets, purchasing, and so forth).
Management Expectations		Senior company managers expect only financial returns from IT and simple ROI-based measurement of its alignment and affordability.
It Ain't Broke		Business and IT managers get what they need from current processes, and they resist new processes that appear to make it more difficult to obtain what they need.
Multiple Perspectives		The company does not speak with one voice.

EXHIBIT 13.8 To-Be Goals

Practical Problem	To-Be—IT Impact Management Goals
Process Disconnects	Connect and coordinate with company practices—budgets and planning. Connect with people performing these practices. Engage management across the company in NIE practices.
Legacy and Entitlement	Examine 100% of IT spend from affordability perspective. Engage management in prioritization and alignment, and alignment assessment for quality and service level.
Management Roles	Management involvement in decision making through prioritization, alignment, budget, and planning.
Company Processes	Employ Strategy-to-Bottom-Line Value Chain from business planning through technology management through corporate budget processes. Engage the corporate process owners (e.g., CFO, corporate budgets) in the NIE practices and the deliverables of the Value Chain.
Management Expectations	Engage senior management and management process owners in strategic intention thinking, through prioritization and IT spend control.
It Ain't Broke	IT Impact Management, a program management approach focusing on management engagement in NIE practices that establishes the basis by which they understand the objectives and outcomes.
Multiple Perspectives	All business units are represented in management groups in each NIE process.

We suggest a company can adopt the goals listed in Exhibit 13.8, which will serve to focus on exactly what needs to be accomplished. While this practical problem approach is not as practice-specific as the other two methods, it works well to establish goals for management process change. These goals can also be established in conjunction with the specific steps to be taken, as identified in the first two methods.

SETTING GOALS FROM A CORPORATE GOVERNANCE AND PROCESS PERSPECTIVE

The focus, until this point, has been on specific IT management processes such as prioritization and alignment, and on IT performance in its role in the company.

An alternative is to view the as-is problems from a corporate or company-wide perspective. The Strategy-to-Bottom-Line Value Chain, introduced in Chapter 6, gives the right perspective on this.

EXHIBIT 13.9   Strategy-to-Bottom-Line Value Chain

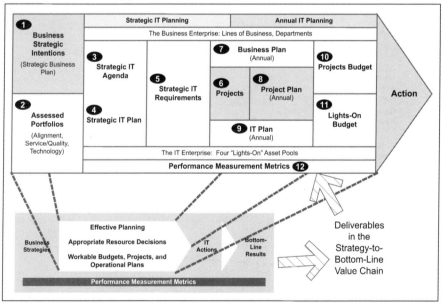

The corporate or company-wide management processes that produce the business strategic plan (Deliverable 1 as shown in Exhibit 13.9), annual plans (Deliverables 7, 8, and 9) and budgets (Deliverables 10 and 11) provide an alternative point for introducing Right Decisions/Right Results and NIE practices. Often, the CFO of the organization, who typically owns these processes, is a good leverage point.

The CFO, for example, should be vitally interested in controlling IT spend and improving IT bottom-line impact. As a consequence, the NIE practices can be supported and encouraged by the CFO as a means for submitting and reviewing IT plans and/or budgets. The core idea is to use the discipline and company-wide standards that come with corporate processes such as budgeting and capital planning as a vehicle for introducing change into IT management methods. This approach also directly addresses the process disconnect problems that we've discussed throughout the book.

The goals for adopting Right Decisions/Right Results and the NIE practices are based on working backward from these corporate process deliverables. (See Chapter 6 for a complete definition of each of the deliverables shown in Exhibits 13.9 and 13.10.)

EXHIBIT 13.10   Establishing the Roadmap

		Deliverable Name	Deliverable Description	Roadmap Perspective	Corporate Process Connection
Strategic Planning	1	Business Strategic Intentions	Mission plus weighted strategic intentions	Required as part of project business case documentation: specifically, how the project supports business strategic intentions.	Capital, corporate budgeting
	2	Assessed Portfolios	As-is alignment, service, quality, technology, use	Required as part of annual plan or budget submission. Required as input to IT project planning, with specific reference to the gaps to-be filled by the project.	Annual plan
	3	Strategic IT Agenda for Use of IT	Strategic Intentions to Strategic Initiatives		
	4	Strategic IT Plan	Strategic Intentions to Strategic Initiatives		
	5	IT Strategic Requirements	Initiatives—3 to 5 years horizon—portfolio format		
Annual/Tactical Planning	6	Projects	Real, doable projects	Business case requires connection to strategic intentions; reference to as-is assessed portfolios.	Capital, corporate budgeting
	7	Annual Project Plan	One year annual horizon—with portfolio format	Prioritized against strategic intentions.	Capital budgeting, corporate budgeting
	8	Annual Business Plan	Documentation according to company practices		
	9	Annual IT Plan	Documentation according to company practices	Strategies and plans connected to business strategic intentions and the Strategic IT Agenda.	Annual plan
	10	Annual and Capital Projects Budgets	Documentation according to company practices	Prioritized against strategic intentions.	Capital, corporate budgeting
	11	Annual Lights-On Budget	Documentation according to company practices	Budgets specifically apply assessed portfolios (through alignment) and business strategic intentions.	Corporate budgeting
	12	Performance Measurement Metrics	Documentation according to company practices	IT metrics consistent with business strategic intentions.	Performance measurement

By focusing on the corporate process connections (capital budgeting, corporate budgeting, annual plan, performance measurement, etc.) and their owners, and by introducing the Value Chain deliverables as components required in their processes, goals, and a specific plan for applying them, can be delivered.

The truly important thing here is that controlled IT spend and improved IT bottom-line impact goals are directly in the interests of the corporate process owners, and they should be interested in helping to achieve the goals.

THE IT IMPACT MANAGEMENT PROGRAM TO IMPLEMENT RIGHT DECISIONS/RIGHT RESULTS AND NIE PRACTICES

We encourage management teams to adopt one or more elements of the Strategy-to-Bottom-Line Value Chain, based on the goals established in the methods described above. However, management teams must understand that, to be effective, outcomes have to connect to budget and management actions for both IT and business. For example, as we have pointed out, prioritization without affecting project budgets, or alignment without affecting lights-on budgets, does not accomplish anything. Planning that does not change projects, or change budgets, does not accomplish anything.

As a result, achieving the management process goals we suggest can require a long-term, possibly multi-phased effort. It is very unlikely, in our view, that company or IT management can accomplish all elements at one time. Given the culture issues, the difficulty of change, and the significant number of players affected, it may make more sense to explicitly adopt a multiphase, multiprocess-cycle approach. This makes a program approach important. (We want to be clear on this. It is very useful for a management team to perform one of the NIE practices, such as prioritization. As we discussed in Chapter 11, this experience can have a major impact on management culture, and encourage further adoption of NIE practices. Accordingly, we do not discourage a management team from considering adopting one practice as a starting point, as a proof of concept. But we also emphasize that, to actually affect the IT spend and IT's bottom-line impact, the connection to corporate processes is needed. Adopting one practice is a starting point but probably will not provide the significant outcomes for which we hope.)

Companies do best by adopting an overall "program" approach to implementing a Right Decisions/Right Results and NIE practices. We introduced IT Impact Management in Chapter 6, and described its role in addressing practical problems in Chapter 7. In addition to thinking through the above suggestions for defining the as-is, and the culture management and maturity model instruments, a program approach establishes an overall framework for the effort. This framework identifies participants, establishes methods for communications, defines overall goals, and generally works to assure that all management groups are on the same page with respect to the need for and the planned changes expected to be implemented. Exhibit 13.11 reminds us of the many groups affected.

EXHIBIT 13.11 Management Processes Involved in the Value Chain

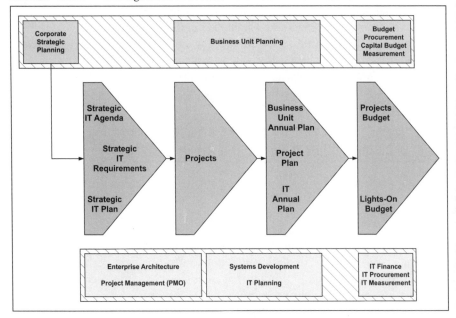

A Program

A program for a particular company will depend on the specific problem and circumstance, as well as its culture and politics. Generally, however, a program consists of four basic elements.

1. Define the program requirements.
2. Manage the program stakeholders.
3. Establish program participants.
4. Create bottom-line impact.

Note that this program discussion does not deal with content—that is, the specific practices or deliverables to be addressed. Those are defined by the roadmap approaches we described above. Here, we assume that we know *where* we want to go (e.g., prioritization, planning); now the issue is *how* to get there, in general terms.

The primary flavor of this program is based on managing the many players and organizations affected. In simple terms, we are dealing with issues that cross the IT and business unit barriers. But within that simplicity, we are dealing with multiple parts of IT (e.g., enterprise architecture, systems development, IT planning, IT financial management, IT governance) and multiple parts of the business (e.g., corporate processes like budget and planning, business unit management, individual user departments).

Also, note that we have dealt with issues of management participation as parts of each individual practice (e.g., in prioritization: who participates in scoring projects, who carries out business case development, what standards are associated with that, etc.). Here, we are focusing on the overall set of activities. We cannot lose sight of the fact that our success is ultimately based on making the connections all the way from business strategic intentions to the actions that ultimately affect the IT spend and IT's bottom-line impact. As we have observed before, it is not merely a question of completing a practice (e.g., prioritization); it's a matter of getting the results of that practice into annual plans, budgets, and ultimately action.

The focus here, then, is on the program approaches that will succeed in making the connections to action and ultimately bottom-line impact. The following discussion will refer back to the Chapter 7 presentation of practical problems as the impediments to success. The IT Impact Management program approach is designed to specifically overcome those impediments. They are in the nature of suggestions, as every company situation is unique. But they are suggestions rooted in the experience of companies that have been successful in adopting the concepts and practices described in this book.

1. *Define the program requirements.* This is the process of defining exactly what can be accomplished and the tasks needed to accomplish it. The key

EXHIBIT 13.12   Establish the Program

	IT Impact Management	Practical Problem Addressed
Establish the program	Build the program to be responsive to the politics in a positive, responsive way. Focus on doing what's practical, in terms of responding to the politics.	Legacy and entitlement Management roles Company processes
	Determine hurdles, impediments, and problems, and strategize to respond to each, with specific program elements.	All
	Establish a phased approach to the adoption of Value Chain and NIE Practices. Plan the program to do something tactical and simple in the short term.	Process disconnects Legacy and entitlement Company processes It ain't broke
	Establish a clear, simple, practical vision of the problem being solved and the outcome to be produced. Establish continuing means for communicating this vision to all managers affected.	Management roles It ain't broke Management expectations
	Establish a clear and simple theme and banner headline (e.g., we're examining lights-on budget, with focus on affordability).	Management expectations It ain't broke
	Focus on measuring outcomes and, if needed, establish a parallel Performance Measurement/ Metrics project.	Management expectations

is to match the program against culture, politics, and practical outcomes. A general framework is shown in Exhibit 13.12.

2. ***Manage the program stakeholders.*** This consists of the actions to keep the program on track and connected to the managers and business units affected by it. The key is to communicate effectively to all managers involved. A general framework is shown in Exhibit 13.13.

EXHIBIT 13.13   Stakeholder Management

	IT Impact Management	**Practical Problem Addressed**
Manage the program stakeholders	Establish one-on-one personal connections to the other corporate and IT process owners (e.g., budgets, CFOs, PMO, performance measurement, enterprise architecture); getting them on board with respect to the problem and outcome.	Process disconnects Management roles Company processes
	Create strawman example of results and management benefits to be derived.	Multiple perspectives
	Conduct continuous communication of vision, outcomes, and intermediate results to peer managers, both within IT and the business.	Process disconnects Management roles It ain't broke Multiple perspectives
	Hold the hands of every IT manager with respect to the process and the outcomes.	Legacy and entitlement It ain't broke

3. ***Establish program participants.*** This consists of a single basic step of establishing workgroups for each practice area. Though simple, this is an underlying foundation, for it addresses most of the major problems in doing this work. Getting management directly involved, from senior to each business unit to each process area, is the core idea for addressing culture and process disconnects and setting management expectations. A framework is shown in Exhibit 13.14.

EXHIBIT 13.14   Program Participants

	IT Impact Management	**Practical Problem Addressed**
Establish program participants	Establish a management workgroup for each practice.	Management roles Management expectations It ain't broke Multiple perspectives

4. ***Create bottom-line impact.*** This is the outcome we're seeking. The key idea is to provide leadership and suggested content, throughout all the practices

and through engaging all managers and workgroups. A framework is shown in Exhibit 13.15.

Although the above IT Impact Management discussion is intended as a framework, with suggestions, experience has shown that they are the kinds of things needed to be successful.

EXHIBIT 13.15   Bottom-Line Impact

	IT Impact Management	Practical Problem Addressed
Create bottom-line impact	Provide the leadership for each workgroup.	Process disconnects
	Develop the strawman inputs to things like Strategic Intentions.	Process disconnects Multiple perspectives
	Use prototype for data collection, analysis, and demonstration of outcome.	Process disconnects It ain't broke
	Persist through several cycles.	Process disconnects Company processes Management expectations

CONCLUSION TO CHAPTER 13

The challenge we address is how both business and IT leadership can work together to *improve* the impact their IT resources have on the financial performance of the company. In simple terms, we answer questions like: "Are we spending our resources in the right places?" and "Are we spending the right amount on IT?" These questions are preparatory to "How can we get results from IT?" and, ultimately, "How can we drive our business strategies to effective IT actions?" These are important, critical issues for management. The key part is that these are practical solutions. Business and IT management can get the answers to these questions and, therefore, produce action and impact—the right business results—from IT. See Exhibit 13.16.

The five NIE practices have developed and evolved in the two decades since the original *Information Economics* book. The core concept has remained as powerful as when we started in 1985: that IT has to fundamentally improve how the business[1] performs, and to do this, business management must be directly involved in IT decision making. The NIE goals further elaborate this core concept, defining exactly what the business goals are, assessing and prioritizing alternatives, and implementing the right ones and measuring the results. The five practices implement the ways and means for achieving the goals.

Right Decisions/Right Results is an integrated approach to connecting and integrating an enterprise's strategic intentions with the IT capabilities and activities that can enable them. New Information Economics is a complete and

EXHIBIT 13.16   IT Improvement Zone

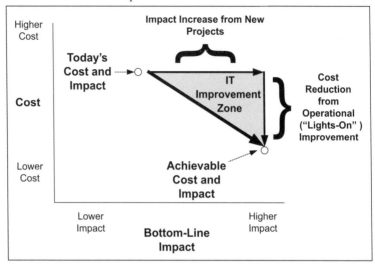

proven suite of tools to coordinate planning, innovation, prioritization, align-ment, and performance measurement activities within the enterprise. We have seen these methods help companies make major advances in their business.

The individual methods can also be applied as stand-alone activities to address specific issues, and they can be applied to all areas of the business, not just IT. All five of the activities use the same techniques to develop management con-sensus and produce implementable action plans that support enterprise strate-gic intentions.

However, even though we offer five practice areas to deal with the issues, this is not merely a management practice book. The basic problems we face, and their solution, are at least as much a management culture problem as a practice problem. Consequently, we address culture directly, and address these problems as being of equal importance. The most elegant and well-defined practice means nothing if the management team is unwilling or incapable of applying it.

In Chapter 1, we set the basic framework for the book, in these terms:

Right Results: The "right results" we want are to control IT's cost and at the same time improve bottom-line impact.

Right Decisions: The "right decisions" lead to the management actions needed to produce the right results. These right decisions lead to:

- Creating better investment alternatives, or in IT terms, creating better ideas for development projects
- Choosing the right investments and projects from the alternatives

- Eliminating nonperforming and poorly performing existing IT resources from current spending
- Improving the performance of the remaining existing IT resources
- Producing the right actions by business and IT managers to implement and follow through on the right investments and performance improvements

The book carries through in presenting frameworks, concepts, and processes to make the right decisions and produce the bottom-line impact and controlled IT expenses.

We expect that companies and management teams can apply the frameworks and processes to place themselves in the IT Improvement Zone. The characteristics of the IT Improvement Zone—the Right Decisions/Right Results Outcomes—are shown in Exhibit 13.17.

EXHIBIT 13.17   Right Decisions/Right Results Outcomes

NIE Practices and Support Practices	Process— Desired Outcomes	Business— Desired Outcomes
Strategic Demand/Supply Planning	IT and business planning are fully connected and integrated.	The company improves strategic and bottom-line impact from its IT investments.
Innovation	IT-enabled innovations impact business planning and offer new strategies.	The company excels in innovating through IT, in products, processes, and performance.
Prioritization	IT investments are prioritized against business strategy.	The company chooses the most valuable IT investments in terms of bottom-line impact.
Alignment	The entire IT spend is aligned with business strategy.	The company improves returns from its IT activities in terms of bottom-line impact. The total IT spend is effectively controlled.
Performance Measurement	IT business and technical performance is tracked.	Performance measures lead to improved IT and business performance.
IT Impact Management	Business and IT management teams execute the processes that improve IT's contribution to business performance.	IT's contribution to bottom-line impact is improved. The total IT spend is effectively controlled.
Portfolio Management	Planning and management processes focus on the entire IT investment.	All IT investments and resources contribute to bottom-line impact.
Culture Management	IT and business managers participate effectively in all NIE-enabled processes.	IT's contribution to bottom-line impact is improved through the effective application of NIE practices.

The Strategy-to-Bottom-Line Value Chain and NIE practices, and the management processes we have introduced, are listed by chapter in the table below.

Chapter	Chapter Title	Key Framework or Process
1	Define the Goals	Right Decisions/Right Results Templates
2	Ask the Right Questions	The Right Questions
3	Connect to the Bottom Line	Shareholder Value and Bottom-Line Principles
4	Understand Costs and Resources	Portfolio Management
5	Focus on the Right Things	Right Decisions/Right Results Goals and Principles
6	Adopt Effective Process to Produce Action	Strategy-to-Bottom-Line Value Chain
7	Tackle the Practical Problems	IT Impact Management
8	Make the Right Decisions	Prioritization and Alignment Practices
9	Plan for the Right Results	Planning and Innovation Practices
10	Keep Score	Performance Measurement Practice
11	Deal with Culture	Culture Management
12	Chart the Path to Implementation	The Business Value Maturity Model™
13	Define What's Next	IT Impact Management
14	Answer the "So What?" Question	The IT Improvement Zone

ADDITIONAL READING

The book's website contains additional information:

Website Note 4: Tests for Connected Business and IT

The appendices also contain related information for Chapter 13:

Appendix A: The Role of Enterprise Architecture in Right Decisions/Right Results

Appendix B: Management Team Roles in Right Decisions/Right Results

Appendix E: The CFO Role in Right Decisions/Right Results

NOTES

1. Although the terminology here and throughout the book is in "business" terms, the concepts and practices apply with equal force to government and nonprofit organizations. While business is concerned with competitive strategy and financial outcomes, government is just as concerned with strategy and performance to organizational mission.

CHAPTER 14

Answer the "So What?" Question

WHY THIS TRIP IS NECESSARY

The Right Decisions/Right Results message is straightforward: First, tell people what the business is trying to accomplish in simple, actionable statements, and second, get business and IT people to use a common and integrated set of management tools to get those things done. The result is also straightforward: The business ends up spending money and focusing people's efforts on activities that most fully support the business's strategies and goals, and stops spending resources on things that don't. The IT budget is more effectively controlled and IT's impact on the bottom line is improved. Using NIE practices moves the company from business strategy to IT action to bottom-line results in an efficient, consistent way.

After almost 50 years of IT being used in business, these messages may be commonly understood but are infrequently put into practice. Companies continue to take an anecdotal, piece-meal approach to IT investments, and the business–IT connection, while improving, remains fragmented in most organizations. However, NIE practices improve the business–IT connection by providing processes and tools for translating business strategies into actionable IT goals, choosing the IT activities that best support those business strategies, and helping IT measure performance against those goals.

Integrating these processes leverages the entire range of IT activities and turns every dollar spent on IT into a carefully considered investment in making the

Control Spending and Maximize Impact on the Bottom Line
1   Define the Goals
2   Ask the Right Questions
3   Connect to the Bottom Line
4   Understand Costs and Resources
5   Focus on the Right Things
6   Adopt Effective Process to Produce Action
7   Tackle the Practical Problems
8   Make the Right Decisions
9   Plan for the Right Results
10   Keep Score
11   Deal with Culture
12   Chart the Path to Implementation
13   Define What's Next
14   Answer the "So What?" Question

company successful. By taking a complete view of IT investment, from business strategy to performance measurement, company management can be sure that IT is doing what the company wants, when it's wanted, and having a significant impact on the company's intended business performance.

FIRST, HIT THE IT IMPROVEMENT ZONE

It is clear what CEOs, CFOs, CIOs, and anyone who is interested in the bottom line of the company want: controlled costs and better results from IT. To achieve that, we need to look at two parts of IT: lights-on expenses and new development projects (including both impact *and* cost). Although we split IT budgets this way, clearly a dollar is a dollar everywhere in the business. Dollars spent on IT are dollars not spent on other parts of the company (and, more critically, are not profit), and dollars spent on unnecessary lights-on expenses are dollars not spent on new projects that will improve IT's impact.

The key to controlled budgets and better impact is hitting the IT Improvement Zone (see Exhibit 14.1). No budget in any company is without "excess" expenses. By focusing NIE practices on the alignment, service level, and quality of lights-on budgets, management can improve the overall cost structure of IT by eliminating or redeploying "excess" resources (and improving the bottom-line impact as well). In conjunction, by focusing all new IT development on the highest bottom-line impact projects, IT's contribution to the business can be increased dramatically.

Obviously, no company will hit the ideal of the "Achievable Cost and Impact" target due to cultural, process, and other constraints. But, by using NIE practices

EXHIBIT 14.1 The IT Improvement Zone

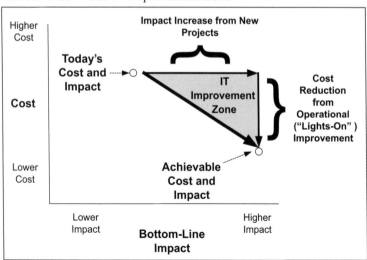

wherever and whenever possible, the company can move from today's situation into the IT Improvement Zone and achieve higher impact with lower costs.

THE "SO WHAT?" FOR THE COMPANY

NIE principles and practices help business get from strategy to IT action to bottom-line impact. Putting these practices in place is straightforward; keeping them in action and having the discipline to follow through is difficult. The hard issues of moving from strategy to action are outside of the processes themselves but are integral parts of the impact that adopting NIE practices can have on a company. NIE practices tackle these hard issues head on and become the tools for solving them.

Cultural barriers loom large in changing any company's processes, especially when a silo orientation gets in the way of company-wide thinking and planning. Using NIE practices forces a company-wide and portfolio-based view of IT investments, effectively changes the cultural issues that obstruct the most effective IT investments, and begins the process of eliminating the silo-think present in many companies. Business management becomes engaged not only in IT planning and execution but also in a company-wide process of evaluating the best places to spend IT resources. The process eventually becomes secondary; the way that management thinks about and acts on IT possibilities becomes the most important impact of adopting these principles and concepts.

NIE practices must also operate in an existing business planning/budgeting/performance measurement environment. The proposed practices tie directly into these parts of the company's management processes and leverage the structures that the company uses for all of its investments in business strategy.

Finally, NIE practices promote a consistent, integrated approach to the five practices in the strategy-to-results chain. Each is helpful on its own, but an integrated adoption of all five can "supercharge" a company's efforts.

Many things work to break the strategy-to-results chain. NIE practices help get rid of these roadblocks and let managers focus on actions, not obstacles.

THE "SO WHAT?" FOR THE CEO

For the CEO, IT is but one tool for implementing business strategies. Unfortunately it is often the least understood tool, leading to ineffective IT investments and misdirected IT resources. Although the business strategies may seem to be clear and adequately articulated, the interpretations of those strategies throughout the company may differ, and this eventually results in poorly focused IT investments. The CEO is left to ask, "Why am I spending so much and getting so little?"

The more appropriate question to ask may be, "Which IT-enabled business initiatives give the most business bang for the buck?" By integrating the strategy-to-results processes, the CEO can have more confidence that the company is spending money where it will have the most impact and is avoiding spending money that won't contribute to business success.

Additionally, by introducing the notion of "affordability," Right Decisions/Right Results puts IT on notice that every dollar is valuable to the company and makes sure that every dollar spent—whether for new investments, infrastructure, or lights-on activities—will be examined, justified, and managed. The result for the CEO is a controlled IT budget and improved business results.

THE "SO WHAT?" FOR THE CFO

For the CFO, IT is also only one possible way to invest scarce dollars to support business strategies. Years of questionable IT results, indefensible ROI methods, and infrastructure "sunk costs" have moved many CFOs into a skeptical posture. The CFO is asking a simple question: By what means can I judge the return on the IT investment?

Again, the better question may be, "How can I evaluate widely different IT investments with a consistent, business-based yardstick?" By giving business management a consistent tool for assessing the business impact of projects across the company and by quantifying an investment's impact on business strategies, the NIE practices and principles give the CFO a solid way to choose IT investments from among a range of IT possibilities.

The CFO is also charged with controlling the expenses and budgets of the company. With IT, it's hard to ensure that all budgets—especially the lights-on budgets that are always defended on "keep the doors open" grounds—are being effectively controlled and wisely invested. The NIE practices give the CFO a tool to set a top-line limit on IT expenses (setting affordability targets) with the assurance that the IT and business managers have the tools and processes to make rational, business-impact-based investment decisions for the entire IT spend. IT expenses are controlled, and bottom-line impact is improved.

THE "SO WHAT?" FOR LINE OF BUSINESS MANAGEMENT

Business management has a simple message for IT: Spend money in the right places (from a business perspective), do what you say you will do for us, and tell us about all of that in words we understand. (And oh, also, get rid of all of our technology headaches in the meantime.) Unfortunately, this message begs important questions: How does IT decide where "the right places" are, what are the best ways to talk about what IT is promising, and what words does business understand?

Again, the fragmented business–IT connection introduces problems in two areas. First, the conversation between business mangers and IT managers occurs anecdotally, often in a business planning vacuum (or, at least, in a context significantly disconnected from business planning processes) and with no common language for describing goals and performance. Second, and sometimes even more destructively, business managers cannot agree among themselves (or simply don't think they need to) about where IT should be spending its resources—again, with no common language for understanding IT activities and alternatives.

NIE principles and practices provide a means for taking business's simple message to IT and making it operational for both business and IT management. Starting with strategic intentions, business management, often for the first time, can agree on the language, intent, and relative importance of the things it is trying to accomplish. This common language provides a consistent way for management as a group to look at IT activities and evaluate their potential impact on the business. These same strategic intentions communicate to IT exactly what the business wants from it, in terms of business outcomes, and gives IT a way to describe to the business how its activities will help achieve those intentions.

Additionally, NIE practices are explicitly intended to tie into the business planning, budgeting, and performance processes already in place in the company. IT planning and execution ceases to become an "over there" phenomenon and starts to be integrated into the business planning and execution fabric of the company.

Finally, and most significantly, the NIE practices produce an important side effect that in the long run may be the most significant result. Companies that adopt these practices and concepts tend to develop a new culture for employing, managing, and leveraging IT, in which IT is an integral part of all business activities. Business and IT managers become partners in employing IT for business results; IT people become active contributors to the business success of the company; and everyone involved communicates in terms of business goals and business performance measures. In short, businesspeople understand what IT can really do for the company, and IT people understand what the business is trying to do in the first place.

THE "SO WHAT?" FOR IT MANAGEMENT

IT asks a simple question of the business: On what basis do we define projects, set priorities, allocate resources, evaluate performance, and help the business innovate using technology? Historically, business answers each question anecdotally, looking at individual initiatives, needs, and business strategies, without viewing all IT activities as a whole that is intended to contribute to business results.

IT can use NIE principles and practices to understand what it needs to do, based on the business results that the company is looking for. The practices help the business and IT, together, understand the business's strategic intentions, use them to assess the value of each IT initiative to the business, and set priorities and resource allocations on a consistent, agreed-on, business-focused basis. The conversation between business and IT changes from "what do we do next" to "what are the best things that IT can do for the business."

Perhaps most importantly for managing IT in the future, the NIE practices provide a disciplined, business-based way to make resource decisions in a cost-control environment. Often IT, and the business, are told to "cut X% of your costs," often in mid-year. The tools of alignment and prioritization give IT a structured way to control costs, with business participation, by focusing on bottom line impact, service and quality levels, and importance to the operations of the company.

THE "SO WHAT?" FOR THE BUSINESS

NIE is a set of practices and principles for moving from business strategy to IT action to bottom-line impact. NIE also requires and promotes a philosophical and cultural change in a company, and this moves the company from anecdotal and technology-focused assessment of IT activities to a holistic, business-results-oriented view of the IT–business connection. By implementing the practices and adopting the principles, the company moves, culturally and managerially, to a position in which IT is an active contributor to the business's performance.

While implementing the NIE practices may seem straightforward, getting results often requires significant change in the company's culture. Changing the culture is difficult at best and, in some cases, almost impossible. Business and IT management must together commit to the NIE principles, suffer the dis-locations in existing planning and execution processes, and work together to implement a new culture and philosophy for planning and managing IT.

CONTINUING DEVELOPMENT

This book is a work in progress. Further research and experience in companies in the United States and Europe will continue to develop these ideas. We expect to update chapter information on a regular basis.

Our websites, *www.NewInformationEconomics.com* and *www.beta-books. com,* contain directions on how to obtain future updates. We can be reached individually by e-mail at:

Bob Benson	*bbenson@aismail.wustl.edu*
Tom Bugnitz	*tbugnitz@aismail.wustl.edu*
Bill Walton	*wwalton@lincoln.midcoast.com*

The Role of Enterprise Architecture in Right Decisions/Right Results

Many companies apply enterprise architecture (EA) as part of their IT management and planning activities. From their perspective, it would seem that EA should play an important role in strategic planning (e.g., strategy demand/supply planning), alignment (e.g., assessment of the as-is IT activities), and prioritization (e.g., deciding on the projects to be implemented). They might see that right decisions means decisions driven by or guided by EA, and that right results means using EA to assure that projects do improve IT's bottom-line impact.

What should EA's role be in Right Decisions/Right Results? We address this in three parts: (1) What is EA? (2) How is EA applied? (3) What role does it play in Right Decisions/Right Results?

WHAT IS EA?

Several years ago, we contributed an EA article to an IT dictionary. Part of it said:

> Enterprise architecture describes the structure of a company in terms of means of production, customer service, strategy and objectives, and use of information and information technology. It provides models to portray component parts of a company and how they work together to achieve its business mission and goals. It connects the company's business structure, use of information and information technology, and the technology architectures needed.
>
> Enterprise architecture is a family of related architecture components. These include information architecture, organization and business process architecture, and information technology architecture. Each consists of architectural representations, definitions of architecture entities, their relationships, and specifications of function and purpose. Enterprise architecture guides the construction and development of business organizations and business processes, and the construction and development of supporting information systems.
>
> Diagrams and schematics are commonly used to represent enterprise architecture. For example, an entity-relationship diagram may portray enterprise information architecture, and an organization chart may portray the enterprise management structure. Such diagrams and schematics come from other disciplines such as organizational design. They have been adapted to describe enterprise architecture.

Enterprise architecture is a holistic representation of all the components of the enterprise, and the use of graphics and schematics are used to emphasize all the parts of the enterprise and how they are interrelated. Data and process models originally designed for computer application development are used in describing information architecture. For example, entity-relationship diagrams that describe information as a set of business entities (e.g., customer and products) and how they relate (e.g., customers order products) can also be used to represent an enterprise information architecture.

Enterprise architectures are used to deal with intra-organizational processes, inter-organizational cooperation and coordination, and their shared use of information and information technologies. Business developments, such as outsourcing, partnerships, alliances, and electronic data interchange, extend the need for architecture across company boundaries.

New technologies add to the need for enterprise architecture. Client-server approaches and related communications networks enable distribution of information and computer applications throughout the enterprise. The need for architecture includes rapid information technology proliferation, incompatible and non-communicating application systems, multiple networks, inaccessible data in parts of the enterprise, piecemeal technical solutions to business problems, uncoordinated developments in common areas of the enterprise, un-integrated data, and inadequate integrity and security of results.[1]

John Zachman is an effective spokesman for enterprise architecture. For over two decades, he has promoted a framework that describes the content of enterprise architecture, the models used, and their purposes. The simple diagram shown in Exhibit A.1 captures his ideas.

EXHIBIT A.1   Simplified Zachman Framework

	Data	**Function**	**Network**
Enterprise Model (Conceptual)	Enterprise-wide data model (e.g., Entity/Relationship model)	Enterprise-wide business process model	Enterprise business model (e.g., logical location model)
System Model (Logical)	Logical data model	Data flows	Geography-based processing model
Technology Model (Technical)	Database design	Process and task specification	System and network model

The chart states our interpretation of the purposes of the framework. While it oversimplifies the full Zachman Framework (for example, his framework has three more columns and several more rows), it does show some of the major components and the levels of models.[2]

The federal government places great emphasis on EA. The diagram in Exhibit A.2 describes the *Federal Enterprise Architecture* which is in the process of development. It is intended to guide federal agencies in the development of their technology plans and projects.

EXHIBIT A.2   Federal Government Reference Models

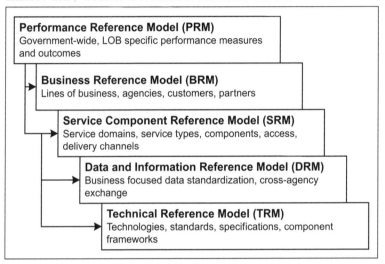

HOW IS EA APPLIED?

Ken Orr describes architectures as critical to managing the IT assets in large complex companies.[3]

We find that companies apply EA in two basic fashions. Most fundamentally, either the tools of EA—meaning the models that John Zachman categorizes in his framework—or the reference models that the federal government is defining, are used to describe the enterprise in an "as-is" and a "to-be" context.

The as-is is used in a documentation and knowledge management fashion; defining exactly how it is that the current enterprise functions and interrelates. Companies differ as to which elements of the models will be applied; most tend to focus more on the technology issues and much less on the business process and data aspects.

The to-be is used as a target definition for a future state. Again, companies differ as to which elements will be defined; most tend to focus on the technology to-be.

The as-is and, if available, the to-be architecture definitions are then used as a standards-enforcement tools for assessing proposed projects. If the to-be exists, then the projects can be fitted into a future-looking architecture. The as-is provides current standards and definitions. These are helpful for interoperability, interchange of information, and integration of the business processes. Again, the EA application is a standard or a framework with which to assess new projects and investments. See Exhibit A.3.

EXHIBIT A.3   Strategy-to-Bottom-Line Value Chain

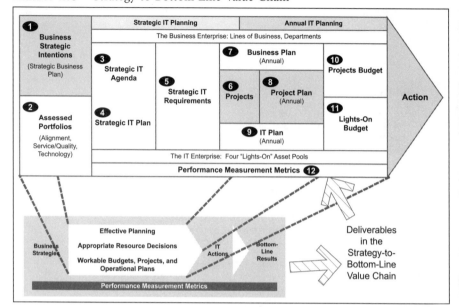

A second, much more dynamic use of EA is to generate better projects. In this role, EA provides insight into what those projects should be, by doing gap analysis between the as-is and to-be architectures. This use of EA makes it a strategic planning tool—in the sense that the decisions of the to-be models, particularly the data and function models in Zachman's terms, represent a strategic design for what the enterprise should look like. Hopefully, this occurs in response to business drivers and strategic intentions.

WHAT IS THE ROLE OF EA
IN RIGHT DECISIONS/RIGHT RESULTS?

In the context of the Strategy-to-Bottom-Line Value Chain shown in Exhibit A.3, EA can provide many of the key inputs into the processes that produce the deliverables. The important objective is the consistent connection of those processes and the consistency of the deliverable. What we do not want is a duplication of effort and multiple voices about planning, projects, prioritization, and annual plans. This can happen if the EA role isn't considered in the context of the Value Chain deliverables.

This very much depends on the role EA plays in the IT organization. Exhibit A.4 suggests some of the considerations. As every company situation is different, there are no absolute rules about this. But the questions about EA roles need to be answered.

Exhibit A.4 also suggests EA roles. Again, this is highly dependent on the company situation and role and capabilities of EA.

EXHIBIT A.4 Enterprise Architecture Role Template

		Deliverable Name	EA—As-Is Technology Focus	EA—To-Be Technology Focus	EA—with Business Process and Data Focus	EA To-Be with Gap Assessment for Projects
Strategic Planning	1	Business Strategic Intentions				
	2	Assessed Portfolios				
	3	Strategic IT Agenda for Use of IT				
	4	Strategic IT Plan				
	5	IT Strategic Requirements				
	6	Projects				
Annual/Tactical Planning	7	Annual Project Plan				
	8	Annual Business Plan				
	9	Annual IT Plan				
	10	Annual and Capital Projects Budgets				
	11	Annual Lights-On Budget				
	12	Performance Measurement Metrics				

NOTES

1. Robert J. Benson, "Enterprise Architecture," in *Blackwell Encyclopedic Dictionary of Management Information Systems,* edited by Gordon B. Davis (Oxford, UK: Blackwell, 1997), pp. 71–73.

2. There are many references to the Zachman model. Among the first is John A. Zachman, "A Framework for Information Systems Architecture," *IBM Systems Journal,* vol. 26, no. 3, 1987.

3. For a very good discussion of EA, see Ken Orr, "Frameworks and Processes for Developing Enterprise Architectures," *Cutter Executive Report,* vol. 6, no. 2, 2002.

Management Team Roles in Right Decisions/Right Results

This appendix discusses the relationship of Right Decisions/Right Results to the company's IT governance processes. It focuses on how governance processes are affected and in particular, how they cope with the complexities of modern corporations in terms of multiple business units and multiple lines of business. This appendix makes the basic point that the management roles in Right Decisions/Right Results is IT governance. One of our colleagues remarked, "It's not portfolio management, it's managing the place."

The thrust of Right Decisions/Right Results is the set of goals, principles, and management processes needed to control IT spending and improve IT's bottom-line impact. The Strategy-to-Bottom-Line Value Chain and the NIE practices define how these goals can be reached and how to reach them. See Exhibit B.1.

EXHIBIT B.1   Deliverables in the Strategy-to-Bottom-Line Value Chain

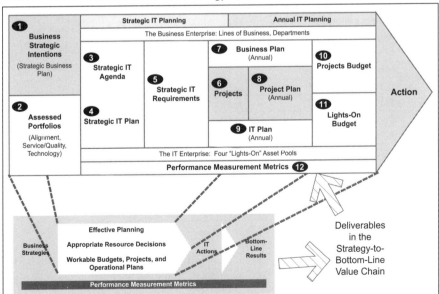

Throughout the discussion of the Value Chain and the NIE practices, management roles have been defined. Overall, we have defined a standard view of these roles (see Chapters 4 and 11) for each of the leadership teams.

These roles are specified in terms of the deliverables in the Value Chain (shown in Exhibit B.1). These deliverables are created in the company processes that deal with the topic. For example, the strategic intentions and the strategic IT plan deliverables are a result of the company processes that do business and IT planning. In Chapters 6 and 11, we discussed at length the cultural impediments involved and, in Chapter 14, how to address them.

To review, the leadership teams are defined in Chapters 6 and 11 as:

- *Senior Leadership Team*—typically comprised of the CEO and direct reports. These direct reports can include the chief executives of lines of business as well as functional ("CxO") reports.

- *Business Leadership Team*—typically made up of direct reports to the senior management team.

- *Technology Leadership Team*—typically the CIO and direct reports.

In addition, there's the team responsible for the Right Decisions/Real Results processes.

These teams are described as enterprise-wide. For example, the Business Leadership Team represents all the business functional areas and the key lines of business (if they are free-standing SBUs). Examining the roles we've identified for each of these teams looks a great deal like the governance role these groups should play in the management of IT. See Exhibit B.2.

EXHIBIT B.2   Senior Leadership Team Roles

	Deliverable Name	Senior Leadership Team
1	Business Strategic Intentions	Approve and weight strategic intentions
2	Assessed IT Portfolios	Review
3	Strategic IT Agenda for Use of IT	Approve
4	Strategic IT Plan	Review
5	IT Strategic Requirements	Review
6	Projects	Review, approve large projects
7	Annual Project Plan	Make decisions or approve funding
8	Annual Business Plan	Approve
9	Annual IT Plan	Approve
10	Annual and Capital Projects Budgets	Approve
11	Annual Lights-On Budget	Review
12	Performance Measurement Metrics	Approve

The role of the Senior Leadership Team is to review and approve the basic resource allocation and budget decisions made through the Right Decisions/Right Results processes. See Exhibit B.3.

EXHIBIT B.3   Role of the Business Leadership Team

	Deliverable Name	Business Leadership Team
1	**Business Strategic Intentions**	Revise and review strategic intentions
2	**Assessed Portfolios**	Assess portfolios/alignment, service, quality
3	**Strategic IT Agenda for Use of IT**	Develop IT agenda
4	**Strategic IT Plan**	Review IT plan
5	**IT Strategic Requirements**	Develop requirements Prioritization Recommend decisions
6	**Projects**	Create project requirements and business cases
7	**Annual Project Plan**	Prioritization Recommend funding
8	**Annual Business Plan**	Review IT plans Establish business unit plans
9	**Annual IT Plan**	Review
10	**Annual and Capital Projects Budgets**	Develop budgets
11	**Annual Lights-On Budget**	Review
12	**Performance Measurement Metrics**	Establish business performance metrics

The role of the Business Leadership Team is to operationalize the main activities, ranging from assessing the current as-is portfolios in the lights-on budget through creating and prioritizing projects and establishing budgets. The core of these activities is the business-driven establishment of requirements through projects, and then the determination of the financial resource allocations to realize them. See Exhibit B.4.

EXHIBIT B.4   Role of the Technology Leadership Team

	Deliverable Name	Technology Leadership Team
1	**Business Strategic Intentions**	
2	**Assessed Portfolios**	Contribute to portfolio development Assess portfolio/technology
3	**Strategic IT Agenda for Use of IT**	Participate in IT agenda process
4	**Strategic IT Plan**	Develop IT plan
5	**IT Strategic Requirements**	Participate in IT requirements process
6	**Projects**	Form detailed projects and technical requirements
7	**Annual Project Plan**	Establish annual project plan and schedules
8	**Annual Business Plan**	Advise
9	**Annual IT Plan**	Develop IT plans, establish budgets
10	**Annual and Capital Projects Budgets**	Participate in budget planning
11	**Annual Lights-On Budget**	Develop budget Initiate plans
12	**Performance Measurement Metrics**	Establish IT performance metrics

The role of the Technology Leadership Team is to support the process and generate IT plans and projects consistent with the business requirements established by the Business Leadership Team. See Exhibit B.5.

EXHIBIT B.5   Role of the Value Chain Process Owner

	Deliverable Name	Value Chain Process Owner (IT Impact Management)
1	Business Strategic Intentions	Create initial draft Strategic Intentions (strawman)
2	Assessed Portfolios	Manage portfolio development Manage the assessment process
3	Strategic IT Agenda for Use of IT	Create the initial drafts (strawman)
4	Strategic IT Plan	Create the initial drafts (strawman)
5	IT Strategic Requirements	Drive the process
6	Projects	Assure that project formation works right
7	Annual Project Plan	Drive the process
8	Annual Business Plan	Assure this happens
9	Annual IT Plan	Assure this happens
10	Annual and Capital Projects Budgets	Create initial draft (strawman)
11	Annual Lights-On Budget	Create initial draft (strawman)
12	Performance Measurement Metrics	Assure this happens Create initial drafts (strawman)

The role of the Right Decisions/Right Results team is to drive the process forward, work out the organizational, cultural, and political deals, and "make it happen." Chapter 14, "IT Impact Management," gives guidance on how to do this.

THE CHALLENGE OF MULTIPLE LINES OF BUSINESS AND GLOBAL BUSINESSES

Most reasonably sized companies have multiple lines of business. How do the management roles play in this situation?

The problem is most severe when each line of business has bottom-line, profit/loss responsibility. Typically, this means that centralized, or single-focus, planning and prioritization processes don't work well if they attempt to ration or allocate financial resources across the lines of business. The reason, of course, is that the chief executive of each line of business is essentially free to make his or her own decisions on resource allocation.

Companies that deal with this problem, particularly global companies where the problem is complicated by multiple-country operating locations and the likelihood of profit/loss responsibility devolved to the county level, have evolved a balance between central governance and the business units that has decentralized financial responsibility.

The corporate center's role is to establish standards and processes. These can include:

- *Definition of standard strategic intentions*—A corporate-wide set of strategic intentions, at least in terms of basic themes, can provide important guidance to the individual lines of business

- *Expectations of standard processes*—The corporate center can encourage and support each line of business to conduct the planning through bottom-line processes discussed in this book.

- *Preparation of standard budgets*—A standard budgeting format, focusing especially on costs within the lights-on portfolios, helps in company-wide communications and management.

- *Use of enterprise architectures and CTO roles*—This can help drive the planning processes in each line of business.

- *Definition of standard roles for management teams*—Perhaps the most important, this encourages each business unit to follow through on business-driven processes such as those stated above.

Viewed from the individual business unit perspective, they carry forward with Right Decisions/Right Results by doing some or all of the following:

- *Adjustment of the strategic intentions to the local business unit requirements*—Although the corporate framework might be appropriate, the specific details in terms of goals and weights are more likely to be different for each line of business.

- *Establishment of prioritization and alignment processes*—This is the basis for understanding the as-is IT spend and making the appropriate decisions for the to-be projects and ongoing lights-on budgets.

- *Establishment of planning process in the Value Chain*—Understanding the connection between strategic intention and bottom-line results, and taking action consistent with this understanding. This is how the business unit can control IT spend and improve IT's bottom-line impact.

- *Establishment of portfolios*—Understanding the total IT spend, particularly in the lights-on, is important to effective business-driven management. It is the basis for applying the basic NIE practices.

- *Implementation of management roles*—This is critical.

The Strategy-to-Bottom-Line Value Chain and the management roles provide for a way for both the corporate center and each business unit to think about and understand IT governance, as well as the connections to controlling IT spend and maximizing IT's bottom-line impact. The Value Chain provides the foundation for: (1) establishing the standards, (2) providing for cross-line of business issues (e.g., corporate-wide initiatives), and (3) enabling effective governance processes that connect from planning to the bottom line.

The Development of Strategic Intentions, with Examples

Appendix C's purpose is to discuss how "strategic intentions" can be documented for a company. A colleague wrote to us as he reviewed Chapter 3, saying: "Most IT professionals do not understand how to derive the strategic intentions of an organization through what management thinks is important. Management's actions and decisions outline their strategic intentions; we have to be smart enough to determine what that is and how we communicate IT's support of it."[1]

The problem in many companies is that there is little awareness of exactly what the company's strategic intentions are. (Note that strategic intentions do not equal strategy. Strategic intentions are what management intends to do, over time. Strategies are one of the means they have available to do them.) Most companies do have formal mission statements, often with a high-level strategy statement. For example, we worked with a financial services company that proudly pronounced its mission and strategy. Its stated mission: to provide a complete set of personal and corporate financial services in its region. Its stated strategy: to offer the highest quality services at the lowest costs possible, to the most customers in the region. However, what we really need to know is what management intends to do—that is, what its strategic intentions are. *How* will the company offer the highest quality services? *How* will those services be offered at the lowest costs possible? And so forth.

In another consumer products company, the overall enterprise goal was to improve relationships with customers. To achieve this, senior management developed strategic intentions for each area, such as customer service (e.g., establish call centers and manage them for improved customer relations), finance (e.g., improve all aspects of customer contacts for billing and collections), and marketing (e.g., develop comprehensive customer information). These strategic intentions were the basis for developing implementation strategies. Unfortunately, in this particular case the strategic intentions were not consistent with each other or with the overall goal. This is why clear strategic intentions are so important, and why it is critical that they become the organizing principles around which business units and IT focus their activities. This is why we use strategic intentions in each of the NIE practices, throughout the Strategy-to-Bottom-Line Value Chain.

Often, companies do have well-thought-out statements of management's strategic intentions. Where this is the case, we can adopt these statements directly and apply them throughout the NIE practices. If a company does not have a clear statement of its strategic intentions, then a management that is interested in applying NIE practices and the Value Chain needs to develop one, using what management is intending to do as a basis.

DEVELOPING STRATEGIC INTENTIONS

From a process perspective, we suggest a five-part approach:

1. Develop strawman statements of strategic intentions.
2. Review strawman statements with individual CxO and line-of-business chief executives.
3. Submit a revised statement to the senior leadership team.[2]
4. Circulate the revised statement to the business leadership team.
5. Agree on this statement as the basis on which to go forward.

It sounds simple, and it can be. Our experience has been that: (1) senior management teams do not invent strategic statements very easily, but (2) they respond very effectively when presented with strawman statements. Furthermore, there are plenty of clues as to what the strawman statement should contain. These include senior management messages to the company, budgets, significant programs and initiatives, annual reports, and any other indicator of what management is actually doing. By "doing," we emphasize those things on which senior management is, or is proposing to, spend money on.[3] Strawman statements also come from the management culture. See Chapter 13 for ideas on how culture can be defined.

A complicating factor can be the degree of independence of individual business units, particularly when they view themselves as conducting significantly different business activities from other business units. A large holding company with various business units is a clear example of this.

On the one hand, it is questionable whether IT is to be managed centrally in such a situation. Typically, a shared service organization provides data center and perhaps systems development services to the business units. But the drivers for determining IT spend and development investments may be unique to each business unit. In this case, the Real Decision/Real Results activities are most likely focused on each individual business unit. Then, the issue of strategic intentions is a business-unit-level issue. On the other hand, it may be company culture to use common strategic intentions for all business units but to allow those units to vary their relative importance (e.g., weighting for prioritization) and goal-setting (e.g., for establishing performance metrics). Finally, some companies have chosen to mix the two, using some corporate strategic intentions (with a predetermined weight relative to business unit strategic intentions) combined with strategic intentions specific to each business unit.

A WORKSHOP APPROACH

An alternative is to conduct a workshop, primarily with the Business Leadership Team. This workshop can be part of the Innovation practice activities, part of strategic planning, or part of the IT governance process. For example, some companies regularly convene an IT management committee as a steering committee to oversee IT activities. This group can participate in this workshop activity.

An example of a workshop agenda follows:

1. Introduction and expectations.

2. Facilitated discussion of issues and opportunities, enabled by "strawman" inputs developed by the facilitator prior to the workshop.

3. Focus on management strategic intentions, based on competitive conditions, strategy development.

4. Develop consensus on the most pertinent and important issues and opportunities.

5. Create preliminary strategic intention statements.

6. Closure based on crystallizing the results and positing the next steps to be accomplished.

Examples of questions for issues and opportunities include:

- What are the key business and competitive drivers affecting my markets, my industry, and my business? What are the key opportunities presented by the business change in markets, industry, and business?

- What are the critical things the management team intends to do: What are the most likely scenarios that describe what my company would need to do to respond to business changes and technology opportunities?

- What are the major initiatives that we'd need to undertake to meet these strategic intentions?

- What are the major hurdles that stand between my company and accomplishing any of these scenarios?

Examples of questions that can be used in developing strategic intentions include:

- What are my company's goals and strategies? What are the initiatives on which we're currently working?

- What are the basic principles on which my company rests?

- What major initiatives are most likely to be undertaken in the coming one to two years?

- What are the major initiatives that most likely would be necessary to achieve the scenario?

- What are the strategic intentions that best synthesize my company's goals, strategies, initiatives, and principles?

- Given these strategic intentions, which of the scenarios are most likely for my company? What is the priority of the scenarios, compared against the company's values and business goals?

Generally, such a workshop can be successful in producing a first round of strategic intentions statements suitable for use in the NIE practices.[4]

EXAMPLES OF STRATEGIC INTENTIONS

Several examples of strategic intentions were included in this book's chapters. They are repeated here for reference. Following these, several other examples are provided.

From Chapter 3

EXHIBIT C.1   Strategic Intentions 1

Strategic Intention Name	Strategic Intention Goals	Strategic Intention Metrics	Weight
Focus on Specific, Narrow Markets	• Focus on markets in which the company can profitably compete • Build strategic partnerships with key customers	• Market share in specific markets • Profitability in specific markets	30
Improve Efficiency through Common Business Practices	• Employ best practices throughout the company • Reduce the unique systems and processes in each operating location	• Percent of standard systems used throughout the company • Percent of standard processes in use throughout the company	10
Be the Lowest-Cost Supplier in Focused Markets	• Reduce the administrative, manufacturing, and operations costs of the company • Optimize purchasing power	• Production throughput • Net delivered cost of product	40
Grow through Acquisition	• Increase the capability of the company to rapidly integrate new applications and operations, with decreased cost	• Time to integrate a new acquisition or operation	20

From Chapter 8

EXHIBIT C.2   Strategic Intentions 2

Category		Standard Information Economics Strategic Intentions	Company One Example	Company Two Example	
Measurable Business Performance	A	Return on investment	Internal rate of return	Profitability index	
	B	Competitive impact	Effect on market share	Customer satisfaction	
Management Agenda (connection to business strategic intentions)	C	Management information	Connectivity and decision support	Product shelf life improvement	
	D	Strategic alignment	Quality performance	NA	
	E	Competitive response	Manufacturing cycle reduction	Empowered employee	
	F	IT strategic alignment	Comprehensive management system	Point of sale global	
Risk and Uncertainty	G	Project and organization risk	NA	NA	
	H	Definitional uncertainty	NA	NA	
	I	Technical uncertainty	NA	Project milestone achievements	
	J	IS infrastructure	NA	Enterprise network installation	
			Total weight	100	Total weight	100

From Chapter 8 *(Continued)*

EXHIBIT C.3   Strategic Intentions 3

Strategic Intention	Description	Goal	Key Metric	Weight
Wholesale Market Share	Attract, retain, and provide high-quality service to wholesaler	Strengthen the product line available to dealers Build the relationship based on wholesaler financial incentives	Wholesale market share Wholesalers satisfaction	50
Retail Market Share	Attract, retain, and provide high-quality service to end customers	Improve ease of doing business Provide effective products and financial incentives	Retail market share Customer satisfaction	20
Securitization/ Funding Efficiency	Capability to securitize receivables	Reduce cost of funds	Time to market Cost of funds	15
Reduce Losses/ Improve Portfolio Quality	Receivable portfolio quality and collection efficiency	Reduce collection losses Improve collection efficiency	Collection losses Wholesale losses Residual losses	10
Reduce Administrative and Operating Costs	Management and performance of all organizations and functions	Reduce the total cost of doing business	Administration percent of revenue	5

Other Examples

EXHIBIT C.4   Strategic Intentions 4

Strategic Intention Name	Strategic Intention Description
Support Business Growth	The Company will be capable of sustaining efficient operations during high business growth periods, such as that caused by mergers and acquisitions.
Intimate Knowledge about Customer and Producer Requirements	The Company will develop and maintain knowledge about the needs and requirements of its target producers and high end customers.
Complete and Integrated Management Information	The Company will develop complete and integrated information about products, producers, and customers and make it available throughout The Company and its distribution networks.
Simplified, Common Business Models and Processes	The Company will increase its efficiency by reducing the complexity and variations of its internal management and systems processes. The Company will move to a single business model and standard processes across the organization.
Strengthened Distributor Relationship	The Company will build and strengthen its relationships with highly productive producers.
Superior, Touch-Point-Sensitive Service to Producer and Customer	The Company will improve its services to producers and customers through improved systems capabilities and interfaces, particularly in key touch-point areas.

Other Examples (*Continued*)

EXHIBIT C.5 Strategic Intentions 5

Strategic Intention Name	Strategic Intention Description	Candidate Measure	Weight
Customer Request Response	The Company will respond to customer requests better than any competitor.	Customer satisfaction	15
Customer Product Response	The Company will lead the market in customizing products and responding to customer requests for new products.	Market share	9
Customer Relationships	The Company will lead the market in customized business and management relationships. [Providers will choose and remain with The Company because of these innovations.]	Customer retention	27
Management Information	The Company will lead the market in creating and using the best information to manage the Company business.	Benefit and utilization cost	9
Bottom-Line Performance	The Company will add $XM to the reserve.	Addition to reserve	18
Customer Growth	The Company will achieve 10 percent growth in customers.	Customers	11
Cost per Customer	The Company will reduce the rate of growth of cost per member by 50 percent.	Cost per customer	11

EXHIBIT C.6 Strategic Intentions 6

Name	Management Factor Description	Metrics	Weight
Customized Product Delivery	The Company will connect, and customize, the best channels for delivering product to each customer.	Revenue and profit	22
Customer Information Services	The Company will provide personalized information services to provide exactly the information the customer wants, when wanted.	Customer base	21
Product Development Time Cycle	The Company will continuously reduce the time from product conception to implementation.	Elapsed time and deadlines	19
Market-Driven Initiatives	The Company will create new products and services based on market demands.	Number of projects	17
Knowledge about Customer	The Company will develop complete information about its customers and markets.	Percent coverage consumers and markets	15
Virtual Enterprise	The Company will connect with Company suppliers and alliances to create seamless information services for customers.	Percent supplier costs via connection	7

NOTES

1. Thanks to Tom Porter, Rollins Corporation.
2. See Chapters 6 and 12 for the definition of the leadership team and the role its members play.

3. For those old enough to remember, we remind you that Deep Throat advised, during the Watergate investigation, to "follow the money." We believe that executive spending patterns are a significant indicator of what managers believe is important and, hence, what their intentions are.

4. There are some parallels between our approach to developing strategic intentions and the approaches taken for the development of "business maxims" as described in Peter Weill and Marianne Broadbent, *Leveraging the New Infrastructure: How Market Leaders Capitalize on Information Technology* (Boston, MA: Harvard Business School Press, 1998).

Applying Strategic Intentions in Prioritization

In a number of sections of this book, we referred to the concept of "cause and effect" as a way to determine the bottom-line impact of a proposed new investment on the set of strategic intentions. We tried to answer the question "if we undertake Project X, what will be the impact on Strategic Intention Y?" We repeated the question for each strategic intention and developed an overall assessment of the bottom-line impact of the project.

Using the same assessment scale for each project is key to this concept and to the Prioritization practice. First, we want to be sure that there is a level playing field for all projects and that all are assessed against the same yardstick. Second, we want to be sure that every manager involved in assessment uses the same vocabulary and means the same thing when he or she describes the bottom-line impact of a project. Finally, we want to add substance to the assessment and take it beyond simple "this is 3 on a scale of 0-5" answers to a scoring system that has a specific definition for each level of potential bottom-line impact.

We propose the scale in Exhibit D.1 as an example of a scoring tool for a specific strategic intention. Using a simple 0-5 scale, we use a consistent definition of bottom-line impact, varying by degrees the specific impact that the project will have on various characteristics specific to the strategic intention. Take the example of a bank that had as one of its strategic intentions an e-commerce initiative to provide services electronically while helping the bank improve its competitive position.

Strategic Intention: The bank will improve its competitive position by providing its services and products to customers through e commerce channels, including the Internet and all of its connection options (wireless, home, office, wireless phone, PDA, etc.).

In most cause-and-effect scales, 0 and 5 are easily defined: 0 is a project with no impact, while 5 is a project that is critical to the initiative. Note that in the example, though, scores 1–4 vary according to the impact of the project on competitive position and the type of services the bank can offer.

We propose that all scoring scales follow this format, so that managers can look at a project and use clear criteria, rather than intuition or gut feeling, to assess the impact of proposed projects.

EXHIBIT D.1 Cause and Effect Used in Prioritization

Cause-and-Effect Language	Score	Effect
• The Project has no relationship to electronic commerce objectives.	0	None
• The Project is indirectly related to providing electronic commerce-based products and services.	1	Minor
• The Project will enhance existing electronic commerce applications or products and services in a minor way, but will not measurably impact the bank's electronic commerce offerings.	2	Small
• The Project will create a new electronic commerce product or service, but will not significantly change the bank's competitive position in electronic commerce.	3	Important
• The Project will create a new electronic commerce product or service, which will provide a significant improvement in the bank's competitive position in electronic commerce, or provide a broad-based competitive advantage.	4	Very Important
• The Project is critical for implementing electronic commerce-based products and services, or is itself an important electronic commerce product or service. This project is critical to establishing or maintaining the bank as a major player in the electronic commerce area, and represents a major advance relative to competitors.	5	Critical

The CFO Role in
Right Decisions/Right Results

Increasingly, the CFO is responsible for IT plans and budgets and is being asked to ensure that the IT investments are improving shareholder value. The CFO, in turn, is asking IT people hard questions: How do we justify new IT investments? Are we balancing our resources between requests for new investment and the needs of existing IT activities? How do we know IT is contributing to our business success? How do we measure and report the business return on IT investments? Overall, the CFO should also be asking, "How can I evaluate widely different IT investments with a consistent, business-based yardstick, and ensure that they produce predictable, consistent results for the company?"

In the past, senior management teams have looked to IT management for answers to these IT value questions. However, the questions are not simply about IT but are connected to business as well. IT is, fundamentally, an enabler of business activity, enabling managers to make better decisions using information. It may also, for example, enable marketers to target more profitable markets, or may enable the reengineering of a business process to reduce time cycles. In all of these cases, IT's contribution is to enable a more efficient or effective business activity, which in turn results in improved profitability. IT is a partner in the bottom-line result, but it isn't the only determining factor.

Traditional IT financial analysis works to translate IT's enabling contributions into concrete estimates of reduced cost or increased income and, thereby, produce a measure of IT's contribution to profitability, or ROI. Clearly, the financial community needs new ways to assess IT bottom-line impact. Whatever we do with IT, we do it with the expectation of directly or indirectly improving financial performance. The problem is, what constitutes a "direct contribution to" profitability?

First, IT can enable improvements in a company's operations (operational effectiveness). If these business operational improvements reduce cost or improve revenue, the benefits may be directly measurable and an ROI can be calculated. In other cases, the connection to profitability may be less clear (e.g., improves customer satisfaction) and ROI is difficult. IT can also enable the success of a company's strategy (strategic effectiveness). For example, if a key strategy is increasing customer loyalty through improved customer service, IT has value when it provides tools and information for improved customer service.

In this context, the CFO plays a critical role, not only in understanding and communicating IT value but also in shaping the way a company uses IT. By insisting on a consistent, business-based yardstick for measuring all IT investments (new and ongoing support for existing IT activities), the CFO can bring rigor to an historically political, informal process of making corporate decisions about IT. By making operational and strategic effectiveness the basis for this yardstick, the CFO can also inject a business-results rationale for assessing all IT investments.

Unfortunately, many companies lack IT and business planning processes that follow these principles and, hence, cannot produce IT plans and budgets that consistently support business strategies. For companies to effectively answer the hard questions posed above, the CFO and the rest of the senior management team needs to work not only to adopt the principles but also to implement process and culture changes to explicitly link IT investments and business strategic intentions.

We want the CFO to be able to say: (1) We are able to translate our business strategies into IT actions; (2) We are investing new IT resources in the right places; (3) We are getting sufficient value from our existing IT assets and resources; and (4) We are spending the right amount on IT. Any company can learn and implement these practices. With effective management leadership, proper training, and a focus on adapting these practices to fit the company's culture, the CFO will answer the value questions with confidence.

The Details of the Business Value Maturity Model™

Chapter 12 introduced the Business Value Maturity Model™ and described the six basic levels, shown in Exhibit F.1. Definitions for the areas covered by NIE practices are given in Exhibits F.2–F.6.

EXHIBIT F.1 Business Value Maturity Model™

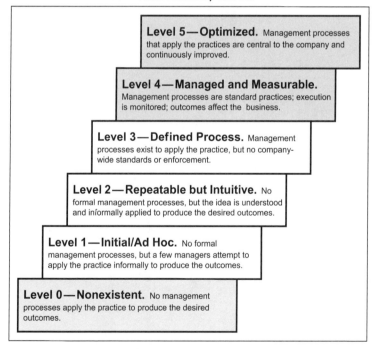

Level 5—Optimized. Management processes that apply the practices are central to the company and continuously improved.

Level 4—Managed and Measurable. Management processes are standard practices; execution is monitored; outcomes affect the business.

Level 3—Defined Process. Management processes exist to apply the practice, but no company-wide standards or enforcement.

Level 2—Repeatable but Intuitive. No formal management processes, but the idea is understood and informally applied to produce the desired outcomes.

Level 1—Initial/Ad Hoc. No formal management processes, but a few managers attempt to apply the practice informally to produce the outcomes.

Level 0—Nonexistent. No management processes apply the practice to produce the desired outcomes.

EXHIBIT F.2 Strategic Demand/Supply Planning

		Maturity Level Description	Practice Outcomes	Business Outcomes
0	Nonexistent	There are no company management processes to produce IT performance measures that are connected to business impact.	None	None
1	Initial/Ad Hoc	The need for demand/supply planning is recognized by IT but there is no structured process in place. It occurs only in response to a specific business requirement and is driven by IT management. IT plans are rarely discussed at business management meetings. Risk and alignment are handled at the project level.	IT initiatives and projects are driven by IT in response to general business requirements. These requirements are typically based on automating existing business processes or enhancing/extending current systems.	IT's role is limited to "squeaky wheel" initiatives and incremental process improvements.
2	Repeatable but Intuitive	IT management understands demand/supply planning but the process is not documented. It occurs on an irregular cycle. No process for communicating changes in business and IT plans and requirements. Some local integrated planning occurs between IT and the business.	IT has a transactional strategy that is driven project by project. Lack of coordination between individual projects creates multiple push/pulls on IT architecture. There is little involvement from the business in capturing the value of a project (IT projects *happen* to the business). Project duplication and overlaps commonly occur.	Some projects are roaring successes, but too many others are dismal failures. No coordination between initiatives limits value across the enterprise. IT experiences an increase in infrastructure complexity. Management attention is given to the application development process. IT alignment and TCO become a business management issue.

EXHIBIT F.2 Strategic Demand/Supply Planning (*Continued*)

		Maturity Level Description	Practice Outcomes	Business Outcomes
3	Defined Process	A policy defines when and how to perform IT/business strategic planning. Management buy-in and support is enabled by a documented methodology for joint IT/business strategy development, the support of validated data, and a structured, transparent decision-making process. Local managers do have local control over the implementation of the process and there are no procedures for examining process results.	IT strategic plan is translated into roadmaps and initiatives (projects). Increase in the percentage of IT budget that is actively championed by the business. The planning process still happens at the business-unit level.	Increase in the percent of business units that have clear, understood, and current IT capabilities. Management attention is placed on project formation process and identifying project (ROI).
4	Managed and Measurable	Demand/supply planning is a standard practice and management notes exceptions. Demand/supply planning is a defined management function with senior level ownership and responsibilities. The process and its results are measured and monitored (e.g., percent of plan converted to initiatives, percent of IT budget connected to process outcomes).	Increased coordination between IT strategy and business strategy at the enterprise level. Better projects that are more closely connected to business objectives and direction.	Closer connection between IT and business processes at the enterprise level (cross-silo). More successful projects due to greater business involvement through the entire project lifecycle. Increased leverage of new and existing infrastructural elements.
5	Optimized	Methods of integrating IT and business planning are continuously improved with best practices, industry comparisons, and tools and automation.	IT and business planning are fully connected and integrated.	The company maximizes strategic and bottom-line impact from its IT investments and capabilities.

EXHIBIT F.3 Innovation

		Maturity Level Description	Practice Outcomes	Business Outcomes
0	Nonexistent	There are no management processes to consider new opportunities created by IT capabilities.	Planning is top-down, and IT planning is reactive to business tactical planning.	IT is seen as a support function only. Limited innovation.
1	Initial/Ad Hoc	IT-based innovation opportunities occur based on unstructured individual insight within the business. Business does not view innovation as something to be managed.	Individuals and departments drive innovations. IT is continually reacting to vendor-driven "flight magazine" innovations based on new technology. Business asks, "Why aren't our IT guys looking at this technology?"	Innovations occur as isolated incidents. Innovations have only loose and incidental connections to business strategy. Follow-through on these ad hoc innovation initiatives is limited due to lack of management commitment.
2	Repeatable but Intuitive	Individual business managers monitor new IT capabilities within the company as well as within specific competitors and the industry. IT is invited to present new capabilities. Outside research views are included as part of the innovation process.	Innovation is viewed as being "environmentally" managed (i.e., if the right elements are present and the culture is supportive, innovation will happen).	Specific managers and business units gain a reputation for being consistently innovative and IT-savvy.
3	Defined Process	A documented process exists for communicating IT capabilities and exploring their impact on existing business processes. This involves a structured visioning and scenario development processes. The implementation of the innovation process is left to the discretion individual managers and innovation results are not specifically monitored.	IT capabilities are used as input to the business's innovation thinking. IT begins to be recognized for its active role in business innovation (inward and outward view). Better (higher value) projects, including cross-silo innovations, are formed.	New IT-driven opportunities are proposed and considered to support existing strategic intentions. New IT-driven capabilities influence the development of new strategies and business innovations. IT evaluates architectural decisions in terms of future business capabilities.

EXHIBIT F.3 Innovation *(Continued)*

		Maturity Level Description	Practice Outcomes	Business Outcomes
4	Managed and Measurable	There is a regularly executed process for communicating IT capabilities and exploring their impact on existing business processes. There is a stated innovation strategy with specific goals. Continuous innovation is expected of all business units. It is measured and is part of individual managers' performance evaluations. Managers are expected to follow the process in their business planning activities and there is a defined process for monitoring compliance. Ownership of the innovation practice lies with a manager who is responsible for documentation, training, process support, compliance, and measurement of results.	Levels of innovation become part of management's performance criteria. Innovation initiatives are managed as an identifiable portfolio (or portfolio subset). Innovations are selected and prioritized based on a multidimensional set of criteria including connection to business strategy and the ability of the organization to implement (change).	Percentage of revenue from new products and services increases. Number of cross-functional innovations and process improvements increases. Organizational change management becomes a critical management issue.
5	Optimized	Methods of driving continuous IT-driven innovation are continuously improved with best practices, industry comparisons, and tools and automation.	IT-enabled innovations impact business planning and offer new strategies.	The company continually improves products, processes, and bottom-line performance through IT-based innovations.

EXHIBIT F.4 Prioritization

		Maturity Level Description	Practice Outcomes	Business Outcomes
0	Nonexistent	There is no defined process for prioritizing projects.	None	None
1	Initial/Ad Hoc	New IT investments are approved individually based on local operational justification. Prioritization is loosely performed by the IT organization in response organizational pressures.	Projects are isolated from other projects and are treated individually. Priorities within a business unit are informally negotiated between business sponsors and IT. Development managers establish priorities across silos based on business unit clout and noise.	Because there is no way to assign value to strategic projects, tactical and operational projects rise to the top. Management views IT exclusively in terms of labor and cost savings.
2	Repeatable but Intuitive	Each IT initiative has a required financial business case that is based on local operational justification. An IT governance board individually approves projects primarily based on projected ROI but with the consideration of other unspecified management factors. An IT governance board manages prioritization, but it is accomplished through a political process of argument and debate. Once approved and started, projects generally run to completion. Resource priorities for running projects are determined by IT.	IT investments are viewed and managed as a project list. Tactical projects and projects to "fix what's broken" dominate the list. Projects qualify for consideration based on ROI projections, but priorities are negotiated based on informal "soft" benefits and management factors. Once a project is approved, it runs to completion.	Large numbers of projects are in crisis. This is due to changing tactical requirements during the development phase. Management attention shifts to improving the development process and managing scope creep. Project benefits are organizationally isolated.

EXHIBIT 1.4 Prioritization (Continued)

		Maturity Level Description	Practice Outcomes	Business Outcomes
3	Defined Process	Each IT initiative has a required project description that includes ROI projections, nonfinancial benefits categories, and risk assessments. An IT governance board approves and prioritizes new projects primarily based on projected ROI but with the consideration of other unspecified management factors.	Project justification and prioritization occur on a regular schedule. New IT investments are described in business terms. In-process projects regularly have their value cases reexamined. IT assigns resources and begins to manage projects as a portfolio.	Management attention moves to the project definition phase and the resource allocation process. IT investment decisions are made by business management rather than IT users.
4	Managed and Measurable	Company strategy is explicitly defined in understandable terms. There are defined processes to justify and prioritize IT-related investments, tied to the company's strategic intentions and business processes. Each proposed investment has a standard business case and project description. An IT governance board approves and prioritizes projects based on a standard multi-dimensional set of value criteria. An IT governance board manages resources at a portfolio level across the company. Projects already in development are regularly reexamined and resources reallocated as necessary. Responsibility for executing and managing the prioritization process has been clearly assigned,	The goal is a balanced project portfolio. This means that IT resources and investments are allocated across a range of different projects—tactical and strategic, with different risk/reward profiles. The process provides early justification for canceling problem projects.	The connection of IT investment resources to business objectives can be clearly communicated. Increase in overall project success and value delivery due to increased business management buy-in and participation. There is a greater business involvement in the full project life-cycle.

EXHIBIT F.4 Prioritization (*Continued*)

	Maturity Level Description	Practice Outcomes	Business Outcomes
5	Optimized	The prioritization process is an integral part of IT management and, through the IT governance board, provides the critical forum for communicating with the business. Prioritization is an ongoing process that is continually reexamined and upgraded.	IT investments are prioritized against business strategy.	The company maximizes bottom-line impact and return on its IT investments and capabilities.

EXHIBIT F.5 Alignment

		Maturity Level Description	Practice Outcomes	Business Outcomes
0	Nonexistent	There are no company management processes to assess the connection between IT systems and services and the business.	None	None
1	Initial/Ad Hoc	IT systems and services are occasionally assessed at an aggregate level on the basis of customer (user) satisfaction. Lights-on applications are inventoried and examined for special purposes such as establishing disaster recovery requirements.	IT service levels and quality become issues. Service level agreements begin to appear. Snap-shot representation of lights-on application status and importance.	IT and business resources are allocated to improving functionality and service levels of tactical applications and IT services.
2	Repeatable but Intuitive	IT systems and services are occasionally assessed at an aggregate level on the basis of business management satisfaction.	High-level issues regarding service level and quality are identified. High-level issues regarding IT's connection to the business are identified.	IT alignment becomes a business management issue.
3	Defined Process	There is a documented process for assessing the connection and contribution of existing IT systems to strategic intentions and key business processes. There is a documented process for assessing the service level, quality, intensity of use, and other key attributes of existing IT systems. The assessment process supports a portfolio view for managing IT resources.	Application-by-application information becomes available regarding annual cost, business impact, quality, and other key attributes. IT uses this information to communicate with the business about managing IT demand.	The business begins to understand where IT resources are spent and the budget impact of lights-on systems. Specific business units begin to evaluate their lights-on applications and make informed retire/replace decisions.

EXHIBIT F.5 Alignment (*Continued*)

	Maturity Level Description	Practice Outcomes	Business Outcomes
4	**Managed and Measurable**	Company strategy is explicitly defined in understandable terms. The organizational responsibility for the execution and monitoring of the alignment process is clearly defined. The results of the alignment assessments are used as important input to the planning process.	Poorly performing and nonaligned systems are removed or replaced. Resources are assigned to maintenance and enhancement projects based on connection to strategic intentions and gaps in service and quality levels of high-connection systems and services.	Budgets and resources for lights-on systems and services are planned and assigned based on connection to strategic intentions and gaps in service and quality levels. The percentage of the IT budget allocated to legacy systems is maintained or reduced.
5	**Optimized**	The alignment practice is an integral part of IT management and, through the IT governance board, provides critical data for communicating with the business. Prioritization is an ongoing process that is continually reexamined and upgraded.	The entire IT budget is aligned with business strategy.	The company maximizes return from its IT activities and capabilities in terms of bottom-line impact. The total IT spend is effectively controlled.

EXHIBIT F.6 Performance Measurement

		Maturity Level Description	Practice Outcomes	Business Outcomes
0	Nonexistent	There are no company management processes to produce IT performance measures that are connected to business impact.	None	None
1	Initial/Ad Hoc	The tracking of IT operational and cost measures occurs. These measures are used for IT operational decisions and are not regularly communicated to the business. External benchmarking is done to answer specific performance questions. Key development projects are 'project managed.'	Value is connected to operational efficiency only. Use of portfolios is limited to key development projects. Activities and resources are directed at operational and maintenance priorities.	IT performance is communicated in IT terms. This lack of relevant performance metrics results in the business perception that IT operates unto itself. Business excludes IT from most planning activities except for large IT-enabled projects (e.g., ERP).
2	Repeatable but Intuitive	The tracking of IT performance, including 'soft' impact measures, occurs regularly but is not connected to strategic intentions. Some IT performance measures (service levels, customer satisfaction) are linked to business impact. Project portfolios are used to track most development projects.	Value is also connected to end-user satisfaction, which is driven by availability and service-level considerations. Use of portfolios extended to most development projects. Service-level considerations impact budgets and actions.	By focusing on end-user satisfaction and service levels, IT brings attention to tactical and legacy-driven priorities. Although IT is trying to respond to business requirements, senior management continues to wonder if IT is working on the right things. IT management is unable to answer these questions.

EXHIBIT F.6 Performance Measurement *(Continued)*

		Maturity Level Description	Practice Outcomes	Business Outcomes
3	Defined Process	The tracking of IT performance occurs regularly through documented measurement processes for which training and support are available. IT management has made a commitment to one or more process maturity models (SEI/CMM, COBIT, others). IT management has made a commitment to use portfolios to manage IT activities and resources. Alignment with the business emerges as a key performance target.	IT performance measures are linked to business impact using cause-and-effect linkages and alignment assessments. Portfolios are used to manage all IT resources and activities. Alignment considerations impact IT's planning and budgeting processes.	IT's efforts to build cause-and-effect linkages to business performance drivers increases the level of trust and collaboration with the business. The conversation between business and IT begins to shift from system requirements to business goals.
4	Managed and Measurable	Management regularly tracks the connections of IT performance measurements to business requirements and strategic intentions. The validity of cause-and-effect linkage assumptions is regularly checked. Responsibility for the ongoing management of performance measurement is clearly defined.	IT value is based on IT's impact on business plans and performance. IT performance measures are coordinated and managed through one office. Connections to business planning processes are coordinated and IT portfolio resource management decisions actively involve the business. Processes for updating portfolio data are defined and implemented.	IT is able to readily connect business priorities to its portfolios. IT managers are evaluated (measured) on their ability to connect IT resources with business goals and priorities. Business managers begin to understand the importance of sharing their goals and strategies with IT.
5	Optimized	Methods of tracking IT performance related to business requirements and strategic intentions are continuously improved with best practices, industry comparisons, and tools and automation. Key IT measures are related to agility and the time needed to respond to changing business intentions.	IT value is based on IT's ability to change with the business. Resource allocation decisions and priorities are continuously reviewed. Portfolio information is actively used at all levels of IT management. IT business and technical performance are tracked.	IT portfolios are used as an integral part of business and IT planning. The dialog between IT and business is no longer about proving IT value but about the continuous improvement of IT value. Performance measures lead to improved IT and business performance.

bibliography

Alter, Steven L. *Decision Support Systems: Current Practices and Continuing Challenges*. Reading, MA: Addison-Wesley, 1979.

Alter, Steven L. *Information Systems: A Management Perspective*, 3rd ed. Reading, MA: Addison-Wesley Longman, 1999.

Amran, Martha, and Nalin Kulatilaka. *Real Options: Managing Strategic Investment in an Uncertain World*. Boston: Harvard Business School Press, 1999.

Andrews, M., and R. Papp. "The Application of IT for Competitive Advantage at Keane, Inc.," in *Annals of Cases on Information Technology Applications and Management in Organizations*, Volume 2. Hershey, PA: Idea Group Publishing, 2000.

Applegate, Lynda M., Robert D. Austin, and F. Warren McFarlan. *Creating Business Advantage in the Information Age*. New York: McGraw-Hill Irwin, 2002.

Applegate, Lynda, F. Warren McFarlan, and James McKenney. *Corporate Information Systems Management: Text and Cases*. Boston: McGraw-Hill, 1999.

Austin, Robert D. *Measuring and Managing Performance in Organizations*. New York: Dorset House, 1996.

Barker, L., and R. Rubycz. *Performance Improvement in Public Service Delivery: A Tool-Kit for Managers*. Marshfield, MA: Pitman Publishing, 1996.

Berghout, Egon. *Evaluation of Information System Proposals: Design of a Decision Support Method*. Ph.D. dissertation, Delft University of Technology, 1997.

Black, Andrew, Philip Wright, and John Bachman. *In Search of Shareholder Value*. Marshfield, MA: Pitman Publishing, 1998.

Boar, Bernard H. *Practical Steps for Aligning Information Technology with Business Strategies: How to Achieve a Competitive Advantage*. Hoboken, NJ: John Wiley & Sons, 1994.

Boar, Bernard H. *Strategic Thinking for Information Technology*. Hoboken, NJ: John Wiley & Sons, 1996.

Bonczek, Robert H., Clyde W. Holsapple, and Andrew B. Whinston. *Foundations of Decision Support Systems*. New York: Academic Press, 1981.

Boulton, Richard E.S., et al. *Cracking the Value Code: How Successful Businesses Are Creating Wealth in the New Economy*. New York: Harper Business, 2000.

Bridges, William. *The Character of Organizations*. Palo Alto, CA: Davies-Black, 2000.

Brooks, F.P. *The Mythical Man-Month: Essays on Software Engineering*. Reading, MA: Addison-Wesley, 1982.

Cairncross, Francis. *The Death of Distance: How the Communications Revolution Will Change Our Lives*. Boston: Harvard Business School Press, 1997.

Cash, James I., Jr., Robert G. Eccles, Nitin Nohria, and Richard L. Nolan. *Building the Information-Age Organization: Structure, Control, and Information Technologies.* New York: Richard D. Irwin, 1994.

Cassidy, Anita. *Practical Guide to Information Systems Strategic Planning.* Boca Raton, FL: CRC/Saint Lucie Press, 1998.

Central Computer and Telecom Agency (CCTA). *IS Strategy: Process and Products.* Norwich, UK: Format Publishing, 1999.

Central Computer and Telecom Agency (CCTA). *Managing Change.* Norwich, UK: Format Publishing, 1999.

Cortada, James W. *Best Practices in Information Technology: How Corporations Get the Most Value from Exploiting Their Digital Investment.* Upper Saddle River, NJ: Prentice Hall, 1997.

Curran, Thomas, and Gerhard Keller. *SAP R/3—Business Blueprint: Understanding the Business Process Reference Model.* Upper Saddle River, NJ: Prentice Hall, 1998.

Currie, Wendy. *The Global Information Society.* Chichester, UK: John Wiley & Sons, 2000.

Daniels, Caroline. *Information Technology: The Management Challenge.* Wokingham, UK: Addison-Wesley, 1994.

Davenport, Thomas H. *Mission Critical: Realizing the Promise of Enterprise Systems.* Boston: Harvard Business School Press, 2000.

Davenport, Thomas H. *Information Ecology: Mastering the Information and Knowledge Environment.* Oxford, UK: Oxford University Press, 1997.

Davenport, Thomas H., and John C. Beck. *The Attention Economy: Understanding the New Currency of Business.* Boston: Harvard Business School Press, 2001.

Devaraj, Sarv, and Rajiv Kohli. *The IT Payoff.* Upper Saddle River, NJ: Prentice Hall, 2002.

Dickson, Gary W., and Gerardine DeSanctis, eds. *Information Technology and the Future Enterprise: New Models for Managers.* Upper Saddle River, NJ: Prentice Hall, 2001.

Earl, Michael J. *Corporate Information Systems Management.* Homewood, IL: Richard D. Irwin, 1983.

Egan, Gerard. *Adding Value: A Systematic Guide to Business-Driven Management and Leadership.* San Francisco: Jossey-Bass Publishers, 1993.

Fleming, Quentin, and Joel Hoppelman. *Earned Value Project Management.* Newtown Square, Pa: Project Management Institute, 1996.

Flowers, Stephen. *Software Failure: Management Failure.* Chichester, UK: John Wiley & Sons, 1996.

Galliers, Robert C., and Walter R.J. Baets, eds. *Information Technology and Organizational Transformation.* Chichester, UK: John Wiley & Sons, 1998.

Galliers, Robert, Dorothy Leidner, and Bernadette Baker. eds. *Strategic Information Management: Challenges & Strategies in Managing IS,* 2nd ed. Oxford, UK: Butterworth-Heinemann, 1999.

Gardner, Christopher. *The Valuation of Information Technology.* New York: John Wiley & Sons, 2000.

Gilder, George. *Telecosm: How Infinite Bandwidth Will Revolutionize Our World.* New York: Free Press, 2000.

Hamel, Gary. *Leading the Revolution.* Boston: Harvard Business School Press, 2000.

Hares, John, and Duncan Royle. *Measuring the Value of Information Technology.* New York: Wiley & Sons, 1994.

Hewitt, Morrison W. *How to Succeed in the Information Systems Profession: Ten Personal Success Factors.* Whitney House, 1990..

Hogbin, Geoff, and David Thomas. *Investing in Information Technology: Managing the Decision-Making Process.* New York: McGraw-Hill, 1994.

Hoque, Faisal. *The Alignment Effect.* Upper Saddle River, NJ: Prentice Hall, 2002.

Kaplan, Robert S., and David P. Norton. *The Balanced Scorecard.* Boston: Harvard Business School Press, 1996.

Kaplan, Robert S., and David P. Norton. *The Strategy Focused Organization: How Balanced Scorecard Companies Thrive in the New Business Environment.* Boston: Harvard Business School Press, 2001.

Labovitz, George, and Victor Rosansky. *The Power of Alignment: How Great Companies Stay Centered and Accomplish Extraordinary Things.* Hoboken, NJ: John Wiley & Sons, 1997.

Lacity, Mary C., and Leslie P. Willcocks. *Global Information Technology Outsourcing: In Search of Business Advantage.* Hoboken, NJ: John Wiley & Sons, 2001.

Lucas, Henry C. *Information Technology for Managers,* 6th ed. New York: McGraw-Hill, 1997.

Lucas, Henry C. *The T-Form Organization: Using Technology to Design Organizations for the 21st Century.* San Francisco: Jossey-Bass, 1996.

Luftman, Jerry. *Competing in the Information Age: Practical Applications of the Strategic Alignment Model.* New York: Oxford University Press, 1996.

Marchand, David A., ed. *Competing with Information.* Chichester, UK: John Wiley & Sons, 2000.

McNurlin, Barbara C., and Ralph H. Sprague, Jr. *Information Systems Management in Practice,* 5th ed. Upper Saddle River, NJ: Prentice Hall, 2002.

McTaggart, James M., Peter W. Kontes, and Michael C. Mankins. *The Value Imperative: Managing for Superior Shareholder Returns.* New York: Free Press, 1994.

Money, Arthur, Alan Twite, and Dan Remenyi, eds. *Effective Measurement and Management of IT Costs and Benefits.* Oxford: Butterworth-Heinemann, 2000.

Neuhauser, Peg, Ray Bender, and Kirk Stromberg. *Culture.com: Building Corporate Culture in the Connected Workplace.* New York: John Wiley & Sons, 2000.

Nolan, Richard. *Dot Vertigo: Doing Business in a Permeable World.* Hoboken, NJ: John Wiley & Sons, 2001.

Parker, Marilyn M. *Strategic Transformation and Information Technology.* Upper Saddle River, NJ: Prentice Hall, 1996.

Parker, Marilyn M. *Theory and Practice of Business/IT Organizational Interdependencies.* Ph.D. dissertation, Katholieke Universiteit Brabant, 1999.

Parker, Marilyn M., and Robert J. Benson, with E.H. Trainor. *Information Economics: Linking Business Performance to Information Technology*. Englewood Cliffs, NJ: Prentice Hall, 1988.

Parker, Marilyn M., and E.H. Trainor, with Robert J. Benson. *Information Strategy and Economics: Linking Information Systems Strategy to Business Performance*. Englewood Cliffs, NJ: Prentice-Hall, 1989.

Pearlson, Keri E. *Managing and Using Information Systems: A Strategic Approach*. Hoboken, NJ: John Wiley & Sons, 2001.

Peppers, Don, and Martha Rogers. *The One to One Future: Building Relationships One Customer at a Time*. New York: Doubleday, 1993.

Porter, Michael. *Competitive Advantage*. New York: Free Press, 1985.

Porter, Michael. *Competitive Strategy*. New York: Free Press, 1980.

Power, D.J. *A Brief History of Decision Support Systems*. DSSResources.COM. Available at: *http://DSSResources.COM/history/dsshistory.html*, version 2.0, 2002.

Power, Daniel J. *Decision Support Systems: Concepts and Resources for Managers*. Quorum Books, 2002.

Rappaport, Alfred. *Creating Shareholder Value: A Guide for Managers and Investors*. New York: The Free Press, 1998.

Reddy, Ram. *From Supply Chains to Virtual Integration*. New York: McGraw Hill, 2001.

Remenyi, Dan, Michael Sherwood-Smith, and Terry White. *Achieving Maximum Value from Information Systems: A Process Approach*. Hoboken, NJ: John Wiley & Sons, 1997.

Renkema, Theo J.W. *The IT Value Quest*. Chichester, UK: John Wiley & Sons, 2000.

Robson, W. *Strategic Management and Information Systems: An Integrated Approach*. London: Pitman Publishing. 1994.

Shapiro, Carl, and Hal R. Varian. *Information Rules: A Strategic Guide to the Network Economy*. Boston: Harvard Business School Press, 1999.

Software Engineering Institute, Carnegie Mellon University. *The Capability Maturity Model: Guidelines for Improving the Software Process*. Reading, MA: Addison-Wesley, 1995.

Sprague, Ralph H, and Hugh J. Watson. *Decision Support Systems: Putting Theory into Practice*, 3rd ed. Englewood Cliffs, NJ: Prentice Hall, 1993.

Strassmann, Paul A. *The Squandered Computer: Evaluating the Business Alignment of Information Technologies*. New Canaan, CT: Information Economics Press, 1997.

Strassmann, Paul. *Business Value of Computers*. New Canaan, CT: Information Economics Press, 1990.

Swanson, Richard A. *Analysis for Improving Performance: Tools for Diagnosing Organizations & Documenting Workplace Expertise*. San Francisco: Berrett-Koehler, 1996.

Tapscott, Don. *Digital Economy: Promises and Perils in the Age of Networked Intelligence*. New York: McGraw-Hill, 1996.

Tapscott, Don, David Ticoll, and Alex Lowy. *Digital Capital: Harnessing the Power of Business Webs*. Boston: Harvard Business School Press, 2000.

Thorp, John, et al. *The Information Paradox: Realizing the Business Benefits of Information Technology.* New York: McGraw-Hill, 1998.

Turban, Efraim, and Jay E. Aronson. *Decision Support Systems & Intelligent Systems.* Upper Saddle River, NJ: Prentice Hall, 2000.

Turban, Efraim, Ephriam McLean, and James Wetherbe. *Information Technology for Management: Making Connections for Strategic Advantage,* 2nd ed. Hoboken, NJ: John Wiley & Sons, 1997.

van der Zee, Han. *In Search of the Value of Information Technology.* Ph.D. dissertation, Katholieke Universiteit Brabant, 1996.

Ward, John, and Pat Griffiths. *Strategic Planning for Information Systems,* 2nd ed. Chichester, UK: John Wiley & Sons, 1996.

Weill, Peter, and Marianne Broadbent. *Leveraging the New Infrastructure: How Market Leaders Capitalize on Information Technology.* Boston: Harvard Business School Press, 1998.

Weill, Peter, and Marianne Broadbent. *Leveraging the New Infrastructure: How Market Leaders Capitalize on Information Technology.* Boston: Harvard Business School Press, 1998.

Weill, Peter, and Michael R. Vitale. *Place to Space: Migrating to eBusiness Models.* Boston: Harvard Business School Press, 2001.

Wigand, Rolf, Arnold Picot, and Ralf Reichwald. *Information, Organization and Management.* Chichester, UK: John Wiley & Sons, 1997.

Willcocks, Leslie P., and S. Lester, eds. *Beyond the IT Productivity Paradox.* Chichester, UK: John Wiley & Sons, 1999.

Wysocki, Robert, and Robert L. DeMichiell. *Managing Information Across the Enterprise.* Hoboken, NJ: John Wiley & Sons, 1997.

Journal Articles

Alster, Norm. "After the Deluge: Despite a Torrent of Interest in ROI, Truly Workable Solutions Are Just Beginning to Emerge." *CFO IT,* October 15, 2002.

Ambrosio, Johanna. "What to Count?" *Computerworld,* July 16, 2001.

Amram, Martha, and Nalin Kulatilaka. "Disciplined Decisions: Aligning Strategy with the Financial Markets." *Harvard Business Review,* January–February 1999, pp. 95–104.

Atkinson, Anthony A., John H. Waterhouse, and Robert B. Wells. "A Stakeholder Approach to Strategic Performance Measurement." *Sloan Management Review,* Spring 1997, pp. 25–37.

Bartlett, Christopher A., and Sumantra Ghoshal. "Changing the Role of Top Management: Beyond Systems to People." *Harvard Business Review,* May–June 1995, pp. 132–142.

Bartlett, Christopher A., and Sumantra Ghoshal. "Changing the Role of Top Management: Beyond Strategy to Purpose." *Harvard Business Review,* November–December 1994, pp. 79–90.

Barua, Anitesh, et al. "Driving E-Business Excellence." *Sloan Management Review,* Fall 2001, pp. 36–50.

Beer, Michael, and Russell A. Eisenstat. "The Silent Killers of Strategy Implementation and Learning." *Sloan Management Review,* Summer 2000, pp. 29–40.

Bensaou, M., and Michael Earl. "The Right Mind-set for Managing Information Technology," *Harvard Business Review,* September–October 1998, pp. 119–128.

Berry, John. "ROI: Whose Job Is It, Anyway?" *Computerworld,* March 3, 2003.

Betts, Mitch. "Do the Math: An ROI Guide," *Computerworld,* February 17, 2003.

Broadbent, Marianne, and Peter Weill. "Management by Maxim: How Business and IT Managers Can Create IT Infrastructures." *Sloan Management Review,* Spring 1997, pp. 77–92.

Campbell, Andrew. "Tailored, Not Benchmarked: A Fresh Look at Corporate Planning." *Harvard Business Review,* March–April 1999, pp. 41–50.

Carr, Nicholas. "IT Doesn't Matter." *Harvard Business Review,* May 2003.

Chabrow, Eric. "The Buck Stops Here," *InformationWeek,* April 15, 2002.

Christensen, Clayton M. "The Past and Future of Competitive Advantage." *Sloan Management Review,* Winter 2001, pp. 105–109.

Colkin, Eileen. "Getting Tough on ROI." *Information Week,* October 21, 2002.

Collins, John, and Darren Smith. "Innovation Metrics: A Framework to Accelerate Growth." *Prism,* Quarter 2, 1999, pp. 33–47.

Courtney, Hugh, Jane Kirkland, and Patrick Viguerie. "Strategy Under Uncertainty." *Harvard Business Review,* November–December 1997.

Cross, Robert L., and Susan E. Brodt. "How Assumptions of Consensus Undermine Decision Making." *Sloan Management Review,* Winter 2001, pp. 86–94.

Deschamps, Jean-Phillipe. "Half of Your R&D Is Wasted —But Which Half and On What?" *Prism,* Quarter 2, 1999.

DiRomualdo, Anthony, and Vijay Gurbaxani. "Strategic Intent for IT Outsourcing." *Sloan Management Review,* Summer 1998, pp. 67–80.

Dixit, Avinash K., and Robert S. Pindyck. "The Options Approach to Capital Investment." *Harvard Business Review,* May–June 1995, pp. 105–115.

Earl, Michael J., and David Feeny. "Opinion: How to Be a CEO for the Information Age." *Sloan Management Review,* Winter 2000, pp. 11–23.

Earl, Michael J., and Jeffrey L. Sampler. "Market Management to Transform the IT Organization." *Sloan Management Review,* Summer 1998, pp. 9–17.

Earl, Michael, and Bushra Khan. "E-Commerce Is Changing the Face of IT." *MIT Sloan Management Review,* Fall 2001, pp. 64–72.

Earl, Michael, and David Feeny. "How to Be a CEO for the Information Age." *Sloan Management Review,* Vol. 41, No. 2, Winter 2000, pp. 11–23.

Eisenhardt, Kathleen M. "Strategy as Strategic Decision Making." *Sloan Management Review,* Spring 1999, pp. 65–72.

Evans, Philip B., and Thomas S. Wurster. "Strategy and the New Economics of Information." *Harvard Business Review,* September–October 1997, pp. 71–82.

Feeny, David F., and Leslie P. Willcocks. "Core IS Capabilities for Exploiting Information Technology." *Sloan Management Review,* Spring 1998, pp. 9-21.

Feeny, David. "Making Business Sense of the E-Opportunity." *Sloan Management Review,* Winter 2001, pp. 41–51.

Froot, Kenneth A., David S. Scharfstein, and Jeremy C. Stein. "A Framework for Risk Management." *Harvard Business Review,* November–December 1994, pp. 91–102.

Garvin, David A. "The Processes of Organization and Management." *Sloan Management Review,* Summer 1998, pp. 33–50.

Garvin, David A., and Michael A. Roberto. "What You Don't Know about Making Decisions." *Harvard Business Review,* September 2001, pp. 108–116.

Garvin, David. "Leveraging Processes for Strategic Advantage." *Harvard Business Review,* September–October 1995, pp. 77–91.

Ghoshal, Sumantra, Christopher A. Bartlett, and Peter Moran. "A New Manifesto for Management." *Sloan Management Review,* Spring 1999, pp. 9–20.

Hagel, John, and John Seely Brown. "Your Next IT Strategy." *Harvard Business Review,* October 2001, pp. 105–113.

Hammer, Michael. "The Superefficient Company." *Harvard Business Review,* September 2001, pp. 82–91.

Haspeslagh, Tomo Noda, and Fares Boulos. "Managing for Value: It's Not Just about the Numbers." *Harvard Business Review,* July–August 2001, pp. 65–73.

Hoffman, Thomas. "CFOs Demanding Detailed IT Project Info." *Computerworld,* April 18, 2003.

Huy, Quy Nguyen. "In Praise of Middle Managers." *Harvard Business Review,* September 2001, pp. 73–80.

Jensen, Michael C. "Corporate Budgeting is Broken—Let's Fix It." *Harvard Business Review,* November 2001, pp. 95–101.

Joachim, David. "The Fuzzier Side of ROI." *Computerworld,* May 13, 2002.

Katzenbach, Jon R. "The Myth of the Top Management Team." *Harvard Business Review,* November–December 1997, pp. 83–91.

Kellog School of Management and DiamondCluster International, Inc. *IT Portfolio Management,* Spring 2003, *www.kellogg.northwestern.edu/IT/research.*

Kelly, Susan. "Scrutinizing IT Spending." *Treasury and Risk Management,* February 2002.

Kersnar, Janet. "ROI: The Age of Reason." *CFO,* July 16, 2002.

Kim, W. Chan, and Renee Mauborgne. "Fair Process: Managing in the Knowledge Economy." *Harvard Business Review,* July–August 1997.

Kim, W. Chan, and Renee Mauborgne. "Strategy, Value Innovation, and the Knowledge Economy." *Sloan Management Review,* Spring 1999, pp. 41–54.

Kwak, Mary. "Spin-Offs Lead to Better Financing Decisions." *MIT Sloan Management Review,* Summer 2001, pp. 10.

Kwak, Mary. "Commitment Counts." *MIT Sloan Management Review,* Summer 2001, pp. 8–9.

Lee, Hau L., and Seungjin Whang. "Winning the Last Mile of E-Commerce." *MIT Sloan Management Review*, Summer 2001, pp. 54–59.

Lenatti, Chuck. "Grinding Away on ROI." *CFO IT*, June 16, 2003.

Low, Jon, and Pam Cohen Kalafut. "ROI Valuation," *Optimize*, June 2002.

Luehrman, Timothy A. "Strategy as a Portfolio of Real Options." *Harvard Business Review*, September–October 1998, pp. 76–88.

Luehrman, Timothy A. "What's It Worth? A General Manager's Guide to Valuation." *Harvard Business Review*, May–June 1997, pp. 132–142.

Luehrman, Timothy A. "Using APV: A Better Tool for Valuing Operations." *Harvard Business Review*, May–June 1997, pp. 145–154.

Luehrman, Timothy A. "What's It Worth? A General Manager's Guide to Valuation." *Harvard Business Review*, May–June 1997, pp. 132–142.

MacCormack, Allan. "Product Development Practices that Work: How Internet Companies Build Software." *Sloan Management Review*, Winter 2001, pp. 75–84.

Markides, Constantinos C. "A Dynamic View of Strategy." *Sloan Management Review*, Spring 1999, pp. 55–63.

Mayor, Tracy. "A Buyers Guide to IT Value Methodologies." *CIO*, July 15, 2002.

McKinsey & Company and CIGREF. *The Dynamics of Relationships between CEOs and CIOs in Major French Companies.* November 2002, *http://www.cigref.fr.*

Mintzberg, Henry. "The Pitfalls of Strategic Planning." *California Management Review*, Fall 1993, pp. 32–47.

Mintzberg, Henry, and Joseph Lampel. "Reflecting on the Strategy Process." *Sloan Management Review*, Spring 1999, pp. 21–30.

Mollison, Caitlin. "ROI." *InternetWorld*, March 1, 2002.

Morris, Virginia, Jonothan Shopley, and Eric Turner. "The Role of Metrics in Sustainable Development: A Progress Report." *Prism*, Fourth Quarter, 1998, pp. 63–78.

Nambisan, Satish. "Why Service Businesses Are Not Product Businesses." *MIT Sloan Management Review*, Summer 2001, pp. 72–80.

Oldfield, George S., and Anthony M. Santomero. "Risk Management in Financial Institutions." *Sloan Management Review*, Fall 1997, pp. 33–46.

Porter, Michael E. "What Is Strategy?" *Harvard Business Review*, November–December 1996.

Prahalad, C.K., and Gary Hamel. "The Core Competence of the Corporation." *Harvard Business Review*, April 2001.

Prahalad, C.K., and Gary Hamel. "Strategic Intent." *Harvard Business Review*, May–June 1989.

Quinn, James Brian. "Outsourcing Innovation: The New Engine of Growth." *Sloan Management Review*, Summer 2000, pp. 13–27.

Rangan, Subramanian, and Rond Adner. "Profits and the Internet: Seven Misconceptions." *MIT Sloan Management Review*, Summer 2001, pp. 44–50.

Rappaport, Alfred. "New Thinking on How to Link Executive Pay with Performance." *Harvard Business Review*, March–April 1999, pp. 91–104.

Ross, Jeanne, and Cynthia Beath. "Beyond the Business Case: Strategic IT Investment." *MIT Center for Information Systems Research,* October 2001.

Schoemaker, Paul J.H., and J. Edward Russo. "A Pyramid of Decision Approaches." *California Management Review,* Fall1993, pp. 9–31.

Sommerlatte, Tom, and Michael Braun. "Systems Innovation as a Source of New Business Opportunities." *Prism,* Quarter 2, 1999, pp. 49–59.

Tapscot, Don. "Rethinking Strategy in a Networked World." *Strategy + Business*, Vol. 24, Third Quarter 2001, pp. 34–41.

Vandermerwe, Sandra. "How Increasing Value to Customers Improves Business Results." *Sloan Management Review,* Fall 2000, pp. 27–37.

Venkatraman, N. "Five Steps to a Dot Com Strategy: How to Find Your Footing on the Web." *Sloan Management Review,* Spring 2000, pp. 15–28.

Venkatraman, N., and J.C. Camilus. "Exploring the Concept of 'Fit' in Strategic Management." *The Academy of Management Review,* July 1984, pp. 513–526.

Williamson, Peter J. "Strategy as Options on the Future." *Sloan Management Review,* Spring 1999, pp. 117–126.

index